WAIT FOR NOVEMBER

WAIT
FOR
NOVEMBER

by
Hans Erich Nossack

Translated from the German by
Ruth Hein

FROMM INTERNATIONAL PUBLISHING CORPORATION
NEW YORK, NEW YORK

Originally published in 1955 as *Spätestens im November*
Copyright © 1955, Suhrkamp Verlag, Berlin

Translation Copyright © 1982 by Fromm International Publishing
Corporation, New York, N.Y.

Printed in the United States of America

First U.S. Edition

Library of Congress Cataloging in Publication Data

Nossack, Hans Erich, 1901–
Wait for November.

Translation of: Spätestens im November.
I. Title.
PT2627.0759S613   1982   833'.914   82-1395
ISBN 0-88064-004-9   AACR2

WAIT FOR NOVEMBER

1

We must be careful not to make any mistakes, I wanted to say to him. But when I looked at him, I did not speak.

No, I have to tell the story in order, in very precise order, more or less the way it happened. Even then it's hard to explain. Some will shake their heads and say, "But that's impossible! People just don't do things like that." And I'll have to agree with them, because I don't know any other answer. It's not that I'm flustered. No, I really don't have the answer. No answers are adequate, though all sound noble.

It began at the "informal reception," as the invitation called it. Or it might have begun even earlier— much earlier. Perhaps it began when I was a little girl. Sometimes it seems as if it had never begun but had always existed, from the very first. But I don't dare think about it; it may all be my imagination.

For the informal reception, tables had been set up in the hall of the art gallery, outside the lecture hall, probably so that we wouldn't have to go somewhere else after the ceremony. Good planning by the staff of the Cultural Affairs Department, for it had been raining for the last half-hour. To one side, where they usually have the coatroom, a kind of buffet with sandwiches and such had been set out. The guests were supposed to help themselves.

I was sitting at a table with the mayor and his wife and the secretary-general of the Industrial Federation. I could not refuse. Max had told me that I would have to stand in for him, that was my job. Otherwise I'm sure I would have left. I knew these people pretty well, but I hadn't the least desire to spend any time with them. And now it was too late for me to leave; I would have been conspicuous.

Our table was in the front row. There was nothing between us and the buffet except a blue-gray rug. The guests walked back and forth, helping themselves to food. They talked to each other, and when they ran into someone they knew, they bowed—cautiously, because of the plates in their hands.

I threw my fur coat over the back of my chair. It was warm enough. I had no intention of staying very long. I crumbled the program I was still holding, but the paper was stiff and snapped open again. I would have had to tear it up, but where to put the scraps? The crinkled paper unfolded in such a way that the name Möncken, printed in boldface, barely showed.

Yes, and he was standing at the buffet with the redheaded Frau Riebow. Both of them were laughing.

She asked him, "Did everything you write about really happen to you?"

And he answered, "What can you be thinking of, my dear lady? All those women and girls! How could I possibly have managed it all?" He was capable of giving such an answer, though that sort of repartee did not suit him in the least.

And she replied, "My husband is head of the press section."

And he responded, "Oh, then I'll have to keep on your good side."

That's what they were laughing about. But how she

2

carried on! I could hear her phony laugh as I sat at the table. She was also made up to the hilt, the paint much too obvious in the fluorescent light. "She's only been a redhead for three months," I told him later. "A fine ornament," he remarked. He did not care, but that was something I couldn't know. After all, I didn't know him at all. I was afraid he would fall for her.

"What may I get you, my dear lady?" the secretary-general asked.

I told him to pick out something, not much. I wasn't hungry. The mayor's wife said what a pity it was that my husband couldn't be there.

The mayor had said the same thing to me earlier; they had to say something of the sort. I answered that my husband was very sorry too, but he would not be back in town until late tonight; he had an important conference in Kassel.

"I see, in Kassel," the mayor said, raising his eyebrows. I don't know why, probably just to be polite. He could not possibly have any interest in Max's conference in Kassel.

I watched the secretary-general go to the buffet. He nodded to Frau Riebow, and he must have said something to her as well. How affected she was as she made a half-turn in his direction!

The secretary-general also nodded cordially to Möncken, I could see. But Möncken jerkily sketched a comic little bow, as if he were startled and had never seen the secretary-general before. And yet they had talked together earlier, had shaken hands. The secretary-general had extended his congratulations.

Of course I was the only one to see it all. The mayor inquired what my husband had said about the jury's selection and whether he was in agreement.

Yes, totally, I answered, adding that Max thought it quite wonderful how the whole thing had been arranged. It was none of their business that Max hadn't given it a moment's thought. I believe he did not even know the recipient's name. Max had other things on his mind; it was not important who won the prize. Only the prize itself—and that it had been endowed at his suggestion; that was very important to him. It was an advertisement for him. Or for his business.

Yes, and then the mayor's wife talked about the book by this man Möncken, and I said yes to everything. I had read it, but that didn't matter one way or the other now. I had to answer the way Max would have wanted. Frau Riebow's goings-on over at the buffet were no concern of mine. I intended leaving soon anyway.

He was thinking exactly the same thing; I could not know that. He felt as if he'd accidentally wandered into a movie in which he didn't have a part, he explained to me later. "That sort of thing can easily happen if you don't watch out. Yes, you've got to be on your guard all the time. And sometimes it's your own fault, because you think you can safely take part for once, just like other people. Yes, why not, after all? It's terrifically exciting. You have to act as if you really belonged all the time, so no one will notice. Because it might be a very nice movie, and you don't want to be a spoilsport. Above all, it's important not to stand aside and pull a long face. You have to keep on grinning, or they'll notice right away. But it makes you very jittery. Do you know the feeling?"

"Oh, yes, only too well."

"You see, you see," he shouted. "Yes, I talked to the right and I talked to the left, like I thought they wanted me to, and all I could think was, How can I get out of here before it's too late? They can eat their canapés without me just as well, and they can toast each other without me. Even better. If only a fuse would blow or there'd be some kind of row. Then one could get away secretly. But that kind of hope is always vain. Everybody was smiling at me; they thought that was how it was supposed to be. I was trapped. Then I saw you." Or maybe by then we were already speaking more familiarly to each other—I don't remember exactly.

"Did you notice?" he asked.

"What?"

"The moment I discovered you."

"Yes. I mean . . . ."

"And do you know what it was I saw first?"

"What?"

"But you mustn't get angry. Your shoulders."

"The dress is cut a little too low for the afternoon," I agreed. "But my husband thought it was right that way."

"Who?" he asked.

"What did she tell you about me?" I asked.

"She—who?" He was puzzled and astonished.

"The redhead."

"She told me your name, but I've forgotten it already. Oh, yes, and that you're rich."

"I'm not rich. My husband may be, but I'm not. She lied on purpose."

"What do we care about the redhead!"

But I have to tell the story in order. We had this conversation much later, at home or on the train. And perhaps even later than that.

The secretary-general returned with plates or with cocktails. The mayor said that he had missed his true calling and that the world had lost a great waiter. Everyone laughed at his joke; even I tried.

"Frau Riebow is monopolizing our author," the secretary-general said.

"Well, then he's in good hands," the mayor's wife assured us.

I gave no sign. But she had not meant it nastily; she didn't know how to be nasty. She was really very maternal; I liked her a lot.

5

"Ah, yes, these creative types," the mayor said. "They have a way with them."

Everyone looked over at the buffet. Then they talked about a play, and then about the exhibition that was to come to town next month. I had to give my opinion on everything.

Ten minutes more, I thought, then I'll get up and somehow excuse myself. "They think you're arrogant," my husband had told me more than once. "That's not good, we cannot afford that. Times have changed, and you must pay more attention to others; you never know when they may be of use to us." Sometimes I believe even Max thinks I'm stuck-up.

At the other tables, too, there was much laughter and chatter. I drank my cocktail and concentrated on fishing out the olive.

But that small, jerky movement he had—I'd noticed it earlier, during his lecture. I'd come a little late and had taken a seat way at the back, so as not to interrupt the proceedings. At the end of the ceremony they rushed up to me and apologized; seats had been reserved for Max and me in the front row. I said it didn't matter, but I hope Max never finds out; it might make him angry at me again. He's very ambitious.

The first speaker was the secretary-general, who talked about the literature prize that was being awarded by the Industrial Federation for the first time this year. Our name was not mentioned, only the Industrial Federation. Max did not want to be named. The whole thing would have to be anonymous, he had said. Many of them already knew that he had instituted the prize and that the money was donated by Helldegen, Inc. And perhaps Max did not want to commit himself.

Then the mayor talked about the city and said that we were not just another industrial town with air polluted by factory smokestacks—that we also considered it a duty to stand alongside other cities that were of

6

similar size and population and furthered the arts. Or something like that. Everyone applauded. And that, he continued, was why he was delighted to be allowed to represent the city in awarding the prize of the Industrial Federation to Berthold Möncken, the eminent author. He reached down from the dais and pulled up Möncken, who was moving toward him. Then he handed him a red-velvet box containing the prize. Berthold told me later that they always use red-velvet boxes when they hand out awards. He placed it in his briefcase, and that night, when we were in the train, he threw the box out the window, laughing. He tore up the prize certificate and threw it out too. I thought you were supposed to keep that sort of thing, but he said it was always the same twaddle.

After the mayor, Berthold himself stepped behind the lectern to talk. I was a little surprised. Since he had been sitting in the front row, I hadn't been able to see him earlier. At first I even thought that it wasn't him at all and that someone else was speaking, because he looked exactly like all the others, with his dark suit and the way his hair was cut. I'd never have believed that he wrote books. He could just as easily have been someone in Max's office or an official of the Industrial Federation. I don't really know what I had expected. Probably nothing at all, and now that I know him, I feel very foolish. Berthold made fun of me, too. "How are we supposed to look? Do you want us to wear velvet trousers and plaid shirts? Bohemianism is something only others can afford, those who have nothing to do with art. An artist's life is messy enough as it is."

I did not listen to his speech. Presumably he thanked them for giving him the prize. I felt a little tired, perhaps because it was spring. But lectures always make me tired; my eyelids start burning, probably from staring at the dais, and to keep others from noticing, I look at my lap or at the program and think about something else. Most of the time what they're saying doesn't matter anyway, and if you really care, you can read it in the paper the following day. But it's a fact that if you think of something else and pay no attention to what is being said, the voice makes you even sleepier. The voice floats around you and through the auditorium, the seats creak softly, and there's the rustle of paper. None of it has anything to do with you, and that's why it's tiring. And sometimes the air in that kind of lecture hall is very stale, too.

Of course I did not fall asleep. "What does the artist have to do with the highly touted preservation of human existence?" I heard him say, and I heard only because he sounded so scornful. "When any one of us warns you about the shining facade, about statistics and the smooth functioning that fails in the face of even a single small human gesture—then he is called a nihilist."

A white-haired little old man with a very pointed nose was sitting next to me. Someone from the newspaper. Though I'd seen him before at other events, I did not know his name. He breathed through his nose, and I asked him in a whisper, "How old do you think he is?"

The little old man stared attentively at the dais, taking his time, and I was beginning to think that he would not answer. Finally he shrugged his shoulders. "He looks extremely unmarried." In order to whisper to me, he held his hand to his mouth. He had bad breath. Perhaps he had digestive problems.

I paid no further attention to him—I felt insulted. After all, that was not what I'd asked him. No sooner do you say something to a stranger, thinking nothing of it, than he starts to take liberties. And there's always the chance that it will get a mention in the newspaper. But surely he had not meant it that way. Because the opinion he whispered to me was absolutely right. Funny that a man would spot something like that; it really was

8

quite impossible to think of Berthold as married. I bet the Riebow woman noticed right away.

I pretended to be listening intently to his speech. And I began to see that he was quite different from what I had thought at first. I even felt a little sorry for him. Not a lot, no, but a little like when you stand at a window in the stairwell and look out at the boys playing in the courtyard below. When I was little, I often stood and watched. My mother would not let me go down and join them; the boys were not refined enough for her taste. My father probably would have let me, but he didn't know, and there wasn't much he could have done if he had known.

Well, one of the boys was rejected by the others; they wouldn't let him play. They shoved him away, made fun of him, and finally acted as if he weren't there. Maybe they had quarreled or something. The boy stood in the corner of the yard and busied himself with something else, acting as if he didn't care. Oh, but how much he wanted to play with the others! Sometimes he squinted in their direction when they weren't looking, but when they ran past him, he acted busy with his own affairs. And later, when his mother called him in to supper, it meant a lost afternoon in his life.

Something like that. You get a good view of all that from the stairwell window. The boy had no idea that anyone was standing there. Nor did Berthold know that I was watching him. Otherwise . . . after all, he did not even know I existed.

You see, he had little gestures that were quite separate from what was going on. The people in the front rows probably never noticed and thought everything was all right. But our seats were much higher, and we had a bird's-eye view of the dais. Sometimes it was his hand; it shot out abruptly, as if to reach for something, to clutch it. But it did not get far; it was immediately ordered back and fastened to the edge of the reading stand. And I think he constantly shifted his weight from one foot to the other and twisted his legs behind the stand. A couple of times he cast a desperate look into a corner of the auditorium, as if searching for something. But there was no one there he knew.

I was afraid that he would lose his train of thought, and in fact he had already come to a standstill and had even forgotten entirely that he was there on the dais to make a speech. Even so, the words kept coming from his lips without hesitation, except that it seemed to me that it was no longer he who was speaking; he himself was standing to one side, far, far away, and had given it all up as lost.

Then he pulled himself together and bowed to the people in the front rows. "Science will refute my words with the claim that a flower blooms even if no one is there to see it. I, on the other hand, claim that the flower will blush with pleasure when you look at it in admiration. And I believe that a woman grows more beautiful when you tell her, 'You are beautiful.' "

The silly women in the audience laughed. They thought he was flattering them, but he wasn't even looking at them. He'd thought the whole thing up at home and learned it by heart. Oh, I was angry.

"Show us your beautiful, human face again, and our song will grow more beautiful." That was the end. He bowed jerkily into the void. The flashbulbs flickered and the people applauded. I was pained.

"And how is our Chairman of the Board?" I heard the mayor ask.

"My father-in-law is very well, thank you," I said.

"We haven't seen him for such a long time," the mayor continued.

"Yes, I asked him to come with me today," I lied. "But he's past seventy."

What else could I have said? It always made me

10

uncomfortable when people asked about my father-in-law. I never knew what was behind the question or whether they were trying to pump me. It had been this way for six months now. I had to be on my guard all the time not to say the wrong thing, something that would harm Max. And I somehow felt that what Max had told me about the incident wasn't the entire truth either. Of course I could not tell him so. Yes, I really liked my father-in-law very much, an affection Max did not suspect.

Surely the people had no evil motives when they asked about my father-in-law. After all, the founder of Helldegen, Inc., was an important man in the town. And what else was there to talk about when you were just gathered casually like this?

Yes, and then it happened.

Now it seems to me as if I was already prepared. It would even have been a disappointment to me if it hadn't happened. Of course I could not know that it would happen the way it did. But I could imagine it more or less, and I wasn't surprised. Wouldn't I have been surprised if I hadn't expected it? But it was almost as if Berthold and I had only parted temporarily to talk to other people—he to the Riebow woman, and I to the mayor—and when he came back to me, I had only to say, "Oh, there you are."

Yet he didn't even know who I was and what my name was. And how was he to recognize me? There were a lot of women there, wives of industrialists and wives of officials. Just like me, they shared little tables with their acquaintances, sipping their cocktails. I could have been any one of them; nothing distinguished me from them. Except that they were cheerfully chattering, and I was sad. Something was constricting my chest. And the table was so small, the people so close to me; when they accidentally touched me, I started.

It isn't easy to tell. Either no one will believe me,

or they'll all think it's silly. Actually it makes sense to me that they find it silly. I can understand that more easily than I can understand what happened. But I had to accept it; I had no choice.

All that time I hadn't lost sight of Berthold. Even as I was talking to other people, I kept my eyes on him. I missed none of his movements. I saw that he emptied several glasses and that the Riebow woman drank right along. I too asked for a second drink, and when I finished it quickly, the secretary-general placed a third drink in front of me. They thought I was having a good time, and that must have pleased them. Max would have been pleased with me too; he always said, "You have to go along to get along."

A couple of times I thought perhaps Berthold was looking at me—and that frightened me. I couldn't bear it. The others mustn't notice. But when I looked up again, he had already turned away. So I had been mistaken. Perhaps he was just staring into the void as he had done earlier, during his lecture, when he really could not have seen me. Besides, he was standing with the Riebow woman, chatting. But finally, after it had happened repeatedly, I decided that he definitely was looking over at me.

Yes, and then he moved as if he were pushing away from the buffet. No, it even looked as if he were pushing the Riebow woman aside. I almost laughed. Probably all he said to her was "Excuse me a moment, please." I bet she was annoyed. But that's beside the point now.

He headed right for me, very slowly and naturally, looking neither right nor left. But how long it took—it was endless. He walked straight on the bluish-gray runner.

Abruptly it grew dark all around; the only light was a pale glow along the line where he moved closer. I did not know whether the light extended to where I sat or whether I was in the dark as well. I reached backward for my fur coat draped over the chair, but then I stopped. It was too late.

I picked up my cocktail glass and stood. "Excuse me," I said to the mayor's wife. Yes, that's how cunning I was. Let her think that I wanted to offer him my congratulations. I had to be considerate of Max. Anyway, I wanted to preserve the amenities as long as I could. Why? It was entirely possible that I'd met Berthold before, and since Max had donated the prize, it was only proper for me to congratulate the recipient.

I walked a few steps toward him, hurrying to get on the runner and away from the table. Everything behind me was submerging. I smiled, I think, but then I stopped; for Berthold was not smiling. In fact, the moment was not appropriate for smiles.

And then we stood facing each other, fairly close. It seemed safer that way, for just as the table sank behind me when I left it, everything else around us now wavered and floated like tatters of fog, barely brushing us; only where we stood was there firm ground.

I wanted to say something to him right away. That was the only thought I had managed to take with me to that spot. I wanted to be the first to speak, so that he would not make a mistake. I wanted to raise my glass and congratulate him; then he would have had to thank me. But I could not get any words to cross my lips; everything seemed so unnecessary.

I simply waited, staring at his tie; it was a gray tie, pale gray silk, the kind everyone wore with a dark suit. The tie had slipped a little to one side, and if I hadn't been holding the glass, I would have straightened it. But where could I have set down the glass? There was no longer a table, and the glass would have fallen into the void.

I'm sure we didn't stand there long; it just seems that way now. For us it was an eternity. When such moments are over, you always long to have them back again, and nothing else suffices afterward. But the world knows nothing.

"You're someone worth dying with," he said. It was as if I'd said it myself, although I would never have used those words. But now it seemed that my own voice was coming back to me. The words were precisely right—to say anything else would have been wrong—and that was why I only said, "Yes."

And I looked at him. I saw his face.

It was the first time I had seen his face. You couldn't always see it, just when you were lucky. He had more than one face. Some that he showed and that all resembled each other and that you could photograph, when he talked to people, to the mayor or the Riebow woman, or walked down the street. I don't know where he got them all—so quickly it could drive you mad. These were faces that looked good, clever faces, alert ones, scornful ones, but all of them shoddy, appearing fleetingly, for just a moment, before they were cast off and new faces were tried on.

But the other face could not be described or photographed. No camera was quick enough. It only existed in the spaces between, only appeared when he changed the other faces, blurred, so that no one noticed. And even if someone had noticed, he would not have taken it for the true face; he'd prefer to think he'd made a mistake.

But I knew that it was the true face, I knew at once. I'd known it even before, and I'd been afraid of seeing it. Not that it hurt—oh, no; but it was so defenseless that it made you totally defenseless too. You lost all sense of yourself; it was almost unbearable. I had to look away quickly.

How alone we were. Altogether outside and alone. I shivered. A pity I hadn't taken my fur coat after all. It's cold here, I thought. Have they suddenly turned off the heat?

14

Out of the corner of my eye I could see that a great deal was swimming around us, outside. Heads and bodies bobbed in their clothes, and when they were swept in close to us, they were bathed in the light we shed. I could even see eyes, wide-open eyes, staring in astonishment at the windowpane. But only for seconds. There was no stopping; the tide inexorably swept them on. Nothing could touch us. There was a gentle roar out there that was no concern of ours either, caused by the waves, by some breeze or other, or by voices.

"I've had three cocktails," I said.

"I drank five of those things," he replied. "That's all they serve here. What does that have to do with us?"

"Where is your coat?" I asked.

"Coat? What coat?"

"Surely you wore a coat."

Finally he understood. "Outside, on the coatrack. My briefcase, too. Come on."

"Act as if it was all planned beforehand," I suggested.

"But why? Everything is clear as day."

"No, I have to get my fur. It's hanging over my chair there. And my purse is still on the table. No, wait," I said. I meant to run back to the table and grab my things. How impatient he was, like a child. "We can't do it your way. Be polite to the people. Shake hands with them and thank them for everything. That's all that's required. I'll think up an excuse."

From then on I had to keep an eye on him; that was my job. And I think we carried it off all right. We held out our hands, and the others, the people on the outside, shook them. Quickly we pulled our hands back. I said that we had to go home, and they probably heard us, but I didn't care. Except when Berthold helped me into my coat, he behaved clumsily. Nothing was quick enough for him. He almost tore off the collar in his haste to pull the coat up when I'd finally found the armholes.

It would have been better if I'd just carried the coat and put it on later, but you can't think of everything.

Then we had to make our way to the door. I took very small steps on purpose, forcing him to adapt to my pace. And all the time it was important to smile the way people smile when they're leaving. But Berthold tore open the door so violently that it flew out of his hand and crashed into the wall.

Outside, on the landing, they had put up two coat-racks, and there was a woman to watch the belongings. "That one over there," Berthold said, rapping a coin against the table. "And my briefcase, please. It's standing against the wall over there. No, not that one—the one over there."

He had a raincoat with a detachable lining, very dirty along the collar and the sleeves. He did not have a hat, only a cap in his pocket, which fell on the tiles when he took out his gloves. He picked it up, shook it, and stuck it back in his pocket.

"Could you get us a taxi?" I asked the uniformed guard who stood by the revolving door. The man ran outside at once and began to wave his arms. The cabs must have been waiting to pick up business, for by the time we stepped outside, one was already at the door. Several drivers were standing by the entrance, smoking. They went with the private limousines and were waiting for their masters.

It was happenstance that I had arrived in a cab. Max had taken the big car, and someone else needed the small car, or else it was in the repair shop. I'd been annoyed at the time, but now I was glad. A taxi was much better, the way things had turned out. I told the driver the address, speaking past Berthold as he climbed in behind me. The driver closed the door, took his place behind the wheel, turned on the meter, and drove off.

It must have been around six thirty or seven. The

ceremony had begun at five. It had rained some more in the meantime. The streetlamps must have just come on. The roads were shiny, and the light was reflected in the pavement.

"Where are you hauling me off to?" Berthold asked at my side without looking at me.

"Home."

"Home?"

"I have to go home first. There's no other way."

Then we were silent. And I came to my senses.

What had I started here? An hour ago—no, half an hour ago—I'd known nothing about any of this. Nothing of the sort had even occurred to me. All had been order and security, and it could still be that way; the decision was up to me. I was sitting next to a total stranger, someone who meant nothing to me and with whom I had no idea what to do now. And it was all my fault, not his; after all, I hadn't been forced to walk toward him, I hadn't been forced to respond. Instead, I was hauling him away, as he put it. Was he reproaching me already?

Yes, I had behaved the way you behave only in dreams, when there's nothing else you can do. Even thinking about it is no help because everything happens by itself, and the only way you can save yourself is by waking up. Then, when you wake up, you're exhausted from the effort, or you're sad because it was only a dream and real life can never be that way. In real life you always have to be so considerate. But the dream is something no one else ever knows about; it remains your secret, and you forget about it yourself as the day wears on. You get up, you shower and dress, still trembling a little because you keep thinking back to it. Then you go downstairs to breakfast, and the others ask, "Did you sleep well?" And for them it's as if nothing at all had happened.

Should I tap the driver on the shoulder and ask him

to stop the car and then ask Berthold to get out? "Yes, see you again soon. Thank you for coming part of the way with me." Or should I drive him to the railroad station? But I didn't know if that was where he wanted to go. Or to his hotel? Which hotel? No, that wouldn't do either. What would he think of me?

I did not know what to say to him, I knew him so little. I didn't even know what to call him. For Berthold is only what I call him now, not then—no, it took a long time before I called him that. And I didn't want to call him Herr Möncken. How silly the name sounds. He wouldn't have been the same person if I'd called him that, not the same man I'd taken along, who was sitting in the taxi with me. I almost believe that if I'd done that, he would have thought I was addressing the driver.

I was cold with perplexity. If only he had said something, the whole thing would have been easier. Instead he sat in his corner staring straight ahead, and I couldn't see his face—that's what it was. Whenever we drove past a streetlight, there was a pale shimmer to my right, no more. I don't know what I expected. Perhaps I thought that he'd put his arm around me right away and pull me close, or something of the sort. Yes, now it seems to me that that's what I was afraid of—and of course I would have had to let him. But it was good that he made no move in that direction. Otherwise he would have been like all the other men, and the reason I'd gone away with him was that he was different.

"Are you cold?" he asked.

"No. Why?"

"Because you're clutching your coat around your knees."

"It's just that I'm a little exhausted," I said.

"Me too. Having to make a speech always leaves me shaky. My legs shake inside my trousers, but no one notices because they're all listening to my lecture . . . . What an ugly city this is."

18

"Yes, it isn't very pretty, but we have some beautiful wooded country to the south."

"Have you always lived here?"

"No, I come from Uelzen."

"Uelzen? I've never been there. The train passes through, mostly at night. Then you can hear them on the platform calling out, 'Uelzen.' "

"There's not much to see there. It's a tiny town."

"I'll buy a used Volkswagen," he said abruptly.

"Yes?"

"That way one can take off at once if one doesn't like it where one is. Drive off to Uelzen, for example. We could take off for Uelzen right away."

I laughed.

"Why are you laughing? Wouldn't you like to go to Uelzen?"

"No, not really. Not there," I said. "What business do we have in Uelzen?"

He was silent. Then he asked, "Tell me, are you a fine lady?"

I did not know what the question meant or what answer I should give.

But then he laughed a little. "I really do believe that you are a fine lady."

"No." I was angry at him. "I don't even know what you mean."

We were silent again. I was wondering what to tell Max and what he would say. Perhaps he'd be pleased that I was bringing this man home. In any case, nothing was as bad as I'd feared at first. And if the people in the art gallery had noticed anything, the fact that he was a guest in our home would silence them.

"Perhaps the word is a little trite," he said slowly, almost as a question.

"Excuse me?"

"The word *fine*."

"Let's just forget it," I said.

"Don't get mad. You do have something about you, something rare. Anyone would notice right away upon meeting you in a crowd."

We were coming to the old railroad overpass. There is a curve just behind it, and the cabbie was driving very carefully. The road was still a little slippery from the rain. A lot of accidents had happened right here; the city wanted to make improvements, but there wasn't enough money, so they had put up warning signs. During the Occupation the center pier had borne a sign with a big skull, and under it the legend DEATH IS SO PERMANENT. Max swore each time we passed it, and each time I laughed at him.

On the main road, the car picked up speed. The pavement ahead was empty, with only a garland of bluish-white lights across the street, and in the far distance a streetcar.

"Do you know what I'd like?" he asked. For the first time he turned halfway to face me. He even raised his left hand a little, and I thought he was going to put it on my knee. Perhaps that was his intention—yes, perhaps he thought I was angry and he'd have to bring me around. But then his hand dropped again.

"Well?" I asked.

"I'd like to go with you to a city—not here, and it doesn't have to be Uelzen—to some city or other, it doesn't matter. Of course, it shouldn't be too small. Yes, and I'd like to walk with you through the main shopping streets, and we'll stop at every shopwindow—holding hands, of course; and as we walk, our . . . hips . . . touch." He slapped his hand against his thigh. "Yes, and then we'll go to a restaurant or to the theater, and the people in the lobby will be dumbfounded."

"Why should they be dumbfounded?" I asked, just to say something.

"Wait and see. They'll break off their conversations in mid-sentence; all heads will turn to stare at us, men

20

and women. How did a guy like him get such a woman? they'll wonder. How?" he asked me.

"Well," I said. "I mean . . . ." I picked up my purse and looked for the keys.

"We're almost there?" he asked.

"Yes, it's not much farther."

Actually I wasn't looking for the keys but for cash. Perhaps he had no money except what they'd given him, and surely that was in the form of a check, which he couldn't use. And I was the one who'd ordered the cab without asking him first. All of it was very embarrassing. I intended, as soon as the taxi stopped, to secretly pass the fare to the driver, reaching across his shoulder. People with such jobs are generally quick and probably used to that kind of thing. I even had an explanation ready: that I'd hired the cab for the whole day and that the factory was paying for it.

But none of it was necessary. He had cash. He carried it loose in his jacket pocket.

We walked up the drive without speaking. Even when I unlocked the front door, we didn't say anything. He stood in the dark, one step below me. Through the frosted panes I could see that there was only a dim light in the living room. So Max was not back yet. Then the door opened. I walked in and flicked the switch in the vestibule. And he followed me, I heard his shoes rub against the scraper. I meant to turn on the light in the coatroom too, but suddenly it was so quiet behind me that I turned around, startled and afraid. Yes, he was in the vestibule, but he had squeezed way into the corner, right by the front door. And the door was ajar; he was still holding the knob.

We looked at each other. I wanted to ask him, "What is it?" but I couldn't manage it. He stood there like someone caught in the act.

"Please forgive me, my dear lady," he began. Oh, the pain that form of address caused me.

"You don't have time?" I asked quickly.

"Yes, perhaps I don't have time—that, too. I have to . . . . Please be reasonable—I have no business here!"

I went to the door and closed it firmly. I couldn't leave him standing there, so helpless. "Come, just put your coat on the chair over there. Surely you can spare me that much time. Of course you can leave soon."

He obeyed, but he moved very slowly. I watched and waited until he had placed his coat and briefcase on the chair. Then, walking ahead, I opened the vestibule door and turned on the light in the living room. "Come in."

Then I had to wait for him again. He turned off the light in the coatroom, then he looked for the switch in the vestibule. He was very neat. Or was he just stalling for time? Before I could say, "Just leave it," he had found the switch. Finally, he stood in the doorway to the living room, but he came no farther. Again we looked at each other, into each other's eyes. I didn't want to ask him again to come closer. If he had turned around then and walked away, I wouldn't have held him back. I don't even know how I could have held him back.

Slowly his glance slid away from me, first to the left, where the armchairs were placed, and then gradually to the right, around the living room to the stairs. I never took my eyes off him. There was no emotion in his face, but I saw what he saw. I saw with his eyes, and it was terrible. Suddenly everything was worthless, all the expensive things, just because he was seeing them. Everything obliterated, everything for show. How much money the things had cost; and yet so cheap. How proud Max was of them; and yet so cold and ridiculous. Like a stage set—everything just right; if you looked at it that way, everything was just as it should

22

be. But from somewhere a draft was blowing through the backdrop. And I'd accepted it all these years, I'd thought that was the way it had to be, I'd been content, I hadn't even noticed the cold wind. The place was always so well heated—how could I have noticed? But now I saw: everything was bare. Fear seized hold of me; what I really wanted to do was run to him. Yes, let's leave quickly, quickly.

Then his gaze held at the top of the stairs. He moved his head a little to indicate to me that there was something up there, and so I looked at the same place and saw Fräulein Gerda leaning against the bronze banister, standing where the stairs turned into a balcony. Max had had it built that way only three years earlier, when the whole house was modernized. The staircase was his favorite part; it made him happy when visitors praised it, and I had been happy for him.

Yes, Fräulein Gerda stood there in her nurse's uniform, holding a tray, staring down at us. There were thick carpets everywhere—how were we supposed to have heard her? So I don't know how long she had been watching us. I don't even know how long we had been standing there. Maybe it was only an instant.

"Good evening. Did my husband call?" I asked her.

And she said, "Good evening, Frau Helldegen," and yes, he had called, Herr Blanck had spoken with him, and Herr Blanck was inside. She pointed to the door of the study, but she never stopped staring at Berthold, and I was annoyed.

I'd forgotten all about Blanck. "Fine," I said. "And tell Günther I'll be right there."

She went away, turning left toward the nursery, but first she looked around once more. She's not a bad person, just terribly tactless and probably not too bright, even though she's a registered nurse.

"Is someone ill?" Berthold asked. He was still

standing in the doorway. He had not taken another step into the room.

"No, why? Oh, you mean her uniform? She's . . . but does it matter? If you're planning to leave at once anyway?" I stepped close to him to at least get another look at him. "I don't want to keep you. I understand. Really."

He did not move from the spot, he only looked at me. Finally he said, "I'll write to you."

"Write?"

"Shall I write to you here? Here?" And he looked around the living room again. "And I don't even know your name."

"Why would you want to write to me?"

"To explain everything. So you won't think . . . ." He faltered and looked at me, perplexed.

I couldn't think of any way out, either. "What's the matter with you?" I asked. "Why have you changed?"

"I'm always like this," he said softly. We were both whispering, not because of Fräulein Gerda—we weren't thinking of her. It just came out that way.

"You were different before," I said.

He shook his head.

"Yes, you were. Altogether different. Is it that you're afraid?" It seemed to me that he started the slightest bit, but I may have been mistaken. "But afraid of what? Of me? Of this house?"

And that may have been something I shouldn't have asked; his eyes flickered back and forth, as if looking for an escape. I should not have asked it for my own sake, either; I myself was afraid, and now I became aware of it, and the realization drove me on. The only thing I didn't know was what I was afraid of—exactly what I was asking him.

As a rule I'm not a fearful person. It must have been his fear that seized hold of me even though I didn't know what it was. It was some obliterating quality in

24

him that made me fearful. By the way he stood in the doorway, reluctant to come in, he was trying to obliterate himself, and if he had succeeded, he would have obliterated me and the house and everything.

Any moment might be the end, leaving only the memory of . . . not of a dream; a dream dissipates like cigarette smoke or like a headache . . . no, of another lost possibility, of the only other possibility. And something like that does not vanish like a headache; something like that stays with you until you perish of it, and it turns everything that comes after into a meaningless substitute.

Into an unbearable substitute—yes. But at the time I could not have explained it the way I can now. And perhaps even now that isn't the correct explanation but only another rationalization.

But is it important to explain this sort of thing? At the time I only knew that it was up to me, and only me, to salvage something, and that I did not have to be clever and I did not have to be cunning—yes, altogether, that it was not important to hold him but only to be entirely myself, very honest, very much the way we aren't ordinarily allowed to be because it is not the usual way and it shocks people.

"Can't I help you?" I asked because I couldn't think of anything else. And when he shook his head, I went on. "Why can't I help you? Is it my fault?"

Again he shook his head. "No, it has nothing to do with you. I'll write to you."

"But why write? I don't want a letter, I want to know now."

"Writing is better," he said.

"Earlier, you were different. Earlier, everything was natural and easy. I understood you at once, I went away with you at once. Don't you even remember what you said to me? You said something to me that no one ever said to me before—at least not in that way. And

I understood you at once, wasn't surprised, wasn't out-raged—it was as if I'd been waiting all my life for pre-cisely what you said, that's why. But you can't say something like that if you don't mean it; you can't do that—it's dangerous. Surely you know that. And you meant what you said; I could tell, otherwise I wouldn't have responded. And now? Now you stand there in the doorway and leave me standing over here, as if nothing at all had happened. And you want to run away and write to me. What good is your writing to me? I want . . . I don't know what I want, I only know that it can't be like this. Or was it merely a poetic expression?"

"I lost control," he said.

"Do you tell other women the same thing? The Riebow woman, for instance?"

"Who?"

"Never mind. No, of course I know you didn't say it to her. And she wouldn't have understood anyway; she would have laughed at you. But I . . . Why don't you say it again?" He shook his head vehemently. "Please. Please. Just that one sentence. Maybe I didn't hear you correctly. There was so much noise. Surely it wouldn't be any trouble to you, would it? Why not? Because if it was only a literary conceit—"

"Please stop," he whispered.

"No. Maybe I want to be able to remember it some-day when I'm sad. You could print it. There's no harm in printing a literary conceit; no one feels personally affected by it. But me . . . it's different with me. I want to be able to tell myself, One single time someone said to me . . . shall I repeat it for you?"

"No. It's not something we're allowed to say."

"Really? But you did say it—to me. How did that happen? And why shouldn't I be allowed to say the same thing to you?"

"Please don't. Not now."

"Not now? When, then?"

"It was a mistake . . . . No, please, words are dangerous. Words are much more dangerous than you think. I know, believe me, it's my profession. Please let me go now."

"Right away, sir, right away. But you can't get off that easy. Before you go, I want to know precisely what you said to me. I want to hear it one more time, and I want you to hear it one more time, so that neither of us can forget it or remember the wrong sentence. What you said to me was—"

He raised both his hands. I thought that he wanted to place them over my lips, and that was indeed what he planned, but he did not dare; he was even more afraid of touch than of words. And if he had, I would have spoken into his palm, and that would have meant even more than saying the words into air. Yes, I was so sure of myself that I stepped even closer to him and offered my lips to make it easier for him. And still he did not dare.

"What you said to me was . . . ." And I smiled. I could not help but smile, for suddenly everything was quite natural and easy again, and his face had returned as well—his real face. He was no longer warding off what I insisted on. "You're someone worth dying with."

The silence returned, the same silence that had enfolded us earlier, in the art gallery. Just the two of us and nothing else. There's no way to talk about it.

At that moment Günther came running from the nursery, barefoot and wearing his light-blue pajamas, calling, "Mama!" He had slipped away from Fräulein Gerda, and she came up behind him and took him by the hand before he could climb up on the balustrade.

"Just a minute, darling. Just a minute," I called. "Be a good boy and go to bed. Mama will be with you in a minute."

27

We watched the two until they were gone. Then we looked at each other.

"Well?" I asked.

"I didn't know," he said.

"Now you know," I said. "Yes, I have to go up and say good night to him, or he won't go to sleep. When does your train leave?"

"My train? But—"

"We can talk about it later if we need to. We'll have plenty of time. But now . . . all right, then, how about your train?"

"Quarter past eleven."

"Do you have your ticket?"

"Yes. Second class. A round-trip ticket. They gave it to me."

"Fine. If necessary, we can get another on the train. Why are you looking at me like that? Quarter past eleven? That means leaving here at ten thirty. So we have plenty of time. Do you have the money?"

"What money?"

"What they gave you. The prize, I mean."

"Yes, I've got it here." He patted his breast pocket.

I could not help laughing. "What a good thing that we've got the money right now. Or would you rather I didn't travel with you?"

He did not know what to say. He had stopped being on the defensive.

"Come on, sit down somewhere. You've got time to think about it. In any case, we have to do some sensible thinking now. And don't worry about me. There's no need to. I know what I'm doing. All right, and now—wait, I have to talk to Blanck first."

I went to the study. Blanck was at the desk, so he hadn't been eavesdropping. He jumped to his feet at once and came outside.

"My husband called?" I asked, not bothering to say hello to him first. Then I remembered that the two had not met, and I made the introductions. "Herr Blanck, my husband's right hand. And this is Herr Möncken. Berthold Möncken. You've heard of him. . . . Well, what did he say? When will my husband be home?"

It took an effort not to laugh in Blanck's face, everything was so easy. I couldn't stand Blanck, and I was always very short with him. He had never done me any harm, and he was extremely competent, according to Max, who thought the world of him. Perhaps that was precisely what made me contrary. I found him repulsive from the first, and I avoided even shaking hands with him; it didn't bother me that I was rude. For his part, he did not notice—or preferred not to notice. He was always very proper—his suits, his bows, his way of answering every question. Nothing of his own, everything the way Max liked it. And his alert brown eyes behind the dark horn-rimmed glasses. And the good-sized birthmark at his temple. I believe he even used the same aftershave lotion as Max, and I didn't like it on Max.

Sometimes Blanck and his wife came to dinner because Max considered it proper to invite them. His wife suited him; everything imitation and ambition. Darting, hard little eyes that missed nothing and sharp, disapproving corners to her mouth. And what exaggerated, honeyed politeness. What could the two of them possibly talk about as they lay in bed at night? Of the next rung they would climb?

I could not say such things to Max. Even his father's remarks invariably annoyed him. "Let's ask Herr Blanck," my father-in-law said whenever we were discussing anything. "He always knows best." And he stressed the word *Herr* with a twinkle in his eye meant for me— even though I'd never talked about Blanck with my father-in-law. What business was he of mine, anyway? I had nothing to do with him. If he was useful to Max in his business, so much the better. It had nothing to do with me.

Blanck informed me that "President Helldegen" would be home around eight, having already eaten. He, Blanck, had taken the liberty of giving the appropriate instructions to the staff.

Around eight. I looked at my watch and then at the English grandfather clock. "We have another half-hour then. Would you excuse me a moment, Herr Möncken? I must put my little boy to bed. I'll be right back. I'm sure Herr Blanck will keep you company until then."

I came close to laughing out loud. The two of them were so funny, standing there. I couldn't imagine what they'd find to talk about. Even Blanck would have trouble thinking of something. I was tempted to ask Blanck if he too would like to die with me. But of course I didn't; it wouldn't have been fair to Berthold. "And if you'd like a drink, Herr Blanck will show you where we keep the stuff," I added as I went up the stairs.

All in all, it was a good thing that Blanck stayed with him while I was gone. That way he could not run from me.

I also sent Fräulein Gerda downstairs, to be rid of her. She was all excited as she asked, "Wasn't that Berthold Möncken?"

I said yes and refused to be drawn into her chatter. I couldn't have endured it just then. I had to be alone. Because I really did not feel as cheerful as I'd pretended to be downstairs.

Fräulein Gerda was only too happy to leave me. She wanted to meet the celebrated writer, she couldn't allow herself to miss such an opportunity. Oh, how stupid the whole thing was! Imagine their faces, hers and Blanck's, if they knew what this writer had said to me. They probably wouldn't even understand. Because I . . . perhaps I, too, had misunderstood.

30

But it wasn't so easy to embarrass Blanck; he was much too smooth and agile. He could come up with a whole slew of polite phrases. He began by . . . .

Should that part be told at all? Now, in retrospect, all of it seems so trivial. They really were just shopworn phrases, of no interest to anyone. All that concerned the two of them was to pass the time until my return. They could not stand around as if struck dumb, but they could just as easily have talked about something else; the result would have been the same. And possibly someone might think that I'm trying to make fun of them when I relate these idiocies. I'm not out to do that at all. I don't have the right.

At the time—that is, right afterward and even in the train—I was so excited that I wanted to know everything. Every word! I questioned Berthold until he grew annoyed. I suspected him of keeping something from me, so as not to upset me. He kept changing the subject and could not understand why I wanted to know all the details. It's true, it was of no importance to him; but I had to know where I stood. Finally Berthold said, "Let's just be glad that that's behind us." And of course he was right.

Well, then. Blanck began by congratulating Berthold on the prize. He could imagine, he said, that it must be a great satisfaction to any writer to see his work finally recognized publicly. Or words to that effect. Yes, Blanck must have said "finally," because Berthold laughed when he told me. "Where does the guy get off? I'm not all that old."

All in all, a splendid introduction by Blanck, except that Berthold did not give him the least help with it. He only muttered, "Yes," so that Blanck had to keep on talking at random. The President—meaning Max—had strongly advocated the prize, Blanck said; he had repeatedly emphasized that nowadays it was the duty of industry to support culture. Industry had to assume the role previously acted by the aristocratic Maecenases.

"Where do you suppose the fellow picked up that damned saying?" Berthold asked me scathingly. He meant Blanck, not Max.

And since Berthold only nodded, Blanck continued. It was truly admirable that a man as busy and under the strain of such responsibility as the President could still find the time to concern himself with such matters. Even Berthold found this admirable, and Blanck asked him if he would care for a drink. To show his eagerness, and probably also because he could not think of anything further to say, he ran at once to the antique cupboard into which Max had had a refrigerator built so that everything would always be on hand for guests. Max was quite smug about the practicality of this device. When the heavy, carved doors were opened, a light automatically came on inside. The refrigerator took up the right half, and on the left there were glasses of every size, olives, crackers, cheese straws, and all the rest, everything easily to hand.

But Berthold did not want a drink, and Blanck concurred: he did not feel like drinking either; there were still a few important documents he had to discuss with the President, nor had they yet gone over the following day's schedule. Whereupon Berthold begged him not to let him interrupt, but Blanck assured him that such was not the case; on the contrary, it was an honor . . . and so on and so on. And surely Herr Möncken was eager to express his gratitude to the President in person. Yes, he might do that, said Berthold, looking at his watch rather rudely. Hm, yes, Blanck said, the President had been away for a couple of days. A board meeting in Kassel, followed by a factory inspection. In general, the President had hardly a minute to himself, and Herr Möncken must understand . . . . Berthold, for his part, assured Herr Blanck that it was not his intention to rob the President of his precious time. But Blanck declared immediately that on the contrary, he had not meant it that way at all; the President was sure to be hugely pleased to shake hands with a representative of the life of the mind.

Fortunately for Blanck, Fräulein Gerda now came tripping down the stairs and immediately began to speak her piece. And once Fräulein Gerda started to talk, there was no stopping her. She went up to Berthold and gave him a hearty handshake. This was her usual practice, no matter whom she was greeting. And at the same time she looked at you so candidly and with such understanding that you were startled the first time, before you became used to her ways. Without stopping for breath, she explained to Berthold that she had never before seen a writer at such close range and that she was proud of the occasion and would tell her fiancé all about it. And that Herr Möncken looked quite different—why was that?—quite different from his picture.

"Which picture?" Berthold asked, appalled.

"The picture in the newspaper," Fräulein Gerda explained, pointing to the evening edition lying on the coffee table. She brought it over and held the picture up to Berthold, and Blanck was drawn into the discussion and was asked whether he hadn't imagined Herr Möncken to look quite different, much shorter, yes, very much shorter, and especially much older.

And Blanck had to take a stand whether he wanted to or not, but Berthold apologized earnestly. The picture was an old one, taken two years earlier; he didn't have his picture taken very often. The newspaper people must have had it in their files.

But she liked Herr Möncken much better in person, bubbled Fräulein Gerda, and she would give her fiancé Herr Möncken's book for his birthday. What a wonderful book—she'd been quite ravished by it. But her fiancé's birthday wasn't for another six weeks, and perhaps Herr Möncken would be willing to write something in her copy—a few words and his name. Her fiancé would . . . .

Yes, yes, that was quite all right, Berthold tried to interrupt, if she'd just give him the book. But of course she didn't have it with her, Fräulein Gerda cried. It was in her room on her night table; she'd been reading in it only last night and hadn't been able to go to sleep. So exciting, and she'd run to get it at once, would Herr Möncken be sure to wait until she . . . .

Then something happened that I hadn't counted on. Suddenly my father-in-law came down the stairs. All three stared at him in surprise. There was no way I could have foreseen such a development, since my father-in-law never went out at night. He had a room on the third floor, one of the guest rooms, with a view of the garden. He had chosen it himself, and he lived there quite isolated. He gave the rest of the house over to us. Max was not at all pleased that his father lived on the third floor, both because of his age and because people might think that Max had elbowed his father aside. But that was the way my father-in-law wanted it, and that's the way it had been for about six months. Since the fight he had with Max.

Now he was slowly making his way down the stairs; he always walked very slowly, though not because of his age—he was not much over seventy. It had simply always been that way, at least in the time I'd known him. He did not speak much, either, so you could not make him out right away. He rarely gave his opinion, but I believe that he was extremely observant. Nor had I ever heard an affectionate word from his lips; it was not his way. But all the same, I think we liked each other quite a bit.

Fräulein Gerda was the first to regain her voice. Was the Chairman planning to go out, she asked. "Yes, my child." That was his plan if she had no objection.

To the mailbox, suggested Fräulein Gerda. No, he could not recall having written a letter. She saw; just a little walk, was that it? Yes, quite right, once along the canal as far as the reservoir and back by way of the park. But the March air was treacherous, Fräulein Gerda observed. Shouldn't she fetch a muffler from upstairs for the Chairman of the Board? "Yes, my child, go ahead if you think it best."

Fräulein Gerda threw a questioning look at Blanck. Then she excitedly ran past my father-in-law and up the stairs.

Now it was Blanck's turn. Would the Chairman of the Board grant him the pleasure of introducing Berthold Möncken, the writer? Herr Möncken had been awarded the prize of the Industrial Federation.

"How much?" my father-in-law asked, turning to Berthold.

"Five thousand." Berthold laughed as he spoke.

"Is that a lot?"

"It will do for a while, thank you."

"Is it a love story?"

"No. Why? It's hard to say."

"Was my question so strange?"

"Not really, no . . . it took me by surprise."

"Hm."

The two of them must have understood each other from the first instant. No, that's a bad way of putting it. They did not understand each other—they came from such different worlds—but they liked each other. That, too, could not have been foreseen. I suspect that they spoke so oddly to each other because Blanck was standing there with them.

"In my day there was a well-known surgeon of the same name. He practiced in Frankfurt, if I'm not mistaken," my father-in-law noted.

"That was my father."

"He's no longer living?"

"No, he died six years ago."

"Hm . . . . My son hasn't come back yet?" He suddenly turned to Blanck.

"The President will be here in half an hour," Blanck replied.

"Hm." And turning back to Berthold, "To the best of my knowledge, this is the first time an author has set foot in this house."

"I am not here as an author," Berthold countered.

"Did I say something else wrong?"

"The title is a little embarrassing, that's all."

"Hm. An insecure field. Isn't that right, Herr Blanck?"

"I'm sorry, sir?"

"Actually, Herr Möncken, I understand that very well . . . . Ah, and here's my muffler."

Fräulein Gerda had stopped to get the book as well. She handed it to Berthold, and he immediately sat down at the coffee table and pulled out his fountain pen to write a few words—and perhaps also because he simply did not want to be standing around idly. For Fräulein Gerda was chattering away in a steady stream while my father-in-law tolerated her wrapping the muffler around his neck as though he were a child. She talked about the March air, which might do him harm; about the picture in the paper, which did not look like Herr Möncken at all; about the book she planned to give her fiancé; and about the fact that she had never before met a real writer and how significant an event it was in her life. And what did the Chairman of the Board have to say?

None of the three gentlemen had anything to say. Blanck would probably have preferred retiring to the study, but there was no pretext on which he could do so. My father-in-law was silent, and Berthold was writing. When he had finished, he snapped the book shut with a fair amount of noise and handed it to Fräulein

Gerda, who immediately stopped fussing with the muffler to reach for it, curious and tactless as she was, and see what Berthold had written.

This action silenced her for an instant. Perhaps she had difficulty making out Berthold's handwriting, which really was illegible. Berthold put on a grumpy expression and stared at the carpet. The whole situation made him uncomfortable. And then, after a short pause, the hue and cry broke out. Fräulein Gerda screeched with pleasure. Even I, upstairs with all the doors ajar, could hear her, and I wondered what it was all about.

"No, but how wonderful. My fiancé will be delighted. I'm so very grateful to you, Herr Möncken. Just look, sir." She handed my father-in-law the open book. He took it and, after a fleeting glance at Berthold, read the inscription. Berthold had written:

I was there when the world was made.
'Tis true we thought some things would be different;
And yet . . .

Just that, and the date and his name. I asked him later why he chose that quotation—it didn't suit Fräulein Gerda at all. He told me that it had first occurred to him to write, "Oh, Mother, why are we not animals?" Anyway, it didn't make any difference. He had a supply of tags from old poems, and when people asked him for an inscription, he just threw in one of them without giving much thought to whether it was suitable. It was hardly ever suitable anyway.

"And yet?" my father-in-law asked when he had finished reading.

"Yes," Berthold answered.

"Isn't it wonderful, sir?" cried Fräulein Gerda, her eyes shining.

"We'll have to ask Herr Blanck," my father-in-law said. "May I show it to Herr Blanck?"

Berthold gestured vaguely, but Blanck was deeply embarrassed. He had to come forward a few steps to take the book from my father-in-law, and he had to pretend to read the inscription with the most profound interest. He stuttered something about great depth and hidden meaning. He cleared his throat several times, but no one helped the poor fellow out. It must have been very funny.

"Nevertheless, if I had any say in the matter, I would endow a prize for a love story," my father-in-law said at last.

"That's an idea worth considering," Blanck interrupted immediately, happy to be able to change the subject.

"How do you mean?" My father-in-law raised his eyebrows.

"Your son, the President, could be won over to such a project," Blanck explained.

"Oh, yes, how wonderful, a love story," Fräulein Gerda cried, clapping her hands.

"Or do you feel that love stories are no longer . . . shall we say, no longer in style?" my father-in-law asked.

"I've never given the matter a thought" was Berthold's answer.

"Hm. In other words, such a question isn't proper to a man like myself?" And since Berthold did not reply, instead standing there like a naughty child, he added, "Because I was not there when the world was made."

Something in my father-in-law's voice must have startled Berthold. He looked up, started to speak, thought better of it, and gave a barely perceptible turn of his head toward Fräulein Gerda and Blanck.

My father-in-law smiled. "Who brought you here? My daughter-in-law?"

"She's upstairs. She's putting Günther to bed," Fräulein Gerda interposed.

38

"Hm. That means she'll be back in a moment to keep you company. All right, then, Herr Möncken . . . ."

"No, please, I beg your pardon," Berthold said abruptly. He even followed my father-in-law, who obligingly stopped. "You mustn't think that I know it all, just because I've written a couple of books."

"Hm. And you mustn't think that I know it all just because I'm twice your age. Well, then, we are agreed. Because the only one who knows it all is our Herr Blanck. All right."

And he left. Fräulein Gerda made as if to follow him, but first she looked questioningly at Blanck. He shook his head and said, "No need."

"Oh," said Fräulein Gerda.

Perhaps it was all for the best that I wasn't there. The whole thing would have been even more uncomfortable for Berthold, and it would have been hard for me to steer the conversation. There's no question that I would have sent Blanck away at once—but why think about it now? Sitting at the side of Günther's bed, I heard the mumble of voices downstairs, and I knew that they were making conversation and that Berthold was still there. I tried to think about myself as I waited for Günther to fall asleep.

I hadn't even taken off my coat because I did not want to waste time. I'd gone straight to the nursery, so as to get back to the living room as quickly as possible. Günther wanted to know where I'd been, and I told him. Then he asked if I was going to go out again, and I said no. I pulled up his blankets, and I carefully smoothed them over his teddy bear, whom he'd taken to bed with him because he loved him so much. The teddy bear was called Jubi.

I said, "Jubi's fast asleep already, he's so tired." But I knew that Günther was waiting for me to sing him his lullaby, as I did every night. It was our habit, but only when we were alone, without Max. For the silly little song was part of my childhood, and Günther somehow understood that we could not have the song if Max was there. Max considered it more proper for Günther to say his prayers. "There's plenty of time for that once he's old enough to go to school," I had countered. I'd even laughed at Max. "You don't pray either, you only pretend at funerals and such, holding your hat." It had been a silly conversation. When I was a child, I'd had to pray too, and it hadn't helped. I was always relieved when my mother finally left the room; that was more important to me.

But Günther asked me to sing. I said, "No, not tonight."

"Why not?"

"Because Mama doesn't feel like it."

"Why doesn't Mama feel like it?"

"Just because."

But it wasn't his fault. I had to sing. I sang more softly than usual, and he listened very carefully to make sure I did not skip any parts. It made me very sad. I kept thinking that perhaps by tomorrow no one would be singing to him. Nobody else could even pronounce the words of the song properly, it was in the northern dialect.

"But now you must sleep. Jubi's been asleep for hours."

I turned off the light, but I stayed by the side of his bed; that way he fell asleep more quickly. He did not notice I was crying.

I did not notice it myself until a tear fell on my hand. I hadn't cried for years and years and years.

It hadn't even happened yet, I could still take it all back. Perhaps I was only upset, and tomorrow I'd be ashamed. I'd never been one to cry a lot, even as a child. They said I was pigheaded, but it was nobody's business if I was sad. I didn't want to give them the satisfaction.

One time everybody surely expected me to cry, they even hoped I would. That was when our dog got run over and was lying in the gutter. And even then I wouldn't give them the satisfaction; I wore a cold expression and turned away. But that night I cried, and for a long time I was afraid whenever I came downstairs, because I thought the dog might still be there and come running up to me as he always had.

Later my mother called me a communist. She didn't mean anything political by it, not what the term means nowadays. She said I'd come to a bad end. Probably Max would have called me a communist too if he'd known what my life was like in those days. Of course I never told him, and my mother was surprised when I married him, even though it was just what she wanted. To the end, she never really believed it, but what could she know about it?

No, I won't go to Uelzen, ever again. Not even with Berthold. But I'll tell him everything—yes, he's the one I'll tell. Even about Arnim.

And suddenly I was crying for Arnim. I was making up for lost time, because I hadn't cried when it happened. Not a single soul suspected what I was feeling inside. They spied on me, everyone knew the story; they whispered behind my back, and when I walked through the town, the women broke off their chatter and turned around to stare at me. Out of envy, I told myself; you silly geese. They were hoping for a scandal, my parents feared one. They worried more about scandal than they did about me. That's how it always is; everyone is like that. I left them guessing to the last minute, let them tremble—I was trembling too, after all.

And how I trembled—I could barely conceal my shivering. It threatened to come over me when I was sitting at dinner with them. How could they eat? How disgusting. I almost threw up, but they'd have thought I was pregnant. My mother's thinking could not get beyond pregnancy—what could she know about it? Sometimes she gave a sideways look at my skirt. But I fooled them all. I simply got married. They were relieved, but they called me a cold fish.

And I? I had expected it to be easier. I hadn't thought about the nights. You get used to it after a while—you have no choice. Perhaps Max thinks I have no talent for it. But something always stays behind, even when you think you've forgotten everything and gotten used to the new way. Somewhere a sigh remains. I haven't forgotten Arnim, and it's been more than seven years.

Some months ago I saw him in the movies, during the newsreel. I was there with another woman, the wife of Herr Behling, our attorney. In the dark I handed her a bag of candy, and as the paper rustled, I heard the name *von Cismar* from the screen. It was like a stab, a piercing stab. They were talking about his brother Carl, the horseman, who was holding a large cup he'd won. But a little way behind him stood Arnim. Then it was gone; everything happens so quickly in the movies. But how fat Arnim had grown, and his face was so bloated. He was once so slender.

When I used to wait for him at the edge of the tree nursery, I was always impatient and annoyed that he hadn't arrived yet. Is his wife keeping him? Whatever can he see in that woman with the boring pale hair? But then I would see him come around the corner of the hedge along the field path, with his calm, slender movements. And when he made his way among the tables in the café in Hanover, people could not help but look at him, whether they wanted to or not. He was always so quiet and a little sad, so different from me. Maybe it's my fault that he's grown so fat—I could have kept it from happening. If we'd stayed together, I'm sure it would never have happened. But of course that wasn't possible. Maybe trying to get used to it gives you a bloated face, and maybe mine will get the same way and I won't even notice.

Yes, and supposing I just let Berthold leave? There's still time, nothing has happened yet. He has to leave in a couple of hours anyway; his train goes around eleven, and he has to take advantage of the ticket. I'll shake hands with him and extend my best wishes. What can he expect of me?

In the meantime Max will come home. Yes, Max will be there with us, and afterward Max and I will talk in our usual way. He will ask about the prize ceremony, who was there and what people said. I won't have to make much of an effort. We'll sit together for a while, and tomorrow morning, when I come downstairs to breakfast, Max will be in a great rush, and everything will be back to normal. He will go to the factory, and I'll be alone with my thoughts.

My tears were not for Günther at all, that was the thing. If I'd been crying for Günther, it would have been all right. But I cried because I had always known that someday it would end like this. I had tried so hard not to think of it; I was careful with everyone I met; I had hoped that I was safe at last. Yes, I'd always known: only if I'm very careful and only if I'm very lucky will I escape it. Then everything will stay the way it is, and no one will have to be upset.

I was playing for time.

But I'd rather tell what happened downstairs. "Your Blanck was making himself scarce," Berthold told me, laughing. He often used such expressions, even though he was a writer. "All of a sudden he couldn't wait to make himself scarce. It often happens to me with people of that sort. They steal glances to every side, they take a few steps backward, and in the wink of an eye they've disappeared around a corner. As if I were out to buttonhole them!"

Berthold described it all very vividly; he made me laugh, too. Blanck talked himself out of the room by saying that he had to sort the President's letters and put them in the folder for his signature. Berthold made a dismissing gesture—"I dismissed him graciously"—and Blanck immediately retired to the study and closed the door. He believed that he had done his duty, especially as Fräulein Gerda was there to keep the guest company.

Berthold asked her immediately, "Tell me, what's wrong with the old gentleman?"

"What do you mean? Why should anything be wrong?" Her words were meant to convey complete astonishment, but Fräulein Gerda was a bad liar. Berthold's question had taken her by surprise, which was why she let the cat out of the bag. "You mean you noticed something?"

Berthold did not reply; he no longer cared, really, and it seemed so silly to be standing around with Fräulein Gerda. He would have liked to leave, but he did not know how to go about it.

"You really wanted to leave?" I asked when he told me the story.

"What was left for me there?"

I admitted that I'd thought about it too, perhaps at the same minute, and wondered whether I shouldn't just let him go.

"Well, you see."

But Fräulein Gerda took advantage of the opportunity to tell him half her life story, in addition to everything she thought she knew about my father-in-law. Berthold was very funny as he tried to imitate her turns of phrase.

In reality, she explained, she was a registered nurse, and her fiancé had only come back a year and a half ago from being a prisoner of war in Russia. She hadn't heard from him in over three years, and she'd given up all hope. Then, quite by accident, just because they were short of nurses, she'd been transferred to the hospital's psychiatric division. That had been a great stroke of luck, because her fiancé was still at the university. He wanted to be an engineer, but when he'd first come back, he'd been very despondent and had lost all confidence in himself. Things were much better now, and the President had promised to give him a job at the plant when he had his degree. Then they'd marry.

And here, in this house, she could earn much more than at the hospital, for in reality she wasn't employed to take care of Günther—that was just what they said because of how people talked and so that the Chairman of the Board wouldn't suspect that they were keeping an eye on him. Professor Meyerbrink had recommended her when the President sought his advice. For reasons of discretion, that is, and because everything should go off unobtrusively. At the time the President had thought that his father . . . well, that sort of thing was called manic-depressive. But in her opinion the old gentleman wasn't sick at all—such a nice old gentleman, always so cordial. And she really did believe that Professor Meyerbrink shared her view; of course he had not admitted as much to her, but she could tell.

"Do you know something?" she burst out. "These are rich people, and it's just a matter of money. They fight about who's to head the factory, that's all. Even the cook, who's been here a long time, thinks so."

Apparently she grew appalled at her own garrulousness. She begged Berthold not to give her away; it was a condition of her employment that she was not allowed to discuss the situation, and she could lose her job, which at present she couldn't afford because of her fiancé. Of course, she could go back to the hospital any time—she had Professor Meyerbrink's promise—but because of her fiancé's future, yes . . . .

45

And explaining that she had not yet had her supper, she said goodbye to Berthold.

Günther had fallen asleep. I went to my room and threw my fur coat across the bed without turning on all the lights. I was afraid of so much brightness. My handkerchief was soaked; I put it in the hamper and got a new one from the dresser.

Then I went to the bathroom. I had to turn on the light over the sink, and I looked in the mirror. My eyes were all red from weeping, anyone might notice. I washed them with hot and with cold water. Then I fixed my makeup a little. I wasn't old yet, and my skin was still much better than most women's, although I didn't do much to keep it that way. You could still tell that I'd been crying, but perhaps only if you stood very close, the way I was standing at the mirror. Quickly I turned off the light. They'd probably just think I was tired or had a headache. I did have a headache; I'm sure it was from the cocktails. Or from crying.

I went back to my room and opened the closet. I wanted to pack a few things now, just in case; yes, just so as to be prepared. If nothing came of it, it wouldn't take long to unpack again. I didn't want to take a lot anyway—what for? Only the bare essentials. I pulled out the small suitcase I kept in the closet behind my clothes. Placing it on a chair, I put a few things in it— underwear, that sort of thing—but without giving it much thought. I simply reached into the drawers, all in the semidarkness.

Then I thought of something else. I looked for my purse, the one I'd taken to the art gallery, and found it on the bed. I sat down and counted the money in it. Then I ran to the dressing table to get the money I kept in the left drawer. There were several hundred marks, which I put in my purse. And my jewelry? I reached for the necklace circling my throat. I was also wearing rings on my fingers, and a pin with a large diamond. I could not take the jewelry with me; it did not really belong to me, even if it had been given to me. To take it would be wrong.

I sat at the dressing table and again could not make up my mind. It would have been better not to have come back to the house at all; we should have taken off at once, when we had nothing else on our minds and everything was clear. Berthold had wanted it that way, too. It was all my fault; I was doing everything wrong. Now I'd have to make the decision alone, without asking anybody's advice. That was the way it would always be from now on.

Of course I couldn't travel in this dress, with its low neckline. Where were we going anyway? To the city where he lived? Where did he live? I didn't even know that much. We hadn't had time to talk about it, and it wasn't all that important. In any case, I'd put on the gray suit for traveling, and my fur coat over it. Yes, and I'd change my shoes, too. I couldn't possibly travel in these.

I decided to change at once so as not to have to waste time later. I took the suit out of the closet. Then I saw myself in the mirror, but because of the semidarkness, I could discern only my outline and the white of my shoulders. Why change now? It can be done in a minute—there is always enough time. And Berthold likes this dress so much, I'd rather not keep him waiting now, we have so much to discuss before Max comes home. How quiet it had suddenly grown downstairs! Might he . . . ?

I ran to the stairs and leaned over the banister. No one was left in the living room; it was deserted, so bright and so empty. So I'd missed my chance again because of my hesitation, because . . . .

But the door to the vestibule stood open. I called softly, "Hello?"

If he'd gone—I don't know what I would have done; it's inconceivable. But he was still there; I'd just had a big fright. And he heard me at once, although I'd called very softly. It was almost like the game you play when you walk down the street with a child. You step behind a tree or into a doorway, or the other way around—the child hides. And you act as if you'd lost him, and you look and look although you know perfectly well that it's only a game and that he can't be far away, and when the hider suddenly comes out of his hiding place, you have to pretend to be very surprised and relieved—that's part of the game. Except that this time I really was frightened.

That was why I could not pretend pleasure when I saw Berthold standing in the doorway to the vestibule again. I tried. I tried to smile, but I don't think I managed. I could not rally myself so quickly. He looked up at me, hesitating in the doorway, just as he had done before, neither all the way outside nor completely inside; but he had not yet put on his coat. He must have felt as I did, because he could not speak at once either. Besides, he was in strange surroundings, you must remember. Surely it was up to me to speak first, but I couldn't, no; my heart was beating so loudly that he must have heard. The banister was shaking with my heartbeat as I clung to it.

"Where have you been all this time?" he whispered at last.

At that, my smile succeeded, and once more I was happy and sure. I knew that he had missed me and had felt alone without me. Everything was as it had been before, in the art gallery. There was no need for thought, no need for caution; whatever we did was the right thing to do.

I started down the stairs, two steps, and he walked

from the door to the foot of the stairs, very slowly. We both moved very slowly, no longer in any hurry. Nothing could disturb us—that was how deep our certainty went.

"I was putting my little boy to bed," I said. "And then I laid out a few things for the trip. Oh, yes, and I washed my face and combed my hair. My dress . . . I'll change later. I didn't want to keep you waiting any longer." Something like that—or perhaps I said something different. It didn't matter what I said. "Yes, and now, sir . . . ." And I continued down the stairs, step by step, very slowly.

I was successful with each step—I could feel it. I was playacting just a little bit, it's true, but not to deceive him or to conceal something, and actually not even for his sake, but because it so exactly suited the moment for me to move down the stairs toward him very slowly and with assurance . . . .

"And now, sir, I'm entirely at your disposal."

And that was right, too. I could tell from his expression. I was standing one step above him; now we were the same height. I should have felt him breathing, we were so close, but I couldn't; he must have been holding his breath.

And the thing is that he didn't smile either; if he had smiled, it would only have been my smile reflected in his face. But I was not in it; his expression was only and entirely one of astonishment, it was dissolved in astonishment, and so guileless—oh, so guileless, so transparent and intangible with guilelessness that it was unbearable, that you wanted to press it close quickly so as not to lose it, so as not to have to see it anymore, yet you didn't dare because it would have been no more than smoke in your hands. There are no words for it. It was recognition without ground or weight, like colors in the ice, not cold, not cold, so delicate and fleeting, oh . . . .

The ticking of the pendulum in the clock was painfully loud. I sidestepped Berthold toward the banister and went down the final steps. I did not want to touch him; I did not want him to touch me. Not now! Not here! Not in this house!

I sat down on the bottom step.

"Do you like to sit on the stairs?" I asked him. "I've liked it since I was a little girl, and I was always scolded for it. My mother said it wasn't proper, but maybe she was only afraid that I'd catch cold; at our house the bottom steps were made of stone. And I should be more careful of my clothes, she said. Why don't you sit here with me? The steps are carpeted, we won't catch cold, and the carpet is vacuumed every morning. Besides, no one will see us.

"At our house the stairs were quite dark. It was an old house with an old and pleasant smell. A large mahogany wardrobe stood in the hall, and jars of preserves were kept on top of it. Once a jar of cherries exploded and left a brown stain on the ceiling. How they wailed! They said it was because it had been a bad year and because of the artificial fertilizer. By and by the stain faded.

"There wasn't much light there, either; only what came through the round window over the front door and from the back, through the door that led to the garden and the laundry shed. I spent a lot of time sitting on those stairs, and no one could see me.

"My father was the county supervisor, and he had offices at the front. I could see and hear everything, and I could make my escape unobserved, too. A bell at the top of the front door pinged when the door was opened. I watched the people; sometimes the dog sat with me, but he kept just as quiet as I did. Some came in fat and blustering and angry and went straight to the offices. Many others spent a long time scraping their feet, clearing their throats, and standing there irresolute. I'm sure they were tempted to turn tail—I understood them only too well—but finally they mustered up their courage and knocked on the door very timidly.

"But I also heard the people passing by outside on the street—their steps and a word or two of their conversations, but never what came next. It was very exciting. I tried to recognize who they were; in a little place like that, you know everybody. But for the most part they were farm women who had come to market. They spoke in dialect. Can you understand the northern dialect? I know a nice little song . . . . No, we can't go on sitting here, it won't do. Come with me."

I got up and walked over to the armchairs.

"Wouldn't it be better to wait in the waiting room?" he asked.

"The waiting room?" I turned to face him, surprised.

"The third-class waiting room is a good place to wait. It's comfortable. The people come, and then they leave by the next train, then another set comes, and they leave. And finally it's your turn. The train is announced over the loudspeaker."

"We have to wait for my husband," I said.

"Oh."

"He'll be here soon, it won't be long. There's no other way. You have to understand. I don't want to simply run away."

He was still standing by the stairs. He must have been disappointed. But there really was no other way.

"Shall I ask them to make some coffee?" I asked. "Or would you like a drink? No? Come, let's sit over there, on the sofa. You have to keep me company. My husband isn't a bad man—I don't want you to think that. Anyway, none of it is his fault. Of course he won't understand, and it will be very upsetting for him; he doesn't suspect, he can't even conceive of there being such a possibility. I . . . . Or would you rather go to the railroad station and wait for me there?"

"If I did, you'd never come."

"Oh, yes, I'll come. Believe me."

"As you wish."

"No, not as I wish, and it's possible you will have left. What's to become of me then? No, please, sit here with me. All I have to do is change my clothes. This dress—it's the first time I've worn it. It was intended for another occasion that was called off because of the flu. Shall I take it along, do you think? It wouldn't take up much room. Why don't you say something? You're letting me do all the talking. Tell me something about yourself."

"What do you want me to tell you?"

"I tell you everything. Or are you bored? I have to go on a little while longer playing the lady of the house entertaining a guest. I've lived more than six years in this place, you see."

"How did you ever stand it?"

"I didn't even notice. I didn't know that there was something to stand. Only through you . . . ."

"I grew up in a house like this. Not quite so lavish, a little more old-fashioned, but otherwise the same. I ran away at a very early age."

"Oh?"

"Yes."

"And then?"

"Nothing. I couldn't stand it. And I don't understand how other people can stand it. But why talk about it! People think it's only natural."

"How old are you?"

"Thirty-four."

"Really? Sometimes you look much older, and then again much younger."

"What difference does it make?"

"I'm twenty-eight. I really am."

He said nothing, he only looked at me. He had finally sat down next to me.

"Don't you believe me?" I asked.

"What?"

"That I'm twenty-eight."

"Why shouldn't I believe you?"

"Just a thought. Because women lie about their age. What do you think of me anyway? I mean, that I just . . . ."

"But it's not your fault," he said. He meant it was his fault because he had spoken to me first. But I'd been waiting for it. Or had it been a literary conceit after all? A sigh escaped me.

"Sometimes," he said as if I'd spoken out loud, "sometimes I'm fed up with always translating the truth into literature. I'd like . . . for myself . . . ." He faltered.

"Yes, I understand."

"No, it can't be. One cannot do such a thing. It isn't meant for me."

"What?"

"Someone like you."

"What nonsense. Just don't start in again about my being a 'fine lady.' "

"But it's true."

"No, it's not true. If I were so fine . . . ."

"But you are. It shows here." He tapped my knee with his finger, and I laughed.

"You certainly notice everything," I said. I thought he was talking about my legs.

"I don't have to notice. It's clear all by itself—the way you came down the stairs and walked through the living room. It's obvious in your walk and the way your skirt moves. One doesn't even have to look at you, one just notices. Everything is so natural. Are you really only twenty-eight?"

"Do I look much older?"

"That's not it. That's not what I meant."

"No woman is fine," I said. "That's just an act."

"You don't know."

"Oh, let's drop it. My husband says people think I'm stuck-up, and yet I'm as shy as a little girl. It's just that I'm good at hiding it. It's so easy to pretend with people. And I'm sure they all envy me and think, What a life she leads, in that house and . . . . Do you know that I went to my wedding holding a bouquet another man sent me? He had an estate near Uelzen. The bouquet was lying on the little table with the mirror, in the upstairs hall on the second floor. Still wrapped in tissue paper, without a card, as we had agreed. The flowers were red carnations, and people were surprised that I didn't carry white flowers at my wedding, as is the custom. I don't know whether Max noticed anything. And even if he had, I would have lied—I would have said that I couldn't find the flowers he'd sent, or something. But he never asked. Perhaps he didn't care. I picked up the flowers, threw the tissue paper on the floor, and put the real bouquet on the table instead. My mother must have seen, but if she'd made even one remark, there wouldn't have been a wedding. She knew that too, and that's why she kept quiet, and that's how it happened. Are you laughing at me?"

"You bit the bullet."

"Yes, I intended to make a go of it. Why? Others make a go of it, and I would have too. It looked that way until today . . . . How come you're not married?"

"I tried it, but it didn't work. It didn't even last a year."

"Really?"

"Yes, it didn't work."

"I could tell at once that you're not married. Even while you were making your speech. I was sitting in the ninth or tenth row."

"You can't see anybody from up there, only heads."

"Were you unfaithful to her?"

"No, not that. She remarried. She lives in Canada. It just didn't work. I don't seem to have the talent for it."

"But I'm sure you have lots of women friends?"

"No, not the way you mean. My so-called women friends don't trust me. Nobody trusts me. It's always been that way. I'm used to it, and I don't want to upset anyone; it's better to stay alone. That's another reason why I left home so soon; I didn't want to cost them a lot of money, because after all . . . but what's the use of talking?"

"I want to know everything about you."

"There's not much to know. It's fairly monotonous. I've written books—to amuse myself, that's all."

We were silent. I didn't know what else to say. He stared into space, thinking of something else, not of me. He had forgotten where he was and that I was sitting by his side.

Finally he noticed that no one was speaking, and his eyes slowly slid upward until we were looking at each other. At first there was mistrust in his eyes, but then it disappeared.

"Is it really true?" he asked in astonishment.

I nodded.

"I don't even know your name."

"Marianne. Don't you like it?"

"I'll have to get used to it."

"I don't like it either. Whenever my mother called me by my name, I'd always been up to some mischief. I made my friends in school call me Marion, which sounded nice and sort of French. I insisted; if they didn't call me that, I simply wouldn't answer. Yes, that's the way I was, but that's all childish nonsense. He called me that too."

"Who?"

"The man with the bouquet."

"Why did nothing come of that?"

"I couldn't do it to my father. We were living in the hinterlands, and there would have been a scandal. As it was, they were talking about us because he was married and the father of two children. His estate bordered my uncle's, where we always went in the summer. I was still practically a child. He told me that his life had no meaning without me. He wanted to give up his estate and everything. We were going to go abroad. I knew his wife, too—a pale blonde from somewhere in Holstein. I think she knew all about us, and that's why I hated her—because she acted as if I didn't even count. Yes, we managed to meet frequently, and any day we couldn't was a day lost. We went to Hanover, too—separately, of course, so as not to attract attention—and we were together there. I'm not fine at all—that's a lot of nonsense. When they asked me at home where I'd been, I lied.

"Later, when I finished school, I took a furnished room in Hanover and got a job as a secretary in the rubber-processing plant. I wanted to earn my keep, just like you, and not depend on others—that's the whole point. But that summer, while I was home on vacation, Max came to visit. He'd been to Uelzen once before; my brother and he were at the university together. My brother has a position now in the Department of Commerce. Max had been in America as a trainee, and in Sweden, too, for a time. My father had a talk with me. He never mentioned Arnim, but I knew what he meant. Anyway, I didn't know myself what was to become of me; everything was so vague. So I gave in. Yes, that's more or less how it was. I'm telling you everything about myself, and I don't know anything about you."

"There's nothing to know about me."

"But things must have happened to you?"

"They don't have anything to do with me. I just happened to be there, and I pretended to take part, so as not to attract attention, but it could just as easily have

56

been someone else. I'd rather listen to you; it's better that way."

"We don't have time now," I said, looking at my watch. "Yes, I think it's time." I got up.

"Where are you going?" he cried, jumping to his feet. He even grasped my arm.

"I just want to change," I explained. "It's better if I change now, so I'll be ready. I just want to put on my suit. And then the suitcase. An interruption later . . . I don't want it to take too long, later."

"But you can't leave me alone now."

"But I'm not leaving you alone. I'll be right back."

"No, you'll stay upstairs. I know you will."

"No, I won't, believe me."

"Yes, you will."

Then I realized that he was jealous of Günther; he thought I'd stay with Günther and forget him. "Why don't you come upstairs with me?" I said. "But you have to be quiet."

I went up the stairs, Berthold at my heels. At the top I stopped and turned around; we almost bumped into each other, that's how close behind me he was. There was something else I meant to say to him. I wanted to say, "Please, not here in the house. Nothing hole-and-corner." But his expression was like that of a little boy whom I was about to forbid something, and I was ashamed of having thought such a thing of him. I said nothing.

I was not able to change right away. Berthold paced the room, looking curiously at everything. He sniffed inside my closet and said, "A fine lady." And he sniffed the bottles on my dressing table and said, "We'll take this one." And I said, "All right," and I put it in my suitcase although it wasn't important. Then he found my nightgown lying on the turned-down bed, picked it up, and wanted me to take it along. But I said no, I had a better one, and when I opened the drawer, he stood right behind me and saw the white silk pajamas, so I had to pack those too—so many unnecessary things, much more than I wanted; the suitcase was almost full.

In all his excitement he did not hear the tires crunching along the gravel and the slam of the car door. Max did not exist for him. But I could even feel the draft when Max opened the front door. I said nothing to Berthold, though; I didn't want to spoil his fun at poking through my things.

Max was extremely punctual, almost to the minute. He always was. When he came home in the evening, he told Gertig, his chauffeur, "You can put the car away. Tomorrow morning at eight, as usual."

I was sure he'd say it this time as well. When we were first married, he used to wait until he'd asked me if we had any plans for the evening, but since I always said no, he stopped. When we did have plans, an invitation to a dinner party or something, it was all arranged beforehand and noted down in his appointment calendar.

Most of the time I was downstairs in the living room when Max arrived, or I came down the stairs to meet him. He liked that; even if he was pressed for time and had other things on his mind, he missed it when I wasn't there. He needed the feeling that everything in the house was in order; that was enough. He habitually asked about Günther and about how I was; his questions seldom varied.

He would be sure to be surprised that I wasn't coming downstairs this time. Would he come up at once to see what was the matter? I was only half paying attention to what Berthold was saying. He moved around my room as if it were his room rather than a strange place. It would not be good if Max came in suddenly and saw this. And I hadn't finished changing

58

either; because of Berthold, I hadn't even been able to begin.

I hadn't heard the front door slam; it had stayed open longer than usual. Even afterward, when it did slam, Max did not come upstairs. As it turned out, there was a ridiculous reason for his delay; it was a matter of a boxing match the following Sunday. No, not boxing—soccer. Some important local championship. They'd been talking about it for days, but how was I supposed to remember that now?

On Sunday afternoons Max often went to the soccer games; sometimes, when there was an important match, he even had Gertig drive him to another town. I never went with him, excusing myself by saying that I would catch cold. I suspect Max was glad that I did not come; perhaps he shouted right along with the others when someone made a goal, and if I'd been there, he would have been embarrassed. Most of the time he went with Gertig and they sat together in the bleachers. People thought Max very clever for this.

So it was only that the first thing Max wanted was to ask Blanck about the tickets for the game. The only reason he left the front door open was so he could tell Gertig at once. But Blanck had probably heard Max drive up and gone to meet him. And as usual, Max would have pretended surprise. "How nice of you to wait for me." I'd heard Max say that a hundred times, although he took it for granted that Blanck would wait for him. Yes, and how about the tickets? After Blanck had told him that he had reserved two seats, Max would have called out to the chauffeur, "Did you hear that, Gertig? All right, then, see you in the morning."

It must have been more or less like that—it was always like that. What would Berthold have said if he had known that the only reason Max was not coming upstairs was because of the soccer game?

And yet the real reason was quite different, as I

only learned many weeks later. The soccer game was a welcome pretext, no more, for Max and Blanck, to keep them from having to talk immediately about the subject that was of much more burning interest to them. That's how they were; when they learned something terribly exciting, something so exciting that they could barely contain themselves, they talked about something inconsequential. Oh, how well I knew them. This day of all days a decision had been taken for which Max had been waiting for months, a decision on which the future of the family business depended—or so he believed. It had nothing at all to do with me, and it was much more important to them than anything else. A strange coincidence!

Or perhaps not so strange; when I thought about it at leisure afterward, it seemed that it could not have been any other way. I don't know what I would have done if I'd known at the time; I was much too preoccupied with myself and Berthold. But it's possible that I would not have gone to the award ceremony if they had taken me into their confidence, and then, of course, everything would have turned out quite differently. It's not my fault that they kept it from me. That was the way they were; they did not want me to interfere.

Now that I know the whole story, I'm not surprised that Max did not come upstairs. I can imagine the two of them downstairs, so excited; I can actually see them. "My wife isn't home?" Max may have asked, and Blanck would have told him that I was upstairs. "Fine," Max would have said. Perhaps he had rubbed his hands. He did that sometimes when he was pleased, and especially when I wasn't there to see, because it was a gesture I disliked. It's possible, too, that this time his hands really were cold from the drive. I mustn't make fun of him.

Yes, and then he must have walked up and down the living room a couple of times. What he wanted most was to disappear into the study with Blanck. But

60

wouldn't he have to come and say hello to me first, for the sake of good manners? He stole glances up the stairs, to see if I was coming at last. And Blanck did not move from the spot; only his head moved to follow Max's movements. Blanck was waiting to be asked a specific question.

The matter was so crucial to both of them that it must have cost them an effort not to let go and gossip about it at once. It had to do with my father-in-law.

Finally Max had to start. Yes, it had been quite right of Blanck to telephone at once, he must have said, and Blanck must have answered that he thought he should inform the President immediately of this favorable turn of events.

Did that mean his father had signed?

Yes, this morning around ten the Chairman of the Board had appeared at the offices of Melchior, the notary, without first making an appointment; he had had them read him the document once more, and at the end he had asked the notary to cross out the paragraph concerning the vote on the Board of Directors. The notary had pointed out that such a course of action was not really necessary; the Chairman was not compelled to cast a vote if he did not care to; that made it much simpler, and besides, the paragraph made the document look much more acceptable. Well, if it was more acceptable that way, the Chairman had said . . . and then he had signed, without further objections and without another word. Thereupon the notary had immediately telephoned Blanck to inform him of the event. By now the written confirmation was lying on the President's desk.

Good. Very good. (This time Max was sure to have rubbed his hands. I can't imagine the scene any other way.) Did Blanck have any idea what could have caused his father, after months of wavering, to sign so unexpectedly?

No, Melchior had wondered the same thing. The Chairman of the Board had been extremely cordial, yes, almost cheerful and in a joking mood, more as if the signing were some quite meaningless formality. At least that was how it had seemed to the notary, although there had not been much conversation and the whole process had not taken long.

Good, good. The main thing was—"Yes, we've weathered a severe crisis—a very severe crisis; there's no doubt about it."

Oh, crisis—what a word! How often I'd had to hear it. And that's why I'm convinced that Max did not miss the opportunity of using it now. Besides, if you looked at it from his point of view, it really had been a severe crisis.

But when I try to imagine them discussing it, I suspect that Max must nevertheless have been displeased with the sudden resolution. He must have asked Blanck if word had already gotten out; perhaps he even motioned upstairs, toward me. And Blanck would have assured him that he had not considered himself empowered to mention a word of it, not before the President . . . .

Fine, Max would have interrupted, then what remained to be done was to compose a short press release. That could wait until morning, but Blanck might think about it in the meantime. Was his father upstairs?

No, the Chairman of the Board had gone for a walk about half an hour ago.

Gone for a walk? Alone?

He, Blanck, had been astonished too, but because of the altered situation, he had had no misgivings about letting the Chairman go out alone. He had also restrained Fräulein Gerda, naturally without revealing his reasons.

"All right, no matter. We'll see." In any case, it was his wish—I'm sure Max grew sentimental at this point—

that both to the world at large and here at home his father continue—with special stress on the word *continue*—to be treated as the head of the firm.

"Of course, sir."

Was there anything else? Blanck should really be getting home to his wife.

No, nothing that couldn't wait. Wednesday of next week there was that conference in Brussels—or was it Antwerp? Blanck merely wished to remind the President of it.

"Wednesday? Fine. Just in case, make a plane reservation for me, will you? Oh, yes, and one more thing . . . ."

This "one more thing" was, I believe, a trick Max used with his employees to confuse them and get them off any subject he was no longer willing to discuss. Apparently he had an endless supply of such "one more things." He used it with me as well, on occasion. Quite suddenly, when we were talking about something quite ordinary, I heard, "And one more thing." It always got him what he wanted, too. He was considered a man who had to handle many weighty problems and who must therefore not be burdened with trifles. At the start of our marriage I felt extremely foolish.

"One more thing," Max would have said tonight. "Do you happen to know what the Tiefenbach Mills closed at today?"

It may have been another corporation, but I think it must have been the Tiefenbach Mills, because later on they were mentioned a great deal and at the time we didn't own them yet. But it doesn't really make any difference.

Of course Blanck would have known the closing price; he was always up to date. "Eighty-two," he promptly replied. Or some other number.

"So they've dropped two whole points since the

middle of February?" Max asked. I'd heard that kind of conversation very frequently.

"Three," Blanck corrected him. Perhaps he expected some recognition of his precision, but Max gave no sign.

"Fine, keep an eye on them. The factory is highly modernized and in splendid running order, as best I could tell from a brief inspection. But the management is overcommitted, they have no liquidity. I expect the stock to come down even further."

Whatever the conversation may have been, they had to break it off because Berthold was coming down the stairs.

Finally I had no choice but to tell him that Max had come home. He wanted to go downstairs at once to talk to him. I tried to change his mind. I wanted us to go down together. He hadn't even met Max. And what was he to talk to Max about? About me? What could Berthold tell Max? He was no match for Max, and the conversation could only come to a ridiculous end. I didn't want Berthold to make a fool of himself.

But he would not be dissuaded—he had this childish idea that it was his business to talk to Max. And actually it couldn't be too bad, because I would be following right away. All I had to do was change my shoes and put on my hat and coat. Yes, and perhaps I'd give one last look to see if Günther was asleep. Berthold did not have to know about that.

But he never got a chance to talk to Max. It wasn't his fault; it was because Blanck was present the whole time, and Berthold didn't know how to get rid of him.

Max gave Blanck a questioning look, and Blanck explained in a whisper that this man was Berthold Möncken, who had been awarded the prize that afternoon.

Of course, Max said, and approached Berthold with

an obligatory smile. "What a pleasure, my dear Herr Möncken, to have a chance to shake your hand personally. Unfortunately I was unable to attend the ceremony this afternoon. It would have meant a lot to me, but one isn't master of one's own time. I am all the more grateful to my wife that she brought you here. Really, such a good idea on her part. I hope everything went with dignity and to your satisfaction."

"Yes, thank you."

"Come, let's sit down. I assume you're spending the night with us."

"My train leaves at—"

"But why? You can leave tomorrow just as easily. I happen to be free tonight, which isn't the case all that often. What a welcome opportunity for me to spend some time with a literary celebrity. I know you think we are philistines—yes, I know you do. I don't mean you in particular, but all artists. And perhaps we industrialists really are philistines. At the very least we're somewhat one-sided, I admit. But you must have some sympathy with us . . . . While I think of it, if you think you'd enjoy it, you could inspect the factory in the morning, to see for yourself how Helldegen products come into being. That couldn't help but be of interest, not only to the housewife who uses our products in her kitchen—I'm sure you're married—but even to a modern writer. No one can live altogether without technology nowadays. How about it, Blanck, do you think you can give Herr Möncken the guided tour? . . . Where can my wife be keeping herself?"

"Your wife is changing her clothes."

"Oh. Good. Won't you sit down?"

"I'm very grateful to you, Herr Helldegen, but—"

"No need to thank me, my dear Herr Möncken, no need at all. I had no say whatsoever in the selection of the prizewinner. I take good care not to venture an opinion in areas where I'm not the least knowledgeable.

65

That's what we have a jury for. And as far as your book is concerned . . . my wife read it, of course, and so did Herr Blanck, didn't you? But I . . . unfortunately I haven't had the time. Please don't hold it against me. I could pretend to be familiar with it, but I always prefer total honesty.

"It's not for lack of interest on my part—oh, no, please don't think that. You have no idea what I'd give just once to have a chance to read a book through in peace and quiet. And of course, now and again I could find an hour or so. It's not a matter of time alone. Anyone who claims he has no free time is just boasting. How much time is wasted on business conferences and the dinners following them!

"No, you must understand: I—and the same is true for most of us—simply cannot afford to be distracted. The Helldegen plant, for example, employs three thousand people at present. Counting their families, that's about ten thousand human beings whose health and welfare depend on our factory's smooth functioning. So you'll understand that even at home we can't free ourselves from our cares. There's too much at stake for someone like myself to concern himself seriously with other problems, no matter how interesting they may be. As I said, we simply can't afford to . . . ah, here comes my—"

Max liked to talk, and he liked to hear himself talk. His words impressed people. He said exactly what they wanted to hear. But in Berthold's case there was the added fact that Max was not precisely certain where he stood. Berthold made people insecure, not on purpose, but by the way he stood and listened and at the same time did not listen; sometimes they didn't believe that he was listening and therefore talked more than they had meant to, also louder. Max must have been having that experience. I assume that he was relieved to see me coming down the stairs; now he could leave Berthold to me. That was why he called, "Ah, here comes my—" But he was unable to complete the sentence.

The three of them stared at me. I had put on my coat. Blanck, the first to collect himself, made a motion as if he intended coming toward me and taking the suitcase from me, but Berthold beat him to it.

I saw how matters stood; Berthold hadn't been able to say anything. "Would you please leave us alone for a moment, Herr Blanck?" I asked.

He sketched a brief bow, threw a look at Max, who was staring at me, and disappeared into the study.

What choice did he have? I followed him a little way to make certain that the door was properly closed. Then I said, "Well, then, Max, you can see—"

"Hello," he interrupted.

"Oh, yes, excuse me. Hello."

"You're planning to go out?"

"Yes, I've decided—"

This time Berthold interrupted me. He took a step behind me and said, "Unfortunately I've had no opportunity to speak with your husband."

Max looked at him, startled, as if he had forgotten Berthold's existence. Or as if he wished to say, "What in hell are you doing here?" Perhaps his expression was meant to insult Berthold.

"I know," I said to Berthold.

"I just sent Gertig and the car away," Max said. "I had no way of knowing you'd be needing them." I'm sure he was just playing for time. Yes, I'm quite certain that he understood at once that something else was going on, though it must have been quite unthinkable to him.

"It has nothing to do with the car," I said as calmly as possible. I even smiled a little. "No, I'm going away with Herr Möncken."

Again Max gave Berthold a disparaging look—two,

really, for he briefly looked at me in between. Berthold's feet made a little sound. I did not want to turn around to look at him; I hoped that he would not interfere. I wanted Max to be the first to speak.

"I had no way of knowing," Max said after a while. His forehead puckered in amusement, an attempt to turn the whole thing into a trifle.

"Of course you didn't," I said. "I didn't know it myself." I responded to his tone, also acting as if we were discussing some trivial whim.

But my response seemed to annoy Max. "You've known this gentleman for some time?" he asked with a great deal more sharpness.

"Not very long. Only since this afternoon."

"Is that right? And the purpose of this exercise?"

"The purpose?" What could I say? I grew nervous. "The purpose? My God, Max—"

"And where are you headed, if I may ask?"

"Anywhere." I shrugged my shoulders. "We don't know yet."

"Is that right? And for how long?"

"Forever."

Now it was out. Somewhat incredibly, I myself was startled when it was suddenly voiced, but at least I had spoken. I did not take my eyes off Max. I had no time to think of Berthold; I even forgot him for an instant. I wanted to know how Max was taking it; after all, he was my husband, and what I was doing to him must have been terrible. It was something he could not even consider.

I must admit that he took it admirably, so admirably that I was ashamed. He stood there and regarded me very calmly, his face impassive, quite blank; he did not even pale. It must be something they learn in the business world, where they have to accept the most devastating news without showing that they are stricken by it. And behind the blank facade of their faces they

68

search for a way out. Only I, who knew him very well, saw that it cost him an effort to maintain his composure. His pupils narrowed, growing hard and pointed.

"I'm really sorry, Max," I said. "But you don't care for empty phrases."

"Are you serious?" he asked, jerking his head in Berthold's direction—a contemptuous gesture.

"I truly am."

"Strange." That was supposed to be another insult.

"What's strange?"

"Not exactly well considered, is it?"

I was about to lose my patience. "Maybe not. But that's hardly your worry."

"Is that right, not my worry? May I at least inquire into your reasons?"

This question confused me because I had not expected it from Max. I thought that he was much too sure of himself to ask such a question, especially in the presence of a third person. "Reasons? My reasons? What's the good of standing here and discussing reasons? The reasons aren't important; perhaps there are no reasons. Let's stick to the facts, as you yourself always say."

"I don't understand." Max shook his head in a studied way. He even turned away a little to take a cigarette from the coffee table as if none of it concerned him seriously, as if it were all over and done with. Or perhaps to indicate that as far as he was concerned, the discussion was at an end. But he did not light the cigarette, he only spent a long time tapping it on the back of his left hand. Quite abruptly he turned back to me, and his voice sounded much more threatening than was appropriate to his game. "And you really think I should just let you run off like that?"

"What can you do to stop me?" I asked. Now I was pretending to consider his options.

Then I heard another movement behind me. Apparently Berthold had sidled nearer and was about to speak.

"What do you want?" Max snapped at him. "If you had the least sense of tact, you'd let me speak to my wife alone. In *my* house, to boot."

I immediately took a step backward to stand next to Berthold. "We'll be leaving *your* house together in a few minutes," I told Max. "We don't have much time anyway. We have to get to the railway station, and we still have to buy our tickets. And most important, Max, we have no desire to stage a scene. We're not in the movies. We're sensible human beings." I felt my composure slipping. Inside, I was shaking like a leaf. "And even if you don't think I'm sensible, it doesn't matter. I'm telling you how it is, Max. I can't do more. I know it isn't pleasant for you—yes, I'm sorry, but—"

"You really never met him before today?" he asked.

"No, why? I swear to you—"

But Max waved my words aside. "Isn't that somewhat—"

"Ill considered?" I interrupted. "Yes, you mentioned that before. What's the point of considering? If you really want to know, I've been considering it for seven years." I shouldn't have said that; I hadn't meant to say it, and I regretted it at once. It just slipped out, it was too late to take it back. Because now Max said something that angered me so much that I lost my self-control.

"Isn't there a simpler way?" he asked.

"I beg your pardon?"

Instead of answering, he cast a disdainful look at Berthold.

"Oh, you mean like you and your what's-her-name?" I suggested sarcastically. I really had forgotten the girl's name. Some blond young thing or other, one of Max's secretaries whom he'd taken along on business

70

trips for a while. I'd never wasted a word on the affair, but I think Max knew that I was aware of the whole thing; he must have thought me very generous because of my silence. But I hadn't taken it seriously; they all did it, so why shouldn't Max? On the contrary, I really hadn't cared at all. Let him amuse himself any way he liked—what did it have to do with me? But a few months ago he had stopped seeing her. He must have been tired of her, or it may have had something to do with the quarrel between him and his father; perhaps he did not want to leave himself vulnerable. What concern was it of mine?

"Is that the reason?" Max asked quickly.

I tried to control myself. "No, that is not the reason. Forgive my mentioning it. I let myself go. You have nothing to reproach yourself with, Max. It's me—I'm at fault. Anyone will assure you of that—any woman, at any rate. I don't want to be right, you see. You can file for divorce tomorrow, and you needn't fear that I'll make any trouble. I won't lift so much as a finger, because I don't want to think about any of it; it's no longer my concern. Let's not quarrel, Max. We've never quarreled. Why start now, at the last minute?"

"And what about Günther?"

"Günther is asleep." Of course I'd expected the question, I'd thought it would come up much sooner. Everyone would ask that question first, surely that was obvious. Whenever I'd read about what was happening to me now or seen it in the movies, that was always the question to which there was no answer. That is, of course there's an answer, as all decent people know. I too had learned it; it wasn't right for me to act as if there were no answer.

"Günther is asleep. He knows nothing. You can tell him tomorrow that I had to go on a trip. Later it will all work itself out. If I were to die, he'd have to . . . ." I was at the end of my tether. Only a little more, and

I'd be crying. I couldn't cry now, or everything would be lost. My hand clutched the strap of my purse. What could I cling to? Berthold was standing behind me, but how far away was he? Perhaps one step only—yes.

So we stood for a while. No one knew what to say; everything had been said.

"Well, then, . . ." I began.

Max's lips tightened in scorn; then he turned toward his study. He won't want to watch me leaving with Berthold, I thought. Really, it isn't easy for him. I was about to head for the vestibule, to finally put an end to it, when Max said quite unnecessarily, "That your behavior is causing me great inconvenience right at this time—you didn't think of that, did you?"

"Is there another crisis already?" I asked. "You always seem to have crises in your business. That's all I ever hear, and I'm sure it won't change. If I were to wait . . . . My going will hardly affect the credit balance of the Helldegen Corporation. I'll resume my maiden name so you won't have any problems from me. At the moment it's all very tiresome for you, I can see, but it won't be for long."

No, surely this exchange was superfluous, just repetitious. We were only trying to cause pain, to wear each other down. Both of us realized quite clearly that we had nothing more to say to each other, and yet it was hard simply to stop.

I don't know what we were waiting for, what else might have been said or who would have been the first to act, because matters took a different turn. We heard the front door slamming at our backs, and all of us turned in that direction.

"What's happening now?" Max asked, his voice somewhat shrill.

Already my father-in-law was standing in the doorway. None of us had given him a thought, and we were surprised to find him among us. Since he had heard voices inside, and probably also because the vestibule door was ajar, he had not taken off his coat. He was still wearing the muffler Fräulein Gerda had fetched for him, but now it stuck up a little from his coat collar. He stood there, staring at us in his calm way. He must have realized that we had argued and that there was a quarrel in the air. Any stranger would have noticed from the way we stood, from the light, the atmosphere in the living room, everything.

I ran to him and hugged him. You see, I needed someone I could say goodbye to. Of course the tears came. He didn't seem at all surprised; he patted my back gently.

Suddenly he was the person I felt closest to. "How nice that I have a chance to see you, Papa," I said. "I would have written you, really I would. I mean, maybe I wouldn't. There's no way of telling beforehand. But I prefer it this way. I want to tell you that I'm going away with Herr Möncken. Yes, I'm leaving Günther and you and Max. I'd so much like to explain it all to you; maybe I could explain it to you. But I can't now— we've already said so much, and it leads nowhere. And there's no more time. I have to go."

"It's all right, it's all right," he said. "It's not nec-essary."

"No, it's not all right. I know that I'm doing a bad thing. I'm doing you an injustice too; I never behaved toward you the way I should have; I never had the opportunity. Oh, Papa, why didn't we talk sooner? I could have talked to you about anything, only to you. Then things would have turned out differently, and I would surely have been able to stand it here. Everybody needs someone to talk to. But I didn't want to be a burden to you. I thought that you cared about the factory and about nothing else and that you thought of me as a luxury item. Don't be mad at me, Papa, it's too late now. I can't help myself. Everything here is so fake, so dead. It's my fault. I was afraid of you."

I could not go on. I remembered that his wife, too, had run away. Max must have been a little older than Günther at the time—seven, I think. And she didn't go off with another man, she just went. They say she died in a sanatorium two years later, I don't know of what. I never saw a picture of her; it seemed there weren't any, but I'm sure one was kept in a folder somewhere.

Max didn't like to talk about her, and when he did mention her, he wasn't altogether truthful, you could tell. He told me only what he wanted me to say in case other people brought up the subject. But perhaps he himself didn't know the real reason; if I know my father-in-law, he buried it all inside, locking it away even from his son.

They said the wife had been sick, but I suspect she killed herself. I think I wasn't supposed to know that, for they themselves did not want to admit it. It was like a blank space when they spoke of the past. Max was very proud of the name Helldegen and thought of the whole episode as a disgrace. He was not at all reconciled to the fact that others knew about it; it robbed him of his self-assurance.

"Papa, I can't help myself," I said again.

"It's all right, it's all right," he repeated, and then, in a quite different voice, so that I could hear it and pull myself together, "Ah, there she is, our lovely Fräulein Gerda."

Yes, at this most inappropriate of all moments she came from the kitchen, where she'd been sitting over her supper for such a long time. She was holding Berthold's book, which she'd probably been showing to the cook, and she said cheerfully, "Well, and how was our walk, Chairman?"

I straightened up quickly and turned to her. "I'm afraid I've suddenly been called away, Fräulein Gerda.

74

Tell Günther . . . take good care of Günther in the meantime. I know I can count on you. My husband will give you any further . . . I think it's best if you go upstairs right now and check whether Günther is asleep. I'm in a great hurry."

I said all that just to get her out of the way. For once even Fräulein Gerda understood that her presence was not desired. Wordlessly and without much ado she went up the stairs. We all watched her go, as if it were the most important thing in the world. Thus I regained my self-control.

"We have to leave now," I said to Berthold. I looked for the suitcase, but he already had it and was walking off with it. "Yes," I said to Max, and in the doorway I turned back to look at him once more. "You can tell people that I had to go away urgently for a rest cure, that my nerves are shot or something like that. They'll believe you, and later . . . ."

A gust of cold air came into the room. Berthold had opened the front door; I saw him standing there and thought that he would leave without me. That would have been the end of everything. Quickly I ran after him.

And even so I felt lost; I did not know what Berthold thought of me. He had hardly crossed my mind though he had been standing behind me all the time. Surely he must have formed an opinion. Perhaps he thought, What do I want with someone like her? Why is she chasing me? Perhaps he would hand me the suitcase and say, "Please, I can't go along with this." I expected something of the sort as we walked down the drive; I wouldn't even have held it against him. After all, I was thinking almost the same thing. I don't know what I would have done, though. I would not have gone back—no, that's one thing I would not have done.

How glad I was that he said nothing at all. Even

if he'd said something altogether different, I would have heard that he wanted to be rid of me. He was walking very rapidly, I had trouble keeping up with him; I tripped along behind him like a little girl who's tired from a long excursion and has to hurry to the railroad station to catch the train that will take her home. Yes, that's how I felt.

But it wasn't because of the train that he was walking so fast; we had plenty of time. It was probably to get away from the house as quickly as possible, first down the drive, then a right turn down our street, then a left to the main street, where there was a cabstand. And if there hadn't been a taxi waiting, we could just as well have taken the streetcar.

Strange, but it occurs to me only now that Berthold chose the right street. He must have been paying close attention on our way here. He looked straight ahead, and I didn't glance at him either. The lighting in our streets isn't what it was before the war; only the main street is a little brighter.

Only once did he say something, sniffing the air. I couldn't quite make out the words, he was mumbling, but I think he said, "There's a smell of snow." I didn't ask him to repeat it, and I didn't say yes, because it didn't matter what he said. I knew that he had said it for me and not because of the snow; he could just as easily have said something else. And it did make me more confident again.

Fortunately there was a taxi at the stand. To the railroad station, please.

But I still did not feel secure; that took a very long time. And basically I didn't really feel secure even then. I just stopped thinking about it so much.

I did not know what action they might take against me. They stood alone in the living room, and Blanck remained in the study. That was dangerous. I was afraid that they might pursue me, to bring me back. I would have liked to look out the rear window of the taxi to see if we were being followed. The only reason I didn't was to spare Berthold.

I had often wondered—even before, before they had the quarrel over the factory—what Max and his father talked about when the two of them were alone, without me. I had a feeling that they could not think of anything to say to each other and that it must have been very awkward for them. They avoided being alone together as best they could. Business discussions, such as they held when someone else was present—those they could not have when they were alone, for no one was listening, and there was no need to repeat any of it to each other. But I'm quite certain that they didn't talk about me either; that wasn't their style—not Max's and not his father's.

Except that this time it was a different matter altogether, much worse for them, and much worse for me. I was the occasion, I had left them alone together; there was no getting around it. What I had done to them! And on top of it all, on a day when they had to exchange a few words anyway, because of their differences. That was what was dangerous.

The taxi was old, and its springs were very bad. I held on to the strap; whenever the car jerked, I thought, Now they're coming.

I could not let myself talk to Berthold about my fear; he did not take any of what was happening seriously. And surely they could not hold anything against him. But against me? What were their plans?

Why did I hear nothing from them for weeks and weeks? Or if not from them, then from an attorney about the divorce? I waited day after day. The uncertainty was the worst. Were they trying to wear me down?

In part that was true, at least for Max. I learned as

much later, from my father-in-law. But at the time, driving to the railroad station, I had no way of knowing any part of the story; I was much too afraid. I tried to put myself in their place, imagining their response in every detail, considering every possibility. Nor did I forget about Blanck and Fräulein Gerda—especially Blanck, for Max could use him to do us harm.

Once Berthold told me that I had an astonishing imagination, I should be a writer. But that was just something to say. And it wasn't imagination, it was fear. I've always been that way: I think up something when I'm alone, and afterward I can't remember whether I just thought it up or whether it really happened to me. But I could swear to it, and the funny thing is that it isn't even a lie; it's the truth, as even others have to admit. If, for example, I were to tell Max and my father-in-law how they acted after I left, they'd cry out in astonishment, "But how did you know?"

Yes, how did I know? I won't tell them. It's none of their business that I know because I'm afraid.

Why is that? What does it matter? So you stay in your living room. You, Max, are annoyed mainly because your father was a witness to it. And you, Papa, you're sad because you can't change anything. Who will be the first to speak? Both of you are almost as afraid as I am.

Of course it was Max who spoke first. He pulled himself together. "I'm so sorry. I wish I could have spared you this scene," he said. When his father did not reply, he continued, "It took me by surprise, too, or I should have found ways and means . . ."

He did not finish his sentence; he must have thought it ludicrous to boast of ways and means. To add to his bad luck, it had been months since he and his father had exchanged more than a few words—only the bare necessities, only to keep up appearances, so that other people, especially their employees and Günther, would not notice that they were in the midst of a protracted quarrel.

All that time my father-in-law had been very correct and just a little mocking—which, by the way, Max could not bear. Perhaps Max was afraid that his father would make fun of him now. He did not know his father very well. He felt inferior to him, though he would never have admitted it; he wasn't even aware of it.

Even outwardly there was an enormous difference between the two. My father-in-law was tall and spare, with long arms and legs, always very calm in his motions and quite taciturn. Max was not short, but he was stockier and had a tendency to put on weight, which grieved him a great deal. He frequently stepped on the scale. His hair was dark, and he already had a bald spot, while my father-in-law still had a full head of white hair. Max must have taken after his mother, but I can't say for sure.

In any case all these factors made it that much more difficult to speak freely, and Max was much too nimble to let it come to an embarrassing remark. He quickly changed the subject. "Yes, and today of all days. I haven't even had a chance to thank you."

"What for?" his father asked.

"For signing the document." Max was irritated, for he believed his father's remark to be a trick—and besides, he did not like to thank anyone. "It saves me . . . please, Father, my only concern is the company. It was not unkindness."

"Do we have to talk about it now?" his father inquired.

Max chose to ignore the question. "Of course your waiver has only a—let us say, an internal significance. As far as outward appearances are concerned, nothing will change. I'll never forget what I owe you. I hope you do not doubt that. Yes, on the contrary, I'd like . . .

forgive me, that's the wrong expression, I'm a little tired . . . I'll make sure that in all crucial matters you are the first to be consulted. I will insist on it, yes." Max grew sentimental; he thought himself exceedingly magnanimous.

His father felt sorry for him. He knew that Max had no choice but to mouth such phrases and that he was doing it chiefly so as not to have to talk about me. That was why he remained silent.

"Don't you want to take off your coat?" Max asked, even hurrying to help his father.

"Then you'd probably prefer me to go on living here for the present?" his father asked.

"What do you mean? Why shouldn't you?" Max was taken aback; he had heard "for the present" and had understood immediately what was at stake. But first he ran to hang up the coat.

"Because of the talk," his father said.

"Because of what?" Max called from the coatroom, although he had heard very clearly. When he came back, he added, "I'd like to see the day when anyone dares to talk about us. Let me worry about that." And to change the topic again, he noted, as if in passing, "Oh, yes, and one more thing. I've inspected the Tiefenbach Mills."

"Hm" was his father's only response.

"It was your idea."

"It was?"

"Blanck found a memo in your handwriting."

"Nothing escapes Blanck's notice," his father said.

"A splendid idea, really. If it hadn't been for you, I never would have thought of it. And it can be brought off if we move carefully. It would save us having to expand and add more buildings here. We could simply transfer the production of certain items. As I said, if it hadn't been for you—"

"Good night," said his father.

80

"You're right, it can wait until morning. Good night."

I believe Max was glad that he would not have to go on talking. But halfway up the stairs his father turned back. There was unusual warmth in his voice as he asked, "What are you going to do, Max?"

"Why? What do you mean?" Max was about to ask if his father was referring to the Tiefenbach Mills, but for once he could not bring off the tone of evasiveness. "Oh, I see," he said instead. "You mean this other matter. Yes, what am I going to do? If I were you, Father, I wouldn't worry about it. It will come out all right."

"You really think so?"

"Why not? You'll see."

"If there's any way I can help . . . ."

"Help? Yes, but it won't come to that. Thank you, Father."

"We're not lucky with women," his father said softly.

"Do we have to talk about it now?" Max asked.

"I think we should, yes."

"On the stairs?"

Giving up, his father walked on a few steps.

They had no practice in talking about such things; they did not know how. Nevertheless, even Max felt that he had been too curt and that he must not let his father leave on this note.

"Please don't misunderstand me, Father. I very much regret this incident, especially for your sake. Of course I'm also thinking of Günther—and as I said, for me too it's an . . . an annoying matter. But the main thing is not to lose one's head, I tell myself. Such things happen in other families as well. And so? Other families have had to learn to handle it. Agreed, something like this is not pleasant, and one would prefer to avoid it. But let's face it, women are sometimes . . . well, unpredictable, if you like, or whatever you choose to call it.

"It's possible that I'm somewhat to blame. Yes, I admit that lately I've had little chance to pay much attention to her; I've had other problems, you know. And women . . . well, it doesn't matter. She'll be back. What can she want with this . . . this . . . it's pure romanticism, nothing more. That's the way women are. In any case it would be exactly the wrong thing at this point for us to also give ourselves up to emotional outbursts. No, we don't need that. What good would it do? We would only risk our existence; I would lose my perspective and capacity for work . . . . I must remain level-headed—that's the most important thing. Even when I was a little boy I admired the way you always came to terms with the facts. That is the secret of your success. Yes, tough and level-headed. Feelings don't last."

Leaning over the banister, his father had listened attentively. Very attentively, so as to understand everything clearly, even the things Max was not saying, and not only the things that perhaps he did not want to say. But apparently he did not hear what he wanted to. It may have been his fault or Max's—it's hard to tell. "Good night, then," he said, going upstairs.

Max ran his hand through his hair, straightened his tie, and brushed the cigarette ash off his suit. He always dressed very neatly. Even the slightest hint of dirt or of something not quite correct about his clothing robbed him of self-assurance. Sometimes he changed his shirt several times a day.

Then he went to the study door—he had already regained his normal manner—and spoke to Blanck. "I'm sorry that I had to keep you waiting so long," he said. "I hope you called your wife at least, so she won't burn your dinner. Yes, we had a private discussion; it couldn't be avoided. All right, then. Oh, and one more thing. Tell me, did we procure any information on this . . . what's his name again, that writer who was here earlier?"

"No."

"No? Why didn't we?"

"We had no business dealings with him."

"That's a mistake. A serious mistake, I'm sorry to tell you. I wish to have information always. See to it that we get some tomorrow. At once. Make it urgent."

"Yes, sir."

"And not just the usual phrases—I want precise facts. I'm less interested in his credit rating than in his past life. Yes, I want information on his whole life—do you understand?"

"Yes, sir."

Meanwhile we were in the third-class waiting room, just as Berthold had suggested, sitting at a large round table because there were no other empty seats. Next to me sat an old woman and a younger one who must have been her daughter. They had unwrapped sandwiches and were eating; at the same time they carried on a conversation in low tones. Across from us a young man slept, his head cradled in his arms; each time the loudspeaker announced a train, he started up and turned sleepy eyes on the clock over the door. At the next table a child, no older than Günther, was screaming because he was overtired. He made so much noise that the adults tried to soothe him by talking to him softly, but they achieved nothing.

People came and went, all of them carrying luggage. Whenever the door to the platforms opened, I was afraid that someone was coming to get me. But who could come?

The waiter had given the table a casual wipe and brought our coffee. But there were still beer and coffee stains. I had a feeling that the waiter was looking at me

impertinently because of my fur coat, but it was probably only my imagination. I had no will of my own—
the way you feel after a huge scare. All that was left
was the trembling no one could see and the fact that I
still did not dare to draw a deep breath. No pain and
no thoughts, only fatigue. Yes, like after an operation.

The suitcase stood between us in the corner, Berthold's briefcase on top of it. I put my toes against the
suitcase—he must have been touching it with his toes
on the other side—so that no one could steal our things.

Berthold looked very pale. I hadn't yet even addressed him by name, for there had not been any reason
to. Perhaps he's always pale, I thought. I bet I look pale
myself. Besides, everyone in the waiting room looked
pale because of the lighting and because they were tired.
Of course Berthold was tired as well; after all, he had
given a speech; that sort of thing wears you out.

I was glad that I could at least see his face again,
though it wasn't the face he sometimes wore. It was
more the face of someone who is just about to leave and
gives a final look back over his shoulder and quickly
nods to you one last time.

Each time our eyes met, I tried to smile; I didn't
want him to think that I was unhappy and regretting
the whole thing. I don't know if I brought it off; he
always looked away quickly, staring around the waiting
room as if there were something of interest there. He
did that so as not to embarrass me, he did not want to
seem curious, and I was grateful; he knew exactly how
I was feeling, and he realized that it was best to leave
it alone now.

But I didn't know how he was feeling. What could
he have been thinking while I was talking to Max and
he stood behind me without my being able to pay him
any attention? Outside you could hear the shunting of
the trains and the childish honking and humming noise

84

of the electrified freight cars; a locomotive was puffing in a self-important way.

"You don't take sugar?" he asked.

"No, thanks," I answered.

"Put it in your purse. For a horse or a dog."

"You're not supposed to give sugar to dogs," I said.

"You don't have a dog?"

"No. My husband . . . that is, because of Günther. Although . . . ."

He looked at the clock. "Twenty minutes more," he said. Then he slurped his coffee and made a long business of looking in his coat pocket for matches to light a cigarette. I would have liked to talk to him, about anything at all, but it was too soon. Even when we talked about dogs or lumps of sugar, the conversation took us in a direction we did not like. Maybe later, in the train.

We had bought me a ticket, and he had it in his pocket. A ticket to D., the city where he lived. There was no question that that was our destination and that I was going along. He had gone to the counter and asked for the ticket while I stood by, entirely unthinking, and let him take care of it all; I even let him pay. The ticket cost sixty marks and change. I thought of it only now. Yes, the ticket was there, but no one was forcing me to use it. Of course I'd have to pay him back the money in either case. I had to offer, preferably at once, but how to broach the subject?

I listened to the women next to me. The younger one asked her mother to give her regards to the relatives. Presumably they came from a village or a small town, but I couldn't make out the name of the place because they spoke a strange dialect. The mother was returning there, and the daughter worked here or was married to someone who lived here. The two of them took it all for granted, though they were a little sad now because they had to part and wouldn't see each other again for a while.

It was different for me. I wasn't being forced to leave, no necessity dictated it. I could easily stay, as I had done all these years. A single sentence had pulled me away. No matter who I told, they'd laugh at me. Because of that single sentence I was now sitting in the third-class waiting room next to . . . next to him, yes. He hadn't even told me that he loved me. For a moment he'd been deeply in love, but so had the others; that doesn't count, that's no reason to run away from everything.

"Those people over there," he said, jerking his head toward a table across the room, where several young men and women were sitting. They looked somewhat suspicious, especially the girls. One of them, with a bloated face and a turned-up nose, leaned against a young man's shoulder. "They're small-time black marketeers or something like that. Or police spies. Or both."

"How do you know?"

"You run across them in every train station. They're nice people."

"Really?"

"Once you get to know them, they're nice to be around."

"Really?" I repeated. I didn't understand what he meant or why he was telling me. Perhaps he wished he were with them instead of sitting with me waiting for his train.

The two women at our table got up, picked up their bags, and moved away. The waiter came at once and cleared their cups. Now there was a great emptiness to my right. I had to find something to talk to him about, I thought, or . . . .

"Can you speak the North German dialect?" I asked him.

"No," he said, looking at me. "I mean, I can read it. Why?"

"Oh, no special reason. It's just that there's a song. It doesn't matter. I only know the song in dialect. A silly little song. A children's song."

"From Uelzen?" he asked.

"Yes. From an old woman who always came to our house on washday."

"I see."

"There's not much to it. A lullaby, kind of. I never heard it anywhere else. She came from the flatlands—the old woman, I mean—but at that time she was living in a cheap cottage in Uelzen. There are narrow little streets there lined with cottages where the sugar-refinery workers live. I went to her house a couple of times; there was an open hearth, and a kettle hung over the fire. There was such a good smell of grain coffee; yes, all the smells were different from those at our house. When it was washday, I always went to the laundry shed with her. Her skin was brown and cracked, and her arms were skinny, as scraggly as heather. When she washed and scrubbed, she sometimes sang the song. My mother didn't want me to spend time in the laundry—she said it wasn't healthy—but the old woman never gave me away. I helped her do the wash and hang the clothes on the line."

"I see."

"No, it isn't true. I didn't help her at all. I was much too little, and I couldn't reach the line. All I did was hand her the clothes and the pins, behind the house, in the little garden. And when she was tired of me, she hit me on the legs with a wet towel."

"And the song?" he asked.

"I just happened to think of it," I said. I wanted to take his mind off it.

"You can sing it to me another time, if you want," he said.

"Yes, it's not important now. By the way, I have to give you the money for the ticket," I said, reaching abruptly for my purse. I was close to tears. Because of what he'd said and the way he'd said it, so casually, not because of the song and not because of Uelzen. But it was important not to cry now, that was why I reached for my purse.

He stopped me, putting his hand on mine. "If I had a wet towel, I'd hit you on the legs with it now," he said.

"It wasn't so bad," I said. "It didn't hurt. It was just cold and revolting. In the cottage there was a cat, too, a gray tiger-striped cat. She sat on the stove, with her feet under her body, staring into the fire."

Then it was time for us to go out on the platform and wait. It had actually begun to snow. Very large, separate flakes floated down onto the tracks and the gravel, melting at once. We looked in the direction from which the train was going to come. Suddenly its yellow eyes turned the corner and approached rapidly.

"Please step back. Watch your step," the loudspeaker blared. I looked at Berthold, he smiled, and I smiled in return. Then he picked up my suitcase and his briefcase.

2

We must have made some kind of mistake after all. I realized it only when my father-in-law's letter arrived. Until then I had refused to admit it. I'd thought, This is a transition period, it's going to be all right.

But what was the mistake?

I had plenty of time to think about it—all the time in the world. But thinking leads nowhere except to confusion. When you think about things, it all seems so obvious and simple. "No wonder," people say, and you say it yourself. No wonder; if you leave your husband and your child, you can hardly expect anything else. Such an action runs counter to the natural order; it is against nature. Some will call it a crime or even a sin, for which one is duly punished.

I know all this myself, I've always known it. I know that I did wrong. All I have to do is compare my behavior with the way other people lead their lives. With my mother and father, for example, or with the people I see on the street. From the outset I had counted on being very sad sometimes; infinitely sad. As punishment if you like, if that's how they want it. I wouldn't have minded the sadness. But . . . .

It's difficult to talk about—perhaps impossible. People think that you want to be in the right in spite of everything, when it's not a matter of right or wrong at

89

all. I don't want to quarrel; but that is not the reason I went with Berthold and left everything behind. No, granted that we are in the wrong, that is not our mistake; I can feel that even if I can't explain it. Our mistake, if we made a mistake, is something else entirely, something that has to do only with the two of us and nothing to do with wrong and sin and punishment, as they call it. Because if it was that, all I'd have to do is accept it, and that isn't hard. That's what everybody does, it's no big deal, they make too much of it. It's the simpler way, and it won't do for me.

Take my mother and father, for example. They lived the way you were supposed to live. It would never have occurred to them to do otherwise. My mother never made the slightest attempt to leave my father; it's odd even trying to imagine, for she could hardly have wanted to. Not because she was so happy; neither my mother nor my father was happy. They weren't unhappy either. I don't know what they were.

Everything was so dead and monotonous, today like yesterday, and tomorrow the same again, and on and on. When there was a war, they were frightened, and when someone in the family died, they were a little sad; and they were a little glad when my father was given a raise, but not very. Everything immediately turned into the ordinary and was neatly hung up in the closet. Even the Sundays . . . .

Each week I thought—and I believe our dog thought the same—Today is Sunday, something special is going to happen. But starting with breakfast, everything was only routine and boredom.

They did not know any better; they knew so little else that they were unable to be unhappy. It was quite impossible; they were in the right.

Sometimes, when I'm deep in despair, I envy them. Why can't I be that way? It's so much simpler. They know what is right and what is wrong, and before going to sleep they say their prayers. They do not ask for more; it's enough to enable them to live.

No, thinking led nowhere, and there was no way of discussing it with Berthold. He made a dismissive gesture and refused to join in, or he laughed while an angry wrinkle appeared between his eyes. "It's always been like that," he said. "There's no point in talking about it. We're outsiders, and that's that."

Once I found an old scrap of verse among his papers. By then I'd read everything he had ever written, and there was a great deal of it that I couldn't understand; still, one likes to know. Most of all I liked to know why he wrote these particular things and why he started writing again. He didn't like me to read his work; it made him nervous. "Why don't you read something sensible?" he said. "All this stuff is out of date, worthless." The couplet read:

That we dream of happiness and know what it is
And yet we have it not—that is our unhappiness.

It seemed good to me. "Yes, that's how it is," I said to him; for even if I didn't know what particular happiness he was dreaming about, I knew the unhappiness, his unhappiness, which was mine as well.

He flew into a rage and tore the paper from my hand. It was a piece of doggerel, he insisted, and that was because of the word *unhappiness*, which should be *misfortune*. But I didn't care about that, and I bet he said it just as a pretext.

And yet we had been happy—he, too, as I knew perfectly well. Even if it didn't last long and was quite a different kind of happiness than I'd imagined, it was happiness all the same. Or even more than happiness, if there is such a thing. It was a total absence, no past and no future. And only because it was true happiness were we so unhappy now; otherwise we wouldn't even have realized it. You see, the way it was before, with

Max, that was only existing and waiting, it wasn't true unhappiness.

I wish I'd died then. All the things people call punishment would have been a comfort compared to the way it was with us now. Everyone probably thought we were very pleased with ourselves; they didn't notice any difference. But for us there was no turning back. No matter how we tried, we remained outside. In that position we floated around things; we reached out to hold on to them, but we were blown onward—very softly, as if by a gentle breeze, but irresistibly—and how much it hurt all the same. So totally without hope and anchor. And neither of us let the other notice anything, so as not to inflict more pain.

Often I thought, Just so long as Berthold isn't wafted away from me, perhaps at night while I'm asleep or when I go out because I want to give him some solitude to work in—yes, and he and his work were wafted away, while I was slowly drifting to the other side. It did no good to stretch out your arms, and you were not allowed to call out . . . .

That's why I said, though I'll be criticized for saying it, that punishment, which people think is so terrible, would be a relief. A reward, even.

My father-in-law's letter arrived in late June. On June 21, to be precise. I remember the date because later I always counted back: on June 21 I saw him for the last time, and now this many days have passed, this many weeks, this many months. I'm getting used to it, truly. Soon I'll be used to it.

Berthold was still in the bathroom when the letter came, and I was in the kitchen getting our breakfast. I was talking to Frau Viereck about the weather, and we agreed that it would be another hot day. The morning paper lay on the kitchen table, and the daily weather report also promised that the good weather would hold.

There had been some accident, too; a freight train had jumped the rails, and people had died. It said so on the front page, but I only glanced at it while the coffee was filtering. Oh, yes, and in the night one of the tenants must have had a nightmare; Frau Viereck apologized because he had shouted for help. Had he woken us up?

Frau Viereck was a nice woman; she did not gossip about her boarders, and she didn't care what they did as long as they didn't bother the others. Nor was she concerned about us. She had come from the East and landed in this town, where she'd been for only a couple of years. She owned the apartment, one of those old-fashioned ones that took up the entire floor, with seven or eight rooms and an endless, long corridor from front to back. All the rooms were rented out; she herself camped out in a cubbyhole without a window. Even the furniture was old-fashioned, scraped together at auctions and the like. And yet Frau Viereck wasn't doing well and had gone into debt. The rents weren't high, for it wasn't a good section of town. We had been living there ever since we came from Ludwigshof.

Somebody had recommended the boardinghouse to Berthold because it was inexpensive, and a room happened to be vacant. He liked it at once. I mean, he didn't even bother to look at it first; he went straight to the window, gazed out at the street, and said, "Yes, this is it. What do you think?"

Of course I said that I agreed. He was pleased that we had found a place to stay so quickly and wouldn't have to go on looking. That was all he cared about. It was a horrible room, so high and uncomfortable and crowded with unnecessary pieces of furniture. Even the view was desolate—an old suburban street, nothing on the other side but red apartment houses with dirty balconies and stores on the ground floor— and it was raining. That was in early May. We had been living there ever since.

Frau Viereck went to the front door, for the bell was ringing and the mailbox lid had clanged. Then she came back to the kitchen with the mail, studied the addresses, and handed me one of the letters. "It must be for you," she said.

I was alarmed. In all this time I hadn't had any mail. Who was there to write me? No one knew where I was, and I hadn't written to anyone, not so much as a picture postcard. I didn't want to bother anyone. I thought it would be better if they forgot about me altogether. Perhaps my mail still came to the house, and people might be surprised that I didn't answer, but what could I have told them? I had to leave it to Max. It wasn't important to me.

The handwriting was unfamiliar. Yes, it's strange that I didn't know my father-in-law's writing. But his name was scrawled on the back of the envelope. "Temporary address, Munich," it said under it. And the front read, "Frau Marianne Helldegen, c/o Herr Berthold Möncken, Pension Viereck," with the right street and number.

Without opening it, I put the letter in the pocket of my robe. I'd had to buy a robe first thing in D. because of the people where I was staying; nothing special, but it would do. Then I went on talking to Frau Viereck as if nothing had happened. I asked her when the laundryman would come by to pick up; I wanted to add a few of Berthold's shirts to the pile. Then I took the breakfast tray and went to our room. Clearing one end of the table, I spread out a napkin and set out the cups.

I intended to leave the letter for later, when I was alone. I tested to make sure it wasn't rustling in my pocket. The letter was thin, I could tell. But this was no time to distract Berthold. Every morning he went straight to work; I think he was already there in his thoughts while he was still in the bathroom. As soon as he finished breakfast, he sat down at his typewriter. He began by flipping through his papers, and though he said a few words to me, this was the signal that he wanted to be left alone. He never said so—on the contrary, he said, "Stay here, don't run away"; but I knew better. And Frau Viereck was not allowed to come in to make the beds; the mess stayed. Only at noon, when we went out to eat, was she allowed to clean. Sundays were no different—day after day the same program.

When he came from the bathroom, we had our coffee. Breakfast didn't take long; he hurriedly swallowed a roll, that was all. He couldn't wait. Work had changed him totally. It had devoured him, and I was superfluous.

"I'm going shopping," I said.

"Yes," he said. He may not even have been listening.

"And afterward I'll go to the museum." I often went to the museum. Not because of the exhibits—I was already thoroughly familiar with them, and the guards all knew me by now—but because there were places to sit; it was free, and it passed the time. On sunny days I sat in the park and tried to read. I couldn't read in the museum because it would have looked odd.

At noon, while we ate, Berthold would ask me what I'd been up to all morning; then I told him whatever I could think of, about the pictures in the museum, the Chinese figurines, or the children and dogs in the park. He found it all very sensible. He was glad that I wasn't more demanding. I don't think he was getting on well with his work, but of course I didn't ask. That would have been a mistake, and though I felt bad about it, there was no way I could have helped him— that's what it was.

I read the letter in the streetcar. It was short. This is what it said.

Dear Marianne,

On the 21st I'll be spending the night in your town, leaving again the following morning. If the two of you have no objection, I'll visit you for an hour around six or six-thirty. If you have other plans, it doesn't matter, but in that case, please leave a message with the desk clerk at the Hotel Europe.

Cordially,
Your father-in-law

I read the note several times. My father-in-law was not fond of writing long letters; it wouldn't have suited him. Besides, what should he have written about? No mention of Günther. Of course not; he was discreet. And he had no way of knowing how I felt about it. If you looked closely, though, there was something about Günther in the letter after all. The phrase "It doesn't matter" could only mean that everything was all right and that his visit had nothing to do with Günther. I studied every word. All in all, it was a very friendly letter; it said, "Dear Marianne" and "Cordially"—yes, and my father-in-law wrote "the two of you." I particularly noticed that one. So in a way he was really writing to Berthold.

But what did he want with us? Perhaps he didn't want anything, perhaps it was only chance, but . . . how did he know our address? I looked at the postmark. The letter really had been mailed in Munich, so he wasn't coming from home; my father-in-law was traveling. Munich? Why Munich? We didn't know anyone in Munich. Or was he on a business trip?

At that, I felt a stab of fear. The date! What was the date? I looked out the streetcar window and searched along the houses sliding by. There were clocks everywhere, on the traffic islands, on the churches, and above the jewelry stores; you could tell the time everywhere, but nowhere was it written what day it was. Finally I asked the woman sitting next to me, and she said it was the twenty-first.

So it was today, and it was already past ten o'clock. I should have opened the letter at home and discussed it with Berthold right away. After all, it was up to him whether he wanted to see my father-in-law or preferred not to. And if I'd shown him the letter right away, it would have been easier to talk to him about it. But it's possible that he would have been upset by it and his whole morning's work would have been spoiled.

Would it be best for me to go back right now and tell him? Oh, but if only I knew why my father-in-law was coming to see us; Berthold was sure to ask. And he probably wouldn't say anything else except that he'd leave the decision to me. If I were to say, "Let's not let him come," he might think that I was giving up the visit only for his sake. And if were to say, "Yes, let's see him," he might think that I was pleased to hear from home and that I was homesick.

No, I had to make the decision on my own. I had to decide first, then stick to my decision. The best thing would be to manage things in such a way that Berthold never knew anything about it. It really had nothing to do with him, so why upset him? It was entirely my responsibility.

At the railroad station I got off the streetcar and waited for the green light. I meant to go straight to the Hotel Europe, write a note for my father-in-law, and leave it with the desk clerk. But what if the clerk should recognize me? Once, three or four years ago, I had stayed there with Max. Desk clerks have such good memories for faces. Every step needed to be thought out.

That's why I first went to the other side of the square and stopped in front of the window of Weyhe Fashions. It was the best shop in town, its reputation even extending beyond the city. I looked at the displays. I'd stood there with Berthold—right at the beginning, when we first came to town. At the time I thought, Now it's almost like you said; we stand outside the stores and look at the displays and touch. An evening dress of silver lamé in the window caught my eye, and Berthold noticed.

"Come on, let's buy the thing," he said at once, pulling me toward the entrance.

"No. It's a designer dress, and it will cost a fortune."

"So what. What do we care about money? We've got it."

"And what do we care about the dress? We have no use for it."

"We'll need it in the fall."

"But not until then," I said. He kept telling me that by fall we'd be out of all this. Berthold was writing something for the stage, and what he meant was that I should wear the dress to the opening night. I was to sit in a box while his play was being performed. He painted a detailed picture. He would make a bow in my direction when he was called out at the end, and everyone would see me sitting there, part of it all. The idea gave him childish pleasure.

It was only with great effort that I finally talked him out of the dress. But that was the way he was. When I was sad, I sometimes thought, He's just trying to make up to me for everything; he thinks that if he buys me beautiful things, I'll be happy and everything will be well. But that wasn't the real reason; it was that having money troubled him. He would have preferred spending what he had on something beautiful, although as soon as he got things, he stopped caring about them and never used them. When there was no more money, he didn't mind. On the contrary, then his restlessness abated. So I always acted very bored when we passed shop windows, or I found fault with everything. He had given me all the money to keep, and there was quite a bit left, but I had to be sensible. He was glad that he no longer had to bother with it.

For example, there was the business with the dog, which happened the first week. It was a puppy, barely ten weeks old, a gray schnauzer, not even purebred, I think. Just because I called to it on the street and the puppy came stumbling up to play with me, Berthold got the idea of buying it without a moment's thought. The woman who was walking the dog did not want to part with him, or at least she said she didn't. Berthold tried to persuade her, he even lost his temper, and my telling him to calm down did no good at all. People were even stopping to listen. Probably Berthold gave the woman far too much. He told me it was just a hundred marks, but I don't think that was true.

And what were we to do with a dog? Anyone could have seen that we couldn't keep him. Frau Viereck made a face when we arrived—of course, because of the other boarders. The dog was high-spirited, still a puppy and he wanted to play; I had to keep an eye on him constantly, to keep him from romping and yelping, which would have disturbed Berthold in his work. We had the animal for barely a week before we gave him away.

And what a lot of trouble we had finding someone to take him; we wanted to make sure that he'd have nice owners and lead a good life. Finally we gave him to some of Frau Viereck's compatriots who lived in the suburbs; they didn't have any money, so Berthold also gave them the dog-license fee for a year in advance. I cried when they came to get the dog; I'd gotten used to having him around. Berthold was sad too; he picked up the puppy and said, "Well, then, little brother." He was upset because it was impossible for us to keep a dog. "Every Tom, Dick, and Harry has a dog except us," he said. Then he sat down at his typewriter and never wasted another word on the matter.

It was high time for the dog to go. Our loneliness was already so great that it wasn't fair to impose it on a dog.

But one thing Berthold did not know; a few times already I'd been on the point of walking into Weyhe Fashions to talk with the manager. I wanted to suggest that they hire me as the receptionist. I still have my looks and good manners—and good taste, too. Of course I'd use my maiden name; then if the ladies who came in to shop were to notice the *von* in my name, they'd be impressed, which would be to the store's advantage.

So that's what I wanted to propose to them. Not because of the money—we didn't need that yet, and they wouldn't pay me much to start with anyway—but because it would have given me something to do; I wouldn't have been reduced to waiting, or the waiting would have been easier to bear. But I never carried out my plan, for fear that they would say no and also for Berthold's sake. He was very sensitive and would have misunderstood. Instead I fed myself with hopes of the fall, as I'd learned to do from Berthold. Everything was put off until fall; one didn't have to endure any longer than that, and there was no point in thinking beyond. When we gave away the dog, the saying was, "By fall we'll definitely get another one." We were going to buy a Volkswagen in the fall, too.

Slowly I walked around the square, past all the stores, to the Hotel Europe. Next to the front entrance there was a hairdressing salon, the window displaying expensive soaps and perfumes. I'd been to the beauty parlor only the week before, and my hair looked all right. I watched the people going in and out of the hotel and getting in and out of the cars that stopped. All of them knew exactly where they were going; they had plans, and some of them were in a rush. The doormen called taxis or, when a car drove up, ran over, opened the door, and took the luggage while the guests rummaged in their pockets for a tip.

In the old days they would have done the same for me when I arrived, and the desk clerk would have waited on me. My name was still the same, I was basically the same person I'd always been for them—and yet I shied away from going into the lobby and talking about my father-in-law with the man behind the reception desk. I'm sure they would have been extremely polite, Madame this and Madame that, but I was afraid that they could tell just by looking at me; and I might have gotten muddled and started to stutter, arousing their suspicion all the more.

I walked back and forth a couple of times outside the front entrance, pretending to be waiting for someone. Finally I felt silly, and strangely enough, my knees were trembling. I thought, My father-in-law hasn't checked in yet, and I've still got time to think it through carefully; there's no rush. That's why I retraced my steps all around the square and then down the avenue to the Café Blüthner. Tables and wicker chairs stood on the sidewalk under the red-and-white-striped canopy. In the mornings it wasn't as crowded as in the afternoons. I sat at a table and ordered a glass of sherry.

Usually I did not frequent cafés in the morning. Though we still had money, I wanted to make it last. When the weather was good, it was just as easy to pass the time in the park across the street, where there was shade and a large fountain and where the benches were never full. When it rained, there was always the museum.

I paid for my sherry right away. The waitresses in the café were in the habit of coming back in five minutes to say that their shift was over and ask whether it would be all right if they brought the bill. Perhaps they had had some bad experiences—people getting up to leave without paying and then mingling with the passersby in the street. I'd been here before with Berthold, and when it happened to us for the second time that the waitress asked us to pay, he grew excited and wanted to lodge a complaint. To avoid such scenes, we preferred to pay at once.

Yes, once in a while we came here in the afternoons when we didn't go to the movies, just to pass the time; there was nothing else to do. But if there wasn't an empty table on the sidewalk, we walked on, disappointed. We absolutely refused to share a table with strangers.

When we did find a table, we might spend as much as two hours there. There wasn't much need to talk, and we watched the traffic, the people and the women and the cars. Through the leaves of the trees you could see the brown gargoyles on the pediment of the opera house. Each time we got up to go back to the boardinghouse, I had a bad feeling, almost a guilty conscience, and I think Berthold felt the same way. At those times we were very careful what we said; we tried to be as casual as possible.

Every now and then Berthold recognized one or another of the passersby. When they were out of sight, he mentioned that it was so-and-so or what's-her-name, writers or artists or theater people. It seemed to me that he knew a great many people, at least by sight; it was hard to find out how well he actually knew them. When I asked if he didn't want to talk to them, he said, "For God's sake, that just turns into prattle."

Yet it would have been good if just once he could have spent time with other people, not always and only with me. I'm sure it would have been entertaining for me too. But there was nothing I could do, that was the way he wanted it. He went so far as to hide, so that his

102

acquaintances might not accidentally discover him—
that's how unsociable he was. I don't know why, but
it wasn't because of me. It was something else, something I didn't understand, and when I asked him, he
was evasive, so I stopped asking.

He was very good at evasion. Before you knew
what was happening, you'd lost him; he was far away,
though he sounded as if nothing was amiss. You felt
like a total fool for having asked your questions, until
you realized that you were quite alone, and that was
his intention.

Of course, I also thought that he was tired of me
and just didn't want to tell me he'd like to be rid of
me—that he was waiting for me to take the first step.
But at the same time I felt sorry for him; it wasn't any
easier for him than for me. I felt sorrier for him than I
can say. He had no one else. I don't know what another
woman would have done.

I realized all this while we were still in D., though
not as clearly as later. At that time we were still
strangers, really. D. was where Berthold had lived before, and we had to return there first, to cash the check
and give up his room and pick up his things. We packed
up everything, and whatever he didn't want to take was
stored with friends.

Berthold didn't own much—a couple of suits, some
underwear, a portable typewriter, and many colored
folders filled with manuscripts. Nothing else. No furniture and no personal belongings; not even books,
which surprised me most. I thought writers always had
large libraries. But Berthold said that if there was a book
you really had to read, you could always borrow it from
the public library. And another time he said, "Posses-
sions lead to sorrow."

D. is a boring city. A lot of artists live there, all of
whom know each other. I thought that was probably

good, but Berthold claimed that it was the worst thing that could happen to them. It was hard for me to understand.

We had to stay in D. for almost two weeks, which was how long it took to take care of things. It was a very bad time for me; from the first moment I had no idea exactly why I was there. If I'd stayed home, then . . . I'd pictured it all so differently, I'd pictured nothing at all; there hadn't been time. And now . . . .

But in D. I wasn't yet ready to think things through so clearly; I was still getting used to the situation. I just wandered about and told myself, "This can't be! This can't be! Perhaps tomorrow . . . ." I decided to wait until tomorrow. It was nothing more than a postponement, then as now.

Berthold found me a place to stay with people he knew. I couldn't stay with him because his room was too small, with just space enough for a kind of cot, a wardrobe, and a table where he worked. I'd assumed that it was for only a day or two. When it took longer, I wanted to move to a hotel so as not to impose on my hosts. But I couldn't, they would have been insulted, and I liked them very much; they were so open. I was made to sleep in the wife's bed while she slept on her husband's couch and he set up a collapsible cot for himself every night. They said they didn't mind, laughing at my concern. Both of them were still very young. He worked for the newspapers and the radio, and she translated books.

Always—yes, even during that time in D.—I felt like an intruder. Some evenings, when Berthold was there too, it seemed that all of us were very cheerful; I tried hard to go along with everything, and I'm sure I succeeded, but later, when I lay in bed, I knew that I was not part of it. I don't know what Berthold told them about me, but I don't think they cared much. They weren't nosy. It was very important to me to know what they thought of Berthold, and I would have liked to talk to the woman about him, but I was ashamed; it seemed unfair to Berthold.

Often he was surly and taciturn, even with other acquaintances we met; I worried that their feelings would be hurt. "We're used to his ways," they said, laughing, whenever I tried to apologize for him. Another time the young man said, "He's his own worst enemy." The hardest part was when people congratulated him on the prize he'd been given in our town. Then Berthold swore and turned away. But I believe everyone thought he was just putting on an act. And I would dearly have loved to know if they thought he was a great writer or what; there was no way I could judge. But to ask would have been betrayal.

I'd already given up all hope. I was living in D. like some relative visiting Berthold for a couple of weeks; that was what was so horrible. A few times, when we were together during the day, we went shopping for me; I'd brought so little. That was the most fun. Berthold took care of everything, and all I had to do was be careful that we didn't buy things I didn't need. In the shoestore he was ready to get five pairs of shoes just because he liked all of them. He needed nothing for himself, but he wanted me to have everything.

I would have liked to give him a present, but I didn't know what; I was afraid of the expression on his face if I walked up with some little gift. It was not possible to give Berthold pleasure. Why had he taken me with him? Was it only pity? Was it because I had chased him? Why wouldn't he talk to me about the one thing that was really important to us?

And yet he took it for granted that we would go someplace together. Often when I was in his room . . . that, too, was different, not at all the way you might think . . . . Most of the time there was something he had to do, not a major work, like now, but letters to be answered, that sort of thing. When he finished, he always said, "And what shall we do now?" Then he brought out a map, and we discussed where we wanted to go. It was on the tip of my tongue to ask, "Wouldn't you rather go alone?"

What use was I to him? Perhaps we'd acted precipitously, but he should not be made to suffer for it; it was my fault. It's always the woman's fault. Women have to think things through more carefully than men do, but I hadn't thought this through at all, I'd just stumbled into it. If only we'd still been like a courting couple, if only for a day or a night. But when I saw him bent over the map, his finger wandering, proposing one or another place, I was too much of a coward to introduce the subject.

I thought him much more self-assured than he was; he was so good at projecting self-assurance, even with other people. He always made light of everything, that's what led me astray. Later, when I asked him why he had been that way, he made fun of me; he said that he couldn't treat a fine lady like any ordinary girl. He was only trying to annoy me—another evasion. He always evaded me; I can't explain it, but it was as if he held a grudge against me.

In the mornings, as I sat on my bed, I thought about it and forgot all about getting dressed. Only because I heard Berthold's friends moving around the small apartment and because I didn't want to upset their routine did I put my clothes on after all. What I really wanted to do was lie down again and never get up. And it was terrible for me to see the others' cheerful faces at the breakfast table, it was almost impossible to bear. How young and carefree they were; even when they quarreled, there was no strain.

Only later did I realize how shy Berthold was, and how insecure. By now I understood, but I didn't let him know I knew. I even loved him all the more for it. But

106

why he was so shy—that I do not know to this day. I never knew there were such men; I thought men were different. All the men I'd ever had anything to do with were importunate and crude, they were hard to keep at a distance. None of them was evasive, none was like Berthold.

And yet my feelings told me that he was much more affectionate than other men. Often I felt like hugging him; I longed simply to put my arms around him— we couldn't go on like this. But each time, quite unintentionally, he slipped away from me. He was looking for something or talking about something else as if he'd just thought of it; he was very clever at this. Then the moment was past, and my arms felt paralyzed. I didn't want to hurt him, and it really did seem that he was afraid of being touched. At the time I didn't understand any of that.

Surely all the people who knew him thought that we were real lovers. When we met in their presence or said goodbye to each other and merely shook hands, they probably thought we didn't want to give ourselves away; I could tell as much from their understanding smiles. Oh, but those two weeks were horrible! Berthold and I did not embrace properly a single time. We didn't kiss, we didn't sleep together, though of course no one believes me.

In the train, going to D. that first night, he put his arm around me lightly, and that was good. I even fell asleep, exhausted by all the excitement. In the morning, before we arrived in D., he brought me a cup of coffee from the dining car.

But everything changed as soon as we got to D. We arrived at dawn. Berthold was a different man from the one who had said that he wanted to die with me. I couldn't possibly remind him of it, it seemed so unreal— even to me. I didn't even dare to think about it, it seemed so dangerous.

But I didn't cry; it just seemed that way afterward. I never cried much, not even at times when other women might have. That's why at home they thought I was heartless. In D., however, I felt paralyzed, as in a dream, when you know that you're only dreaming and you strain agonizingly to wake up and put an end to the misery and uncertainty, but you can't. That's worse than crying.

In reality, though, it may all have been different from the way I'm telling it. It wouldn't even be worth it to remember those two weeks in D. if the present situation weren't so similar—only so much harder to bear, because between that time and this lies the brief period when we were happy.

Even now it would be better not to tell about it, since I'll tell it all wrong and be understood all wrong. And that would be unfair to Berthold—yes, especially to him. There is so much for which there are no words, and that is what's real. It exists, certainly, but you have to experience it yourself. There's no way of communicating it; people only get the wrong idea.

To whom was I talking anyway? I was talking to my father-in-law, and my father-in-law wasn't there; he wasn't even at the hotel yet. I was all alone at my table in the café. People passed by, some swiftly and some dawdling, talking to each other, laughing. Cars and trams ran regularly up and down the street. At the entrance to the café a waitress wearing a small, cute apron leaned against the entrance and watched the tables, and I . . . yes, I was sitting there alone pretending my father-in-law was with me. Was I talking out loud? No, the people at the adjoining tables took no notice of me, so they hadn't heard anything; they thought I was like them.

It was simply that I hadn't talked to anyone for months, for years. I wanted to tell someone the story of my life—not to justify myself, no; just to tell it, that's all, to get rid of it. And as always, there was no one. Even if my father-in-law had been sitting across from me, I wouldn't have told him any of this. We weren't nearly close enough, and he wouldn't have understood. Surely he would have been convinced that I was trying to apologize to him for leaving Günther and Max.

Nor would he have believed that we had been happy after all; he would have thought I was spinning empty phrases. Out of politeness he would have pretended to believe me, but inside he'd have been thinking, How can she talk about happiness when she's so unhappy? Yes, the words are stupid, I agree, useless words. No one knows what happiness is, certainly not I. When I had it, everything seemed so ordinary that I didn't think of it as happiness but as . . . I don't know what; I didn't give it a second thought.

But unhappiness—everyone knows precisely what that is.

There is a great emptiness behind faces and behind everything that happens, an emptiness that questions and questions. During the day you manage not to hear; so much is going on, and then there are all the habits and customs you use to order your daily life. But at night, when you become aware of it by chance—often it's nothing more than a silly song on the radio—then the fear grows and you can't go to sleep. Why is there this emptiness? It wasn't that empty before.

Yes, it seems that unhappiness isn't allowed. That's what they all preach, they preach it to me too; instead they talk about obligations and responsibilities. I never did believe them; I always thought that they talked about such things because they themselves were unhappy and angry and didn't want others to have what they lacked. And I do not believe it to this day, although I find myself in a situation they could use to illustrate their sermons.

Berthold was happy, too. I could not tell him so today, for he would only get angry, and it wouldn't do any good. But that he was happy—I knew that absolutely; otherwise I wouldn't have been so happy.

It came over us at a time when actually it was already too late and everything was hopeless. Quite imperceptibly and without our doing anything to bring it about and without our even being aware of it—suddenly there it was. Suddenly Berthold was the way he really was, and all my misery seemed never to have existed. Because I knew from the very first how he really was, from the very first instant. I'd merely forgotten.

Oh, there's no way to talk about it.

One day we left D. The young couple with whom I'd been staying took us to the railroad station and waved goodbye. The train started, and all at once the weather turned beautiful. It even grew warm, much warmer than was usual for the time of year. It was only mid-April, but when we crossed the Rhine, the fruit trees were in blossom everywhere. Berthold laughed because I was wearing a fur coat. It was a different world. As he helped me take off my coat, we touched. We were alone in the compartment. Suddenly his real face was back. That's how it began.

We did not travel far, only two or three hours, but it would have been all right even if it had taken longer; we weren't tired, we needed only to look at each other. We rode as far as Olmheim. In D. they had told us that Olmheim was a quiet place, but we didn't like it. Nothing but rest homes, everything narrow and a little old-fashioned and dowdy. "How about hopping barefoot in the dew-freshened grass?" Berthold scoffed—because Olmheim was a spa, where people came to take the waters.

We got on a small yellow mail bus that stopped at the marketplace, and we rode on through narrow forest gorges with swampy meadows and a brook running

110

through the center. We were the only passengers. The horn sounded its bright, cheerful two notes whenever we came near a village, until finally we got to Ludwigshof, the end station; that's where the border is.

"This is the end of the line," Berthold said cheerfully. "It seems a nice place." We had no passports. In my hurry I'd left mine behind at home, and Berthold didn't have one to begin with; he didn't like to travel. Occasionally he moved from one town to another, that was all. Perhaps if we'd had passports, we might have gone farther. Even though life on the other side of the border was the same as here, we would have enjoyed finding that out. But we didn't think of that until much later.

Ludwigshof isn't even a village. It's just a tiny border station deep in the mountains, with only three or four houses along the street; that's where the border guards and foresters live. One of the buildings had been destroyed by mortar fire during the war and hadn't yet been rebuilt. And there was a sawmill; you could hear the saws shriek and the logs thunder as they rolled off the wagons. And then, of course, there was the inn, two hundred yards from the barrier, where a red light burned all night long. We could see it from our window.

I want to describe every detail, because we were happy there. I'd like to explain why we were happy, so as to prevent anyone's thinking it was only because we finally slept together. No, it wasn't that; it was more a flight from those things for which I can't find words, and I was almost sorry when we had to embrace because we could no longer endure the other things. I felt cowardly and evil, fearing that in this way his face might be extinguished for me forever. Everyone will doubt me, everyone will smile and say it's my imagination; as soon as you talk about it, it's as if it had never been, and yet it's impossible to forget it. It changed me more than anything that ever happened to me. It made me incapable of any other kind of joy.

Often I wondered how his wife could have left him. I think no wife can bear to be looked at that way, but perhaps she was blind to the look or Berthold didn't look at her as he looked at me. I don't know much about it, and I never mentioned it. It wasn't any of my business.

How quiet the nights were. Only the roaring of the water at the sawmill dam, and sometimes an owl chuckling in a wailing sort of way high up in the forest. Outside, the moon shone down on the hollow and on the white apple trees along the road. The chain of hills on the other side of the frontier faded into a gentle mist. Often we stepped to the window and stared out until we were chilled through.

The days were very quiet too. When we were in our room, we could hear the hunchbacked chambermaid grumbling downstairs in the kitchen and the innkeeper muttering. The sounds were the kind that tire you.

There wasn't much traffic on the road outside the inn toward the frontier—only three or four cars a day, a few more on Sundays—but you could hear every car that passed; the road was covered with new gravel, so that every footstep crunched. We always rushed to the window, as if we were expecting someone to pay us a call, but it was just a joke; we had nothing else to do. Most of the time it was one of the border guards going home after work, a sheepdog trotting at his side; we would call to it, and the dog would lift his eyes to us before giving his master a questioning look.

Soon we knew them all, the frontier guards and the dogs. In the evenings we walked to the barrier and chatted with the men, who didn't have much to do. There was a bigger road on the other side of the hills, where traffic was heavier, but ours was too far out of the way.

There weren't any smugglers here, either; it wasn't worth their while. The frontier guards made their rounds through the woods and hills to catch young people trying to cross illegally to join the Foreign Legion. "Surely it isn't hard," Berthold said. "All you have to do is wade across the brook. If you really want to get across, wet feet don't mean a thing." But the frontier guards explained that most people didn't know which was the right brook.

Everyone liked Berthold, who was an altogether different person than he'd been in D. He was so young—that wasn't just my imagination. The dogs went to him at once, and even the white goats staked along the slope liked him to stroke them. And for the whole two weeks the weather was wonderful. The warm spring drifted across the border from the west into our valley. The fruit trees were covered with snow-white wreaths of blossoms. One morning the swallows arrived; they perched along the telephone wire leading from the inn to the sawmill, right outside our window, and when we lay on the bed after dinner, we heard them twittering to each other.

Every afternoon the little yellow bus arrived. Long before it turned the corner by the mountain, it sounded its horn. No one knew where we were, no one could write to us, and yet we were cheered by the mail bus; it took itself so seriously.

Berthold talked to everybody, to the innkeeper and to the innkeeper's wife and to the pale, pregnant housemaid; he had stopped being withdrawn and awkward. He even talked to the only other people staying at the inn, a married couple, both pretty fat; they had a little car and took a lot of excursions, even across the frontier. I thought Berthold wouldn't like them. They were quite different, the husband was a department head in an insurance company. But Berthold listened closely to whatever they had to say, and he laughed and joked with them; he was a changed man.

I noticed the very first night how young he was, not in years—he was seven years older than me—but in his behavior. Very, very young. I noticed it in his movements, in his hands, in everything. So guileless and shy, and so astonished. He moved me. I felt much older. Everything was quite different from what I'd imagined.

We didn't care that we had no passports. As long as the good weather held, the place where we were was quite enough. On the other side, right behind the hills, there was a handsome town, they told us, but we had no need of an old town. We couldn't see it from where we were, for we were in a genuine hollow, the valley ringed with hills as if there were no way out. Right behind this barrier the mountain crest took a sharp turn and hid the view completely, as did the street running alongside below. You could follow it with your eyes for only a little way; very soon it disappeared around the corner, probably through a narrow gorge, the brook always keeping pace.

Just at the corner there was a large red quarry, and next to it a pilgrimage chapel—a tiny thing, like a toy. Sometimes you could see the pale-blue bus that had brought the pilgrims, and you could make out the miniature figures going into the chapel. There was a healing spring there, they said. We couldn't go there, but now and then a black-bearded monk with bare feet in sandals came from the chapel. When we spoke to him, he replied in our language.

But from our window the quarry looked like a wound in the mountain, like raw flesh. Once, early in the morning, there was the sound of blasting, and I started up out of my sleep. "It wasn't a shot," Berthold said.

114

Above the quarry the morning sky was veiled in a cloud of dust.

On the street outside the café there was a screech of tires as a car braked abruptly, and then there was a crash. People came running. I too rose in fright from my chair. But it was nothing serious, only the fenders.

I looked at the waitress and then at my watch. I hadn't been here very long, it just seemed that way. No one could speak rudely to me because I sat too long and had ordered only a sherry. I still had plenty of time to think about everything; I did not have to decide right away.

Maybe I was worrying about nothing. We had been happy, and of course nothing could stay the same forever. Anyone I told my story to would laugh at me. Even my father-in-law.

Berthold had to work—of course he did. It was my fault; I was too impatient. And my father-in-law was the last person I could discuss it with. Perhaps he wouldn't say anything, but he'd think, What does she want anyway, a woman who left her husband and her child, and all because someone said something crazy? It serves her right.

But of course my father-in-law knew nothing of the first words Berthold had said to me, and he wouldn't have understood anyway. Often in our dreams a character says something to us that no one would really say, but we understand immediately, and it touches us so deeply because it is meant for no one else. In the morning, when we get up and go to breakfast, we worry that everyone will notice we've changed completely.

I don't think there was a single time when Berthold told me he loved me. I took care not to say it to him. I was pretty sure he wouldn't like it. Besides, it wasn't necessary—it was something we knew.

One time the fat couple staying at our inn took us

up a mountain in their car. We were very grateful to them, because we couldn't hike far; I hadn't brought the right shoes. We could only walk along the road a little, and even that was painful because of the gravel that pressed through my thin soles. And the forest paths were too sloping, and at this time of year so muddy that I slipped.

The drive up the mountain was steep, always close to the precipice, but a well-traveled road. The top was bare, it was only grass and bushes and a radar station. Oh, and the view we had from there—far, so far. Behind us, to the east, lay the plain from which we'd come, without clear outlines, only mist. And to the west, beyond the border, only woods and one blue mountain chain after another, between them dark valleys with green patches, and wherever the sun penetrated, white villages and old castles, and then more blue mountains. Our mountain was higher than the others. We could see everything.

Berthold took me by the elbow, and I could tell he was happy, because he could not speak; his voice would probably have trembled. I too was speechless.

Impossible to forget such a moment. Berthold won't forget it either. You can't will such a moment, which is worth more than a whole lifetime; you can only wait for it. Soon Berthold too would long to have it back— I was sure he would. And when he finished his work, it would be like that again.

I have to admit that from time to time I grew restless, even then. Especially at the beginning. Or did I say that already? I want to talk about it over and over, until I find the right word—but I can't find it. It was so different from the way it had been with Max or with Arnim. I did not know what it was supposed to mean when he looked at me.

He could look at me for hours; it seemed to be his favorite activity. Well, maybe not for hours—maybe it

116

just seemed that way because it was almost unbearable. He sat next to me in bed and looked and looked, without speaking, without blinking, always straight into my eyes. As if I weren't here at all, as if it weren't me he was looking at. And I could see nothing but his face above me; everything else was as if lost. I thought, What is he looking for?—but he wasn't looking for anything. And I thought, Perhaps he's annoyed, perhaps he has some fault to find with my face, with my body, with me; perhaps I'm not smart enough for him.

Then I wanted to ask, What is it? And as if he knew, a slight smile flitted across his face, not like his own smile, but from somewhere else—a childish amazement, I don't know at what. The amazement took hold of me; it was like floating, and I felt too heavy for it. That's why I found it almost unbearable.

Later I didn't want anything to change. I wanted only the face and the amazement. I couldn't get enough of it, I would have liked to absorb it all; I wanted to be like him, and sometimes I felt as if I were. When he smiled, I had to smile, without any reason. It was like a mirror—no, not a mirror, no glass between us—like one smiling face. Oh, I knew that he loved me, even if everything was strange to me. Once he almost said it, and I think now that meant even more than if he actually had said it.

We were talking about his books, or rather about his writing, and he said, "I had to start on it at an early age."

"But why?" I asked.

"What choice did I have?"

He did not like to talk about his writing, and I was sorry that I'd asked; even if I didn't know why, I always sensed that my questions made him sad. He looked at me a long time, and then he said, "Perhaps if I'd met you sooner, I wouldn't have had to spend my time on that first."

People will say that that's the way all lovers talk and you can't take it literally. Everybody thinks that they've always known each other and only chance kept them from actually meeting. But when Berthold said something like that, it made me feel ashamed and in need of making it up to him. Yes, what's to become of him if I leave him? It isn't thinkable. No one will see his face. It will drift over the heath like the moon, no place to cling and rest, and I am far away and it's all my fault.

Because sometimes I thought . . . and I was thinking it even now, at this very moment, sitting outside this stupid, noisy café, staring at the street, though no one had any inkling of what I was thinking . . . . Yes, and it's almost ridiculous to think anything of the sort; if people suspected or learned, they would screech with mockery, "What? That fellow with the pinched face and the stuck-up manner?" And I'd have to agree with them, because the things I'm talking about can't be seen or shown. And yet . . . .

I would have liked to know what he was like as a child. There were no memories, no pictures of that time; everything seemed obliterated or hidden behind an opaque veil. Sometimes the curtain stirred a little, as if something were there after all, but perhaps it was only a draft and nothing else. Once I asked him about it.

"Like every other kid," he said. "There's nothing to talk about."

That wasn't true—he just did not want to think about it. It must have presented some kind of danger for him. I tried to find out so I could help him, but I didn't succeed.

He still had a mother. She lived in another town, and it had been a long time since Berthold's last visit to her. He wrote her on her birthday and at Christmas— a postcard, that was all. She too wrote now and again. When we were in D., one of her letters arrived. Berthold read it while I was there, then he tore it up and threw the pieces in the wastebasket.

"What does she say?" I asked.

"Nothing special," he replied. "She read in the newspaper that I won the prize, and she's writing to congratulate me."

"But of course she's proud of you," I suggested.

"That's her business," he answered. "It's got nothing to do with me. She has money; what she's hard up for is ways to pass the time. I don't want anything from her—just let her leave me alone, and I won't bother her."

It hurt me to hear him talk like that, although I didn't get on well with my mother either. I thought, How hard he is. Why can't he forgive her? But it wasn't hardness.

There were other children in the family—a brother who had died right at the beginning of the war, and a married sister Berthold knew hardly anything about. When the subject came up, he erased it at once, as if he were cleaning a blackboard. It was that way with everything, and that was what made it so hard to be with him. I never knew what he'd be like from one minute to the next or if he'd even be there at all. You couldn't hold on to him—that's what it was.

Then I remembered something that cheered me up: Berthold liked my father-in-law a lot. He often asked me about him, and I told him as much as I knew. To my surprise, though they had barely met and my father-in-law was a prominent businessman and the two of them were so different, Berthold was actually worried about him. It could do no harm for them to meet again. It would be a change for Berthold; we never saw anyone at all. Perhaps it would allow Berthold to relax and be good for his work. It would be only a brief interruption; my father-in-law would be traveling on tomorrow. So

119

it was just for tonight, for two or three hours. I'd let the two of them talk, and I would listen.

I was glad now that I hadn't left a message at the hotel. Berthold might even have reproached me if I'd turned my father-in-law away. "How could you do that to the old man?" he would have asked. Yet I would have acted only for Berthold's sake, to keep him from thinking that I still had ties. For the same reason I avoided talking about home. I did talk to him about Uelzen and my childhood, but not about my marriage. Even when I recited the lullaby and wrote it down for him, I didn't let on that I'd sung it to Günther every night, but perhaps he suspected. He liked the song though he didn't understand the dialect; it sounded so funny on his lips that we laughed a lot.

But if the meeting with my father-in-law should miscarry—what then? What could the two of them possibly talk about? And Berthold was so distrustful now. I mustn't allow him to realize that I knew how displeased he was with his work. I had to pretend to be invariably cheerful. It wasn't easy; I couldn't always be on my guard, and he was so alert that the slightest change in my voice worried him. Wouldn't my father-in-law notice at once that I was always on my best behavior and how unnatural our life was? And how was I to explain?

I had had no practice spending time with artists. How could I know that they were harder than other human beings? So inhuman in their hardness. Perhaps they had to be for their work, but if they hated their work as much as Berthold hated it, and if they were so tormented by it that there was no recognizing them— how was I to deal with that?

Besides, Berthold told me over and over that he was not really a writer. You couldn't call him that; if you did, his face twisted in disgust. He named a few, living and dead, who were real writers, but he said his

120

case was quite different; the fact that he wrote was mere chance, a pastime to keep him from going crazy with boredom, nothing more. It was just procrastination, he said. He really meant it; yet he did nothing to change the situation. He could have stopped writing, after all. Perhaps the people he named talked the same way; I didn't know and I didn't ask. I only saw how tormented he was and how useless I was.

Sometimes he was like a man who had committed a crime and was trying to hide it from the world and from himself. That was why he was always evasive—so that no one could touch him and lay the whole story bare. Of course I knew that he had committed no crime, that he was quite incapable of it, but he too may have felt the way you feel in dreams sometimes, when you think you've done something terrible and you want to run away but can't. And I stood there shouting, "Come on, I'm here," but he did not see me, and he held his breath in fear and waited spellbound for his pursuer.

Those are words I've never used before, and they aren't really right, but I have no other way of thinking about Berthold. I only sensed that I was not enough, that that was why he tormented himself with his work and pushed me aside. My father-in-law would have said that a man had to work and could not spend all his time worrying about his woman, but that wasn't it; my father-in-law could not understand. It wasn't work the way he knew it; it made no sense, and even if a good line came out of it, it was no more than what someone might say in his sleep when the torment was too great.

I did not want my father-in-law to tell Max that I was unhappy. Berthold was not to blame. I needed only to remember him standing on that bridge—I think it was in Heidelberg, when he was at the university, when he was still very young. I could see him standing there alone, and I understood everything without being able to put it into words. I wanted to run to him and make everything all right, but something held me back, and I hesitated all over again. Might it be that running to him was what was dangerous?

When he first told me about it, it didn't sound as if it had really happened to him. It was more like something the grown-ups had told him or something he'd seen in the movies—that's how casually he spoke about it, in order to mislead me. I wasn't supposed to take it seriously, and I came close to not taking it seriously, to treating it like everything else that happens to us as children and that we've long since gotten over. He told me about it only by chance, because I'd asked him one of my stupid questions. But suddenly I was alarmed. I saw him standing on the bridge, and I understood that nothing had changed from that day to this.

I'm ashamed to talk about it now; it was only a woman's curiosity that made me ask. I wanted to know whether I meant more to him than the other women he'd been with before me. What need did I have to ask! I knew, I could tell from his face, that he was completely committed to me. What more did I want? I had never believed that one human being could commit himself as completely to another as he had. I would only have had to say, "Now let's do this" and "Now let's do that," and he would have agreed.

But what? What should I have said? All I had to offer him was myself.

On the day we met, I asked him if he'd had a lot of girl friends. I did that more out of embarrassment and flirtatiousness. But in D. I watched to see if there might not be a number of women after him. I couldn't imagine anything but that every woman begrudged my having him. Not because he was especially good-looking, but because of his way and because all of them thought he'd be an easy catch. Didn't I think the same thing?

But this time I had another reason for asking. I

122

really wondered about him. Nothing came to him naturally, as it did to other men; he was altogether different. It seemed to me that he didn't have much experience with women, and that's what I was asking about. Why didn't he have any girl friends? And why did they leave him? Something like that.

"They always dumped me," he said.

"Dumped you?"

"I always wanted to marry them. That probably scared them off."

"Why should that have scared them?"

"I don't know. Everybody says that all women want to get married—think of all the jokes on the subject! But there seems to be no truth to it, at least not in my case. I don't think it has anything to do with money or security, as they call it. When I got to know them, they were very nice, ready for anything, but as soon as I proposed marriage, they got scared. Some of them simply laughed at me, as if I were crazy, and others dropped me without a word when they realized I really meant it. I don't think they trusted me."

"Would you really have married them?"

"On the spot. I would have gone straight to city hall without giving it a second thought. I wanted everything to be regularized. But they thought I had a screw loose."

He'd probably been a little childish, he said, and he could understand how the girls felt. But when you're young, you doubt yourself. You think maybe you're not a real man when the same thing keeps happening to you over and over. Now he was used to it he no longer minded; but before . . .

Once he even proposed marriage to a prostitute. "A real hooker," he phrased it. He was less than twenty years old, so legally he couldn't have gotten married. First she thought he wanted to live off her earnings, and she yelled at him a lot. When she understood that he meant it, she got all the girls in the house together and told them about it.

"And all that time I was sitting on her bed while they stared at me and gave me advice; they have more common sense than most people. And they were deeply moved—they almost cried. Finally they ordered cake and ice cream. It's a funny story."

"And you really would have married her?" I asked again.

"I'm sure of it. She need only have said yes, and if she had, I'd have been pleased as punch. Of course it wouldn't have worked out, but I wasn't thinking about that. You know, I didn't have anybody else, and I wanted somebody I could always go back to, something like that. I didn't care about anything else—I mean, that she was a hooker—I don't care to this day. Maybe what they say is true, but that doesn't matter to me. Except that today I'm a little smarter and I know it wouldn't work.

"But in those days the girls were smarter. All I wanted was to share her free time. Of course, the way I thought it would be . . . her in the next room with other men, and me waiting for her to be through . . . all that was impossible. I felt so lost sometimes in those days. But you have to get used to it; later you laugh about it and don't even try.

"Shall I tell you something? I have never been jealous. When somebody leaves me, it makes me a little sad because I'm alone again and have to start from scratch, and also because I can't seem to succeed at what comes so easily to other people. You keep falling into the same trap, you keep trying; you see the way other people live, and you think, I can do that, it can't be so difficult. That's the error. It's hard to realize, and especially if you're tired you commit it over and over. That's why I write—so as not to leave myself open to that. But jealous? I must be lacking the faculty for it.

124

"Even when I was a child, people got angry at my indifference. During the war they thought it was courage, though I'm really a coward. I've given it a lot of thought—time is what I've plenty of, since I'm usually alone. The other people are in the majority, and they're more important to this world than I am, so they're in the right. But what I can't understand is how that can be enough for them. And how hard they work at it! But I can't offer them a better alternative, so I keep my mouth shut and stay on the sidelines. It's better for them to be as they are, with all their games and their ambition. That way they don't notice the sadness . . . . Have you ever been jealous?"

"Yes, very."

"Oh."

"I'd be jealous over you, too."

He shook his head and looked at me in bewilderment. "But you don't need to. It doesn't suit you."

"I don't want to lose you."

"Why should you lose me? I'm so faithful that it might become boring. No, *faithful* is a stupid word; there's no merit to my fidelity—I simply can't be any other way. And even if you were to leave me . . . no, I'm only saying it because that's what I'm used to . . . even that wouldn't change anything. I would wait, and in the meantime I'd write, to make the time pass more quickly. A woman can't be unfaithful."

"But that's nonsense, Berthold. They do it all the time."

"Oh, that's just on the surface. That has nothing to do with what we're talking about. Sometimes it's just an error. But a man . . . yes, that's bad for you. Sometimes a man really is lost and forgets everything. It must be terrible—I feel sorry for you."

"But just the opposite is true."

"No, I know more about it. And the only reason you don't know is that they always told you different.

It's become a habit, and no one dares to work it out for himself anymore. It's gone so far that people can't imagine it any other way; if you begin to question it, they start to scream, and eventually they kill you. But I learned at a very early age, when I was still at home. I always thought, What they're telling me, the way they want me to do things—it can't be right. I tried hard to please them, not wanting to make a bad impression, but they noticed all the same.

"I watched my father—I liked him. Surely it's not possible, I thought, that this is enough for him. Why doesn't he talk to me and explain everything? Then I'll come to a stop, like him. But he was a busy man; even at night he was called to the hospital because of some operation or other, and at home he let things slide. He was probably too tired.

"Once I came home during the holidays; I was already at the university, I think it was my first term. I'd really been looking forward to it, and I thought they were looking forward to it too. But the first time we sat down to dinner, my mother said, 'Isn't it odd, when we're here alone it's so cozy, and no sooner is Berthold back than we quarrel.' But we hadn't been arguing at all, I swear. My father was at the table, and my brother and sister, and we were just eating and talking about this and that.

"No, it was something else. Today I know what it was. People grow uneasy as soon as I'm present, even if I keep my mouth shut and go through the same motions they do. Somehow I make them uncomfortable, and they don't like being uncomfortable. At the time I didn't understand, and I fought it because I didn't want to be different. But one day it got the better of me. On the bridge in Heidelberg.

"It could just as easily have been some other bridge—it had nothing to do with Heidelberg. It was shortly after dark, and I was standing there looking at

126

the water, just like that, for no particular reason. The streetlights had just come on, and the windows in the houses were lit. Most people were probably sitting down to supper and feeling cozy; they thought everything was going fine, just as they wanted it to be. That's when it came over me; that's when I found out. I was still far too young for the idea, and I didn't want to admit it. I fought it, I was so afraid of it.

"And that's why I ran to girls and women like a silly kid—because I didn't want to lose my bearings. But they couldn't help me; they didn't even like me, and they noticed that it was too late, that there was nothing they could do with me now. Yes, it's strange how they noticed at once, long before I realized it myself. Even if you talk their language, they notice. I can read it in their eyes, a little flicker, an uncertainty in their gaze. What does he want with me? Is he making fun of me? And then it's all over, it's no longer their business.

"Today none of that is important to me; I just tell myself I'll have to get along without. But in those days . . . it almost bowled me over. The only thing that saved me was writing. Because it was the realization that everything they'd taught me was wrong—that's the idea that came to me there on the bridge while I looked down at the water and the lights reflected in the river.

"A horrifying thought! Suddenly there you are, completely at a loss, no solid ground, suspended between yesterday and tomorrow, and down there the water flows, headed somewhere or other, without thinking whether it has to be that way. Why did they teach me wrong? Was it intentional? Did they want to hold me on their shore? But they weren't out to mislead me—they just didn't know any better themselves.

"It was my misfortune that I'd gone to the bridge. It wasn't their fault, and it's unfair to blame them. I have their longings and their genes—that's why I understand them so well, and I don't want to upset them.

Only . . . it's as if I'd been poisoned by the thought, and I know that none of it is meant for me."

"None of what?"

"Something like you," he said, touching my stomach with his finger.

"What nonsense."

"Do you remember when you came down the stairs?"

"What stairs?"

"At your house. It was exactly like the fantasies I'd spun sometimes when I was alone, but I never really believed they could come true. It was enough to fantasize. And suddenly there you were, coming down the stairs. I wanted to run away. I didn't want to wake up and find myself standing there alone. By and by disappointment wears you down—I mean, the fact that nothing is ever what it might be. You lose the energy to live like other people. But you . . . ."

The night he spoke of all this, I found the word that explains everything, the word I'm reluctant to say because it's not a common word and doesn't answer anyone's expectations. I saw him standing on the bridge, just the way he described, and he wore the same face that always rendered me so helpless when I saw it, the absent wonder that's so hard to bear.

It does no good to close your eyes—it's still there, and you can sense it right through your lids, you can feel it all over your body. You have no idea what it wants and what it's looking for and what will be good for it. All you have is your arms and your body to hold the face and shelter it, but perhaps that way it will get lost and you'll never see it again.

What remains is a man just like everybody else, not very different from other people, and you think maybe you were mistaken. Trying to come to terms with that thought, you smile at yourself, but all the time you know that something has been lost, has been gambled

128

away. I've beheld the face of an angel; it looked at me and wanted something from me, but I could not bear to see it, and so it vanished. You don't even dare to think the word anymore.

It was the rain that drove us from Ludwigshof. Everything changed, it was no one's fault. The rain washed away the two happy weeks, and the brook carried them off across the frontier. And how cold it got! This was only right, the locals said; it was much too early in the year for warm weather, even for their area. In the large lounge of the inn the sawdust oven was fired up. An electric heater was enough for our room. That was not the problem.

The first few days weren't so bad. Berthold was even pleased with the rain that pattered down outside our window and on the woods, so evenly that you could forget everything and live at the center of a huge silence.

But now we were shut away from everything; what happened on the other side of the rain was none of our business. Though we kept thinking that the following morning the weather would clear, it went on raining steadily. There seemed no end to it. It made Berthold restless, and I grew restless for him.

The mountains were black with damp, and the brook by the sawmill grew sluggish with mud. The wet laundry in the courtyard under our window slapped on the line, and the chickens huddled under the projecting eaves.

Berthold rummaged among the papers he had brought. I didn't know what they were, but I was pleased and thought that it would be good for him to keep busy. I always thought that someday he'd have to start writing again—it was his profession, after all. I had no idea how writers worked. This is what I imagined: they write for a few hours every day, until there's enough for a book; then somebody gives them some money for it; then they write the next book; and so on. I also thought their lives were easier than other people's; they didn't have to work eight hours a day, and they could organize their time any way they liked.

Sometimes Berthold said that if he had a choice, he wouldn't write at all, the torture was too great. He'd prefer to be some insignificant clerk, so that when he came home at night, he wouldn't have to think about work; that was a life to be envied. But I didn't believe him. I thought he only talked that way because he was in love; once he had said that now he wouldn't have to write anymore—now he had me.

After looking briefly at his papers, he put them away again without discussing them with me. He seemed very displeased, but I wasn't supposed to notice. Then he got out his typewriter and wrote a letter to a magazine or perhaps to his publisher. Sensing that he didn't want me to ask, I didn't ask.

He stood at the window for half an hour or more without saying a word, staring out at the rain. Then he drummed his fingers on the windowsill, abruptly turned around, and made some excuse for leaving the room. Before long he was back, and everything was as it had been before. He had only gone downstairs to tap the barometer that hung in the lounge or to buy cigarettes, though he could have sent me.

Or he fell on the bed and pretended to be tired, although he slept badly at night. He didn't fall asleep until near dawn, and when I got up because the innkeeper's wife had asked us to have breakfast by ten o'clock, he stayed in bed. Once he even said, "It's not worthwhile."

If only he had talked to me about whatever was making him uneasy—perhaps it's not possible to talk about such things. He tried to act toward me the same way he had before it started raining, but it was difficult for him and created problems for me too—it was no

130

longer genuine. If I'd been smart, I'd have said right away, "Let's leave here." But I didn't dare, and so we struggled along for a week.

It was the yellow cow that finally made up our minds for us. Wearing our raincoats, we were walking up and down the road outside the inn just to get a breath of air. We couldn't go far; everything was too wet. The cattle were grazing in the meadow by the brook below. Among them was a light-yellow cow we had noticed before. She stood still and stared at us while the other cows cropped the grass and paid no attention. Only the yellow cow was curious. Water running off her back, she turned her head slowly to watch us as we walked on, and when we turned back, she turned her head the other way. When we stopped, her head also came to a stop, and she stared as if she were wondering about us, trying to find out what we might do.

That's when Berthold said, "Why don't we leave?" And he quickly added, "That is, if it's all right with you."

I said it was all right and asked "Where shall we go?" He suggested that we try . . . he named the city where we are now. But then he said, "You know, it doesn't make any difference. We could go some other place, if you prefer."

We returned to the inn at once, as if we had been given new life. We paid our bill and packed our things, intending to leave that very afternoon on the little bus. Just to get away!

In the train Berthold asked, "You're not angry, are you?"

"Why should I be angry?"

"Because of the rain."

"But it's not your fault."

"Yes, it is. I should have known it was going to happen."

He looked out the train window so as not to have

to look at me. And still I hoped that here, in this city, things would get better all by themselves. But by now I realized that it had been wrong of me to come here with him. I should have let him leave alone; we should have separated then, no matter how hard it would have been for me. He mustn't feel tied down—that could only lead to unhappiness. He needed me only for a rest between two works of literature, but the rest was over and I was in the way.

I did not leave a message at the hotel—I was too much of a coward. Instead I persuaded myself that there could be no harm in my father-in-law's spending an hour or two with us. I was glad that I could postpone the decision a little while longer, for how could I have decided? I had no idea what to do with myself; so much thinking had exhausted me.

Nor did I tell Berthold at once about my father-in-law's letter. As always, we met at the little restaurant at the suburban railroad station not far from our boardinghouse. The food was cheap, and the service was fast. Usually I got there first and found us a table; if you came later, there might not be one left or you might have to share.

When Berthold walked in, I saw that I couldn't talk to him right away; he'd have to eat first. We shook hands, and he asked, "How are you?" He immediately picked up the menu and studied it, his pinched face conveying that he was not pleased with his morning's work. Whenever that happened, he looked old and exhausted. Deep lines ran from his nose past the corners of his mouth to his chin, as if he were disgusted—or as if he were a depraved person. And it *was* a depravity, he had once told me laughingly. He meant writing. But it had been a long time since I had dared to discuss that sort of thing.

He asked me how I'd spent the morning, and I told

132

him that I had gone to the Café Blüthner. He found my recital very agreeable and was pleased that I was taking advantage of the good weather. Then the waitress brought our soup, and we spooned it up in silence. I was afraid of giving myself away; the longer I put it off, the less I knew how to begin. Better not in this place, better to wait until we were alone.

I asked him if there had been any mail for us. First he said no, and then he said, "Yes, from the repertory company, and a query from *Sirius*." *Sirius* was a magazine that wanted to buy one of his stories; he frequently received such requests. Sometimes Berthold sent in something and was sent money in return. He always handed the money over to me immediately, and I added it to what we already had.

Nowadays Berthold behaved with me as he behaved with other people, and I understood why they thought he was stuck-up. He was very well-mannered, but the good manners were an insult, as if he were pushing you away with both hands. And if I asked him something he was sure to know—about books, that kind of thing—though he always answered me, it sounded as if he were saying, "Why bother talking about it? One way or the other, it hardly matters." That killed the conversation, for basically he was right, of course; it wasn't the subject we should have been discussing. He did not seem to realize how much he was hurting me with the fact that everything was only a burden and a duty to him.

Yes, it was painful to be alone with him, to live in one room with him and to sleep at his side. He isn't the man with whom I walked away from everything, I thought. This is worse than being married. Here you freeze to death.

Walking back to the boardinghouse, I still did not mention the letter. I wanted Berthold to have a nap first; he looked so tired. Besides, we always rested right after dinner. We lived by a strict timetable, although we didn't need to. One day was like another, even Sundays; Berthold said that otherwise nothing got accomplished.

In the afternoons he fell asleep as soon as his head touched the pillow. The shouts of the children and the trucks passing in the street didn't disturb him. For half an hour and sometimes longer he slept like someone totally exhausted, and afterward he seemed paralyzed.

I rarely fell asleep, but I pretended to because that was how he wanted it. He must have thought, If she can sleep, then everything's all right. That's why I pretended—for his sake. If he had known that I hardly ever slept, he too would have refused to lie down.

But the afternoon hours after our rest were the worst of all. Both of us did all sorts of things to get through them. It was important not to talk much, best not to talk at all; that was the main thing. Neither of us gave a sign, both acting as if this were the way things were all over the world. The hours were so dreadful that any lament was silenced and any effort to escape them vain. If one had wanted to cry, the tears would not have come. Only when darkness began to fall did we breathe more easily again.

And during these dead hours I was supposed to tell Berthold about my father-in-law's letter?

I got up first and made Berthold a cup of coffee. We had a little hotplate so that we wouldn't have to run to the kitchen for everything. This time I made only one cup for Berthold because there wasn't any more coffee left in the jar. I had meant to buy some that morning, but I'd forgotten because of the letter. Berthold didn't even notice that I wasn't having coffee. At least he didn't say anything.

Then I left him alone in the room and went to the kitchen to rinse out some stockings. I also wanted to press a blouse. I had permission to use Frau Viereck's iron.

134

She joined me in the kitchen and told me all about a train wreck in which thirty-two people had died. She had heard the news on the radio. I asked her where it had happened, but it was in another part of the country; it wasn't the train on which my father-in-law was arriving. Frau Viereck complained that nowadays there were so many accidents and people had become so careless. I agreed with everything she said. While she talked, I listened for the sound of the typewriter in our room. But Berthold never wrote at this time of day.

Perhaps he suspects something, I thought. Because that was the way he was. You'd think he didn't care about anything, about any other human being, but he was extremely sensitive when there was something in the air. Every five minutes I looked at the clock on the kitchen wall, and then I delayed a little longer. The clock was rimmed in white china painted with a blue windmill and a sailboat. It ticked very loudly.

"We might be having company later on," I told Frau Viereck. She was surprised, because no one had ever come to see us before, but I didn't tell her who our visitor would be. She asked if I wanted her to prepare anything, perhaps make some tea and set out a tray with cups and plates; and would I like to borrow a white cloth for the little table? I thanked her and said that our company would probably not be staying long, and perhaps we'd all go out to supper; we hadn't decided yet.

I couldn't put it off any longer; I had to bring myself to the point. Berthold was standing at the window staring down at the street; though he didn't turn around when I entered the room, I was sure he heard me. How hard he was making it for me. I had to initiate everything; he never took the smallest first step. And then, if I made a mistake, it was all my fault.

He hadn't touched his work; nothing had changed. The piece of paper in the typewriter hadn't inched up at all. I put the blouse I'd pressed on the bed, to let the dampness go out of it. Then, just in case, I smoothed Berthold's side of the bed. He had already pulled up the covers, but very sloppily. All the time he stayed at the window as if I weren't in the room at all.

I sat down in the chair by my bed, opened the nightstand drawer, and took out the stuff I used to groom my nails. It was very quiet in the room, the only sounds coming from the street and occasionally from the kitchen, where Frau Viereck was bustling about. When a truck passed on the street, the glass prisms on the ugly chandelier tinkled.

Berthold pulled the thin curtain across the window sharply. My corner of the large room was now dark, and I pressed the switch of the bedside lamp.

"Oh, forgive me," Berthold said, about to open the curtain again.

"It's all right, it just makes a glare," I said. We were silent again. I don't know what he was doing. I deliberately didn't look up but kept filing my nails.

"Would you like to go to the movies?" he asked.

"But we've already seen everything. The program doesn't change until tomorrow."

"Oh, yes, right. Well, we don't have to go."

"Why don't you get to work?" I asked. Maybe I sounded a little condescending, I don't know. I was sorry as soon as the words were out of my mouth. Berthold walked slowly to the table and looked at the sheet in the typewriter. He did not sit down.

"Would you like some more coffee?" I asked.

"No, thanks. I mean, I'll make it myself. Would you like a cup?"

I shook my head. I wanted to pretend that I'd had coffee in the kitchen with Frau Viereck, but the words wouldn't come out. Berthold had already gone to the dressing table and turned on the hotplate. Just to keep busy.

136

In my despair I couldn't control myself. "When did all this start to happen, anyway?" I asked. I tried to sound as if we were talking about something unimportant.

"What?" he asked from behind the dressing table.

"All this."

He dropped the metal lid of the coffee jar. It rolled along the floor and came to rest. "Damn!" Berthold shouted.

"What's the matter?"

"There's no more coffee."

"I forgot to buy any. I can't even—"

"Nonsense. I'll just run over to the store at the railroad station and get some."

He went straight to the closet where we kept the money, only too happy about the interruption. But I could not let him run away now.

"Surely we can't go on this way?" I said.

"What?" He stopped at the open closet, as if seeking refuge behind the door.

"Why did you close the curtain?"

"No reason. I can open it again."

"Don't bother. I want to know what you think about when you stare at the street."

"Me? Why? Nothing. At least nothing in particular. I watch the people in the street, that's all." Apparently afraid that I didn't believe him, he began to talk about what went on in the street. "The women go shopping, they hurry to make it before the stores close. Sometimes they stop and talk to each other and exchange bits of gossip. And every five minutes men pour into the street. You can always tell when a commuter train has come in. It's the same thing every afternoon at the same time. Day after day. Funny."

"Why funny?"

"Oh, it doesn't matter. It's got nothing to do with me."

"We go to the movies, and that passes two hours; if we're lucky, there's enough to think about on the walk home. That's funny too."

"Don't you feel well?"

"Oh, Berthold."

"It's a muggy day."

"There has to be a reason. It might as well be the weather."

"Why don't you tell me if there's something you want?"

"What do *you* want?"

"Me?"

"Yes."

"Why me? Nothing. That is, I want whatever you want."

He was still standing by the open closet door, and I was sitting in my corner near the bed. I had turned off the lamp. I didn't need it; I could file my nails in the dark. It was just a pretext anyway. I didn't want to look up, because I knew he was standing there waiting for me to drop the subject.

"Maybe that's the mistake."

"What?"

"That you want whatever I want, as you say."

"What else should I want? I don't have anybody else."

"I only complicate your life."

"Nonsense."

"Don't you ever want to spend some time with your friends?"

"What friends? I have no friends."

"Your fellow writers, or whatever you call them. Why all this hairsplitting? You understand me perfectly well. I don't want you to think that I don't think about it. Perhaps it would be good for your work."

"Fellow writers? What gives you that idea? Either

138

they feel as I do—and those are the best of them—or they talk another language and produce nothing but empty blather. Fellow writers! At least . . . ."

"What?"

"Oh, nothing."

"I'm sure there's a third-class waiting room here too, along with some other dubious establishments. Why not, if it gives you pleasure? Maybe that's the kind of place that's good for your work."

"Nonsense."

"You keep saying, 'Nonsense.' "

"I've got some things on my mind, that's all. But it will change. When I've finished my play . . . ."

He faltered. I wanted to ask when that would be, but then I remembered that the present situation had only been going on for six weeks; surely six weeks was not long enough to finish such a work. So it was all my fault because I wasn't patient enough. That's what always happened when I decided to have a talk with Berthold. Before I ever got to the point I was trying to make, I started to feel guilty and gave up.

"I really want to talk to you, Berthold."

"What is it?"

"No, not like this, not with one foot out the door. There's no point to that. You don't have to worry that I'm going to criticize you."

"I know it's hard on you. But why talk about it? It can't be helped."

"Is it true that it can't be helped? How do you stand it?"

"What do you mean? What is there to stand? It's always like this. It comes with the job."

"Do you think you'll finish the play?"

"What do you mean? What about the play? Why shouldn't I finish it?"

"What do I know about these things!"

"Do you doubt my ability?"

"No, that's not it. Forgive me."

"I'm sure I'll finish it. I have to."

"You have to?"

"Yes, or I'm done for."

I was sorry I'd asked about his work. "All right, we'll stop talking about it," I said. "Forgive me for bringing it up."

"Shall I go for coffee now?"

"Go ahead, if you think it's so important." I was actually considering just letting him go. Perhaps by the time he came back with the coffee, my father-in-law would have arrived and things would run their course all by themselves.

"The coffee isn't important," he said.

"Can you spare me five more minutes, Berthold?"

"Yes."

"No, not like that. Why do you make it so hard for me? All I want is for us to talk just once the way we did with each other two months ago—though at that time we had no need of words because everything was clear. Sometimes I stand at the window and stare at the street the same way you do. I envy the women who go shopping and stop to gossip. I even envy the dogs."

"We simply don't belong, Marion, that's all there is to it. But of course it's all new to you."

"I think I do belong. To the women down there."

"No."

"But that's not what I wanted to talk about. No, it's something else entirely. I've had a letter."

"Oh? From home?"

"No, not from home. From Munich. From my father-in-law."

"And?"

"He's passing through town. Today. He's spending the night at the Hotel Europe. He's probably already there by now—I don't know exactly when his train gets in. Yes, I'm sure he's there now. I could still telephone.

Wait, let me show you the letter. It isn't long. Look in my raincoat pocket."

"What does he want here?"

"He wants to visit us around six or seven."

"But why didn't you say so right away?"

"I didn't want . . . . Just read the letter. I don't want you to think I'm keeping secrets from you. I swear to you, Berthold, it's the first I've heard from home."

He gestured in dismissal.

"No, please, Berthold, read the letter. It's proof that I'm not lying to you. I never wrote to them, either. Not even a postcard to Günther whether they would have let him have it or not. I didn't want you to think . . . I didn't want, behind your back—"

"But the only reason I never asked you was because I didn't want to hurt you."

"And you mustn't think that I wish I were back there. But you could have asked me, even if it had been a little hurtful. Maybe it would have been better. Did you read the letter?"

"He could be here in fifteen minutes."

"We can still telephone. You just have to say. Anything's all right with me. Or we could go out, and Frau Viereck could tell him that we're not home. I meant to go to the Hotel Europe this morning and leave a message for him not to come, but then I didn't. I wanted to talk to you first. Did you read the letter carefully? He writes, 'the two of you.' And he says, 'if it isn't convenient.' No, listen to me, if it isn't convenient for you, we'll just not see him. Let him think we didn't get his letter in time."

"But what's the point of all that?" Berthold sounded confused.

"You mean you don't mind?"

"No, why should I? And the decision isn't up to me."

"You're pleased?" I actually got the impression that he was glad of the visit. I felt very hurt.

"Do you have misgivings?" he asked.

"No, none at all." I stood up. "Please let me get to the closet now."

The space between the closet and the foot of the bed was so narrow that you couldn't get past when the closet door was open. Berthold was leaning against the bedpost, letter in hand, and I was waiting on the other side of the closet door for him to move away. I could see myself in the full-length mirror.

"I wonder what he wants," Berthold said.

"That's what we'll find out. Perhaps he doesn't want anything. He's a lonely person too. Come, let me get at the closet now." I closed the closet door slowly so as not to jam him in, and I squeezed past him. He put up no resistance. I opened the closet door again, so that he was pushed to the other side.

"Wouldn't it have been better if we'd met him at the hotel?" he asked.

"Why?"

"We don't have anything to offer him."

I couldn't help but laugh. "I daresay he's not coming to see us for what we can offer him."

"But when he sees the way you live?"

"The way I live? What about it? What do you suddenly have against the room? It's a handsome room, it's big. Don't worry. I told you that he comes from a poorish family. His father was a shopkeeper, a greengrocer, somewhere in a mining region. He won't be so easily put off. Besides, it isn't that easy to fool him."

I slammed the closet door. I wanted to pick up the blouse I had pressed. I was still in my slip. "All the same, of course, there's no need for him to realize right away how things stand with us. Please make an effort."

"You're changing your clothes?" Berthold sounded surprised.

142

"As you see, sir."

"But he might be here any minute."

"So what? And if he should happen to catch me only half-dressed, he'll think that even in the afternoons we're carried away by passion." I was extremely irritated. But at heart I was sad.

"Would you prefer to be alone with him?" Berthold asked after a while.

"Why would you think that?"

"Perhaps it embarrasses you to have me here."

His question made me even sadder. I did not know how to answer. I didn't want to quarrel with him, and when you're sad, it's so easy to quarrel in an effort to make the other person sad too. Nor did I want to look at him, for I would have lost my composure at once.

I put my blouse on in silence, then I took the suit off the hanger and put on the skirt. I acted very busy, as if he weren't in the room. Then I went past him to the dressing table to comb my hair and fix my face, paying no attention to him at all.

"I asked you a question, Marion," I heard softly from the other side of the room.

"Yes?"

"I asked you if you'd prefer to be alone with him."

"Are you really so naïve or . . . just indifferent? I can't make you out. I think a person could be unfaithful to you and you wouldn't even notice. You'd sit down at your typewriter."

"Buy that's no answer at all, that's just nonsense."

"Why shouldn't we talk nonsense once in a while? A woman needs that, trust me. And besides, it passes the time. Seriously, I wonder what you'll look like." I was so sad and so angry at myself that my lipstick slipped and I had to wipe my mouth clean and start all over again. "I mean, what you'll look like when you're alone again. It's that look that will probably keep me from being able to betray you."

143

"It's not your style, either."

"Not my style?"

"Do we have to talk about it right now?"

"Is that right? It isn't my style? Thanks a lot." I went to my night table to put on my wristwatch. Berthold stood in a corner of the room like a scolded child waiting to be forgiven. "I wouldn't even know who in this whole damned world I could be unfaithful to you with," I said, turning my back to him. I had propped my foot on the chair to adjust my stocking and fasten it to the garter. And then the other stocking. "All right, that does it. What about you? Don't you at least want to put on a tie? And you haven't shaved."

"Why did you put on that suit?"

"Why? Don't you like it?"

"Isn't it too warm?"

"No. Besides, I don't have a lot of choices."

"You'll have to be patient until fall, Marion. As soon as I've finished the play, they'll give me an advance. I could have one now; they've offered, but I don't want to commit myself. I'm superstitious."

"If I cared about that—do you seriously believe I care about that? For that, I could have stayed where I was. There I had it all. You don't understand much about women, do you, Berthold? You bought the whole package—everything they say about us in jokes. You have no idea how little a woman needs. Even less than a writer. It's true. You should make a mental note of it in case you ever have to write about a woman. In your play, for example."

"In which play?" Suddenly his voice was alert.

"You are writing for the stage, aren't you?" My remark was casual; I shouldn't have started. "Strange. I would have thought you'd write another novel."

"I don't have the peace of mind for a novel these days." His voice was testy.

"Does it take greater peace of mind?"

144

"You've been reading my stuff?"

"I just looked at it once, just at the page that happened to be in the typewriter. Wasn't I allowed to do that?"

"Oh, it doesn't matter."

"When I was straightening up or dusting. It's unavoidable. You have to look at something."

"It doesn't matter."

"How was I supposed to know?"

"Know what?"

"That I wasn't allowed."

"It's not a good idea for an outsider to look at unfinished work. It alters it for the worse. It makes you wonder, What will she think of it? with every sentence you write. I can't allow that to happen."

"I only wanted to see what it was you were struggling over."

"It's not a struggle. It's like any other job, no worse. I have to rewrite the whole thing anyway."

"Because of me? Because I looked at it?"

"Because it's no good."

"But you've made five or six fresh starts already."

"Have I? I wasn't counting."

"The page number was always the same."

"And if it was the same a hundred times? Or a thousand! That's my business." Words escaped him.

"Yes, it is your business. Forgive me. Everything I do is wrong."

"Don't get so worked up." He tried to soothe me. "It's got nothing to do with you. Listen to me, Marion. There's no reason to cry."

"Who's crying?"

"I didn't even know that you could cry."

"I didn't know either. It's because of the weather."

"The old man will be here any minute."

"I wonder why he's not here already. He was always very punctual. Maybe he changed his mind. If he doesn't show up—what then?"

"Something might have come up to delay him. Or maybe he's having trouble finding the street. Shall I telephone the hotel?"

"Just tell me a story while we wait."

"What do you want me to tell you?"

"It doesn't matter. Something nice, just to give me something different to think about. In the fall, you think?"

"What about the fall?"

"When you finish the play?"

"Don't you believe me?"

"Why shouldn't I believe you? If you say so."

"November at the very latest."

"And then?"

"They want to have the opening in November."

"Did you promise?"

"I did, but that's not what matters. It's for my own sake, because I want to have it off my chest."

"And then?"

"Why, then we'll attend the opening."

"And I'll be there?"

"What a question. You're the guest of honor. You'll sit in a box. Everyone will stare at you. Me too, when I come onstage at the end. We'll buy you a new dress."

"Do I have to have a floor-length evening gown?"

"I don't know. I suppose it depends on the theater."

"Maybe that other dress would do. It's still brand-new."

"Buy why not a new dress?"

"And then?"

"What do you mean, and then? Then we'll be free again."

"And then?"

"We'll go someplace. Why think about it now? We

146

have plenty of time. If the play is a hit, we can buy a Volkswagen; then there will be nothing to tie us down."

"And then?" I tried to smile as I asked, but Berthold didn't know how to continue. The whole story, up to the part with the Volkswagen, was one he'd told me many times, but he could never get beyond that point. For some time we were silent, not knowing how to go on. Our whole conversation had been no more than a childish game. I no longer believed in it.

"Do you still think about the yellow cow sometimes?" I asked.

"What yellow cow?"

"The cow in Ludwigshof, the one that looked at us. And the way the black mountains wept."

"One must never look back," he said quickly. "It leads nowhere. But you know, we could go back there if you liked it so much."

"Didn't you like it?"

"Of course I did, sure. But the second time around is usually a disappointment."

"No, I don't want to go back there either. It would only make me sad. Tell me another story."

"What can I tell you? You know everything."

"I just want to see the face you wore when you talked to me the first time. At the award ceremony."

"How can I know what I looked like? I'd had it up to here with all the goings-on."

"No, even more the face you wore when I came down the stairs at my house . . . . Sit here with me, Berthold. Why are you always on the go, as if I were going to do you some harm? It won't be long now. The old man will be here any minute . . . . Really, the next time you want to get a woman, all you have to do is look at her the way you looked at me."

"What a lot of nonsense."

"No, I mean it. No woman could withstand it; it's

147

a perfect ruse. I'm only telling you because you won't tell me a nice story. Shall I sing you the song?"

"No, not now. What's the point of all this?"

"Didn't your mother ever sing to you when you were little?"

"No, she never sang."

"My mother didn't either. She didn't even like to hear one of us sing. She must have thought it frivolous. Sometimes my father sang in the bathroom while he was shaving, but not often, and only when he wasn't thinking about what he was doing. Because if my mother heard him, she nagged him afterward, at breakfast. Perhaps she was a very unhappy woman—I don't hold anything against her. And she was right, too. I did turn out very badly . . . . Why do you write if writing makes you so unhappy?"

"Don't start that again. It doesn't make me unhappy."

"It's bent you all out of shape . . . . It's not idle curiosity, Berthold. Really it isn't. I just want to understand the reason, the real reason. It's all so strange to me, can't you understand that?"

"It's my fault, but I can't change it."

"You said it yourself, before—I'm an outsider. Yes, you did, and you were right. I know I am. But why is it that way? It hasn't always been that way."

"It's just my way of living."

"What is?"

"Writing."

"I don't understand. I'm not smart enough."

"If I didn't write, I'd stop existing altogether. There's nothing to understand—that's how it's always been, that's all. The less one talks about it, the better."

"Unfortunately I never learned how to write."

"Thank your lucky stars."

"Why? It might be a good thing if I could."

"No. You don't need to."

"Will you write about me one day?"

"No."

"But why not? You mean I'm not a fit subject? You could give me another name and another husband so no one would ever know it's me."

"No, I couldn't do that."

"But why not?"

"Just because."

"If I could read it, I could remember our time together."

"But you're here."

His expression was so stubborn that I almost laughed. That's how silly Berthold's words seemed to me, and that's how nervous I was.

At that moment there was a knock at the door. Both of us jumped up, startled, and stood there like two people caught in the act. We hadn't heard the front doorbell ring.

I called, "Come in."

I had no specific plan—you mustn't think that. In retrospect it looks as if I knew exactly what I was going to do, but actually I couldn't have said what I hoped for from my father-in-law. My only resolve was to keep him from seeing how things were with us right away. But when I saw him standing in the doorway, I forgot about everything.

He looked so much better than I remembered him, tanned and wearing a light-gray summer suit. His eyes under the bushy white brows were kind. Unable to control myself, I ran to him and hugged him. Perhaps he knew everything that very first second.

"It's so wonderful of you to come and see us," I said.

He said, "But why shouldn't I?" Since he was passing through anyway, it was only natural. And then he said hello to Berthold and immediately added something quite personal. Such was his custom. Max thought it a gambit to disarm people and gain the upper hand. Whenever anyone came to the house on business, my father-in-law began by talking about something else altogether, something personal, and since he had a good memory, he could almost always come up with some remark that could be of interest only to the visitor. On such occasions Max was on pins and needles; he wanted to get down to business at once. I think my father-in-law was sincere and would have been delighted if the callers had responded in kind, but that rarely happened; they were too much in awe of him and his position.

"We only met for a few minutes," he said to Berthold, "and under very confusing circumstances at that. It was a day when I had had to make a rather difficult decision. You probably noticed."

"No. I mean . . . ." Berthold was stammering.

"So much the better. By now I've regained my equanimity. By the way, I read two of your books."

"Berthold is working on something new," I quickly interrupted because I did not want him to talk about Berthold's books. "Please sit down, Papa."

"Yes, please have a seat," Berthold said.

We all sat down. There was an awkward pause. All of us had so much to say, but we didn't want to hurt each other. My father-in-law looked around surreptitiously. Perhaps he did not want to have to look at us.

"Yes, this is where we live," I said. "For the time being, until Berthold finishes what he's working on. Then we'll move on. Berthold thought the room would shock you."

"Me? Why? What's the matter with the room?"

"Berthold has always lived in rooms like this. How did you find out where we were?"

"I'm not a sly old fox for nothing. But all joking aside, it wasn't very hard. I went to a large bookstore in Munich, and the manager was kind enough to call

150

up one of the trade associations. And guess what—they knew where to find you."

"In Munich?" I asked.

"I spent five weeks in Berchtesgaden."

"Alone?"

"Yes, quite alone."

"You're looking well."

"I enjoyed very good weather."

"And when will you be leaving?"

"Tomorrow morning. I'll get home around noon. At my age one doesn't like to travel at night. Besides, I'm in no hurry, isn't that right?" he said to Berthold. "I'm no longer indispensable."

"Does anybody know . . ." I began.

"No, but I'm glad you asked, so we can clear that matter up right away. I assure you that no one knows. And there's no need for anyone ever to find out that I came to see you. At least I've learned to keep my mouth shut," he said to Berthold with a smile.

Turning back to me, he continued, "And now, my child, I will answer the question you need not have hesitated to ask; because surely that's what you want to hear, isn't it? Yes, it is, we don't have to play hide-and-seek. All right, then—Günther is fine. I hear every week. The last postcard I had is four days old. Here, you can read it yourself. Written by Fräulein Gerda, who takes good care of Günther—and only of Günther, I've escaped her clutches. Yes, that's the story. Anything else? Things are more or less the same. My son is successful. Very successful, in fact. He gives me regular accountings of the business, to keep up the amenities. Max is always extremely correct in such matters. Besides, I'm sure he takes pleasure in proving to his father that he does everything right and that I was wrong."

As he talked, my father-in-law was smiling, directing his remarks more to Berthold than to me. I didn't dare look at Berthold.

"All right, that's that. Any other questions?"

I shook my head.

He was silent for a while, as if considering something. "By the way, I still live at home," he said at last.

I did not understand what he meant. "But were you planning to . . ." I began, confused.

Yes, he'd toyed with the idea of retiring altogether, my father-in-law confirmed. But in the meantime he'd realized that such a move wouldn't have been right for him. "Where is there for people like us to disappear to? Can you tell me?" he asked Berthold straight out.

Berthold did not answer. His lips tightened.

"Yes, that was why I read your books—to find the answer," my father-in-law said after waiting a while. "I did not find it there, either. That may be my fault. I'm sure the books weren't written for me."

"You would be doing me a great favor if you'd stop talking about my books." Berthold's words sounded so insulting that I was frightened. My father-in-law was equally taken aback and looked at me helplessly.

"Nor can I believe," Berthold continued, "that you've come to see us in order to talk to me about my books."

"But Berthold!" I cried.

"What? It seems more appropriate to clarify the matter at once. You may think it an affectation on my part, Chairman, but this is how it is: I am disgusted by everything I have ever written. In my line of work one can never rely on past performance; that is a comfort we do not know. Anyone rash enough to rest on yesterday's laurels is done for. But enough of that. I think we'd better talk about the purpose of your visit."

I would have liked to change the direction of the conversation, but it was too late. My father-in-law was

152

looking at Berthold attentively and did not speak for a long time.

"I beg your pardon. I had expected something quite different," he finally remarked, speaking very softly and carefully. His voice sounded sad. "And why do you think I came?"

Berthold shrugged his shoulders. "That's your affair. By the way, I'm in an awkward position in relation to you."

"No, you're not," my father-in-law countered with great determination.

"You're very kind, Chairman, but I'm not in the habit of telling myself lies."

"At the very least, my position is equally awkward."

"Please let us be honest with each other."

"Yes, certainly."

"You came to see how things stand with Marion. That's all."

"There is that aspect of it, yes."

"And whether she might be ready—"

"But Berthold!" I called out again.

"No, no, let him be, my child. Herr Möncken is quite right. He's mistaken on only one point. Of course I'm interested in how Marianne is getting along—even in how you are getting along, although you won't accept that from me. But to find that out, I would not have had to visit. There are all sorts of information bureaus and that sort of thing. I'm sorry that there's such a misunderstanding between us. Didn't Marianne tell you anything about me?"

"Yes, Papa, I did," I said. "I mean, not a lot. I don't know a lot."

"It isn't very important"—he smiled at me—"except that Herr Möncken seems to believe that I'm not sincere. I hadn't counted on that."

"Stop, Papa."

"No, I'd really like to explain why I came to see you. It's a little difficult only because I'm not accustomed to talking about myself. Do you really believe that in my profession we can rest on past performance, as you put it? Perhaps outwardly we can, but . . . . Anyway, my son wanted to have me declared incompetent because for a time I entertained the idea of recanting my so-called achievement. It was all happening just at the time you came to our town. More precisely, on the very day I declared myself incompetent, as it were.

"My son is right, you know; it's too late for me to dissociate myself from my so-called achievement, no matter how I wriggle on the hook. I can't do it by spending money or by giving it away or by destruction. I don't know whether what I'm saying makes any sense. I can only use simple business language; as soon as I try to speak about personal matters, I'm unsure of my ground. I only managed to get through the commercial track in school, as you will long since have noticed by my vocabulary.

"But to cut a long story short, since all I want to do is explain why I'm here—I realized that there's no way out for me. In other words, that I must be what this achievement demands of me, that I must play the part to the bitter end. I have no other choice. Is that clear?"

Again Berthold did not answer, but this time it wasn't because he was feeling superior but because he was at a loss how to respond. He was looking at the floor, not at my father-in-law.

"But that still does not explain why I'm here," my father-in-law continued after a pause, when neither of us spoke. "Quite frankly, I didn't realize until now that my visit would require an explanation. When I decided to come, it seemed to me the most natural thing in the world. Perhaps that was somewhat inconsiderate of

154

me—I understand that now—but I even felt drawn to you, odd as that may sound.

"I hope you didn't read the article that appeared in one of the popular magazines on the occasion of my seventieth birthday. I didn't read it either, but I was told about it. A successful man, and so on. One who by his own efforts worked himself up from nothing to the position of leading industrialist. My son thought I shouldn't be angry about it, even if none of what the fellow wrote was true—by the way, he must have gotten most of his information from the good Blanck. In short, my son thought that in any case it was good publicity and would help our corporation. Of course he was right; it really doesn't matter what they write as long as they mention the name Helldegen. But I didn't mean to talk about that—it really has nothing to do with me.

"Yes, that's the point. I hope I'm not annoying you with my unwelcome revelations? Actually they're unsuitable to a man of my age. One of your fictional characters . . . forgive me, it makes you uncomfortable when I mention your books, but I'm only referring to one expression, a single sentence that caught my eye. Yes, it caught my eye, and it also puzzled me a little. Or made me sad, if you prefer. You have one of your characters say . . . I forget his name— a young man, I believe . . . he says, 'We're entirely lacking in old people.' He says it more or less by chance; it just slips out in conversation.

"Perhaps you had no particular intention when you wrote the sentence, but I felt that it related to me. I don't think of myself as old, in spite of my white hair. I don't even think it's ordinary vanity that keeps me from admitting that I really am quite old—but let others be the judge of that. Incidentally, it's happened that someone took my son to be older than I, or at least wiser. But that's all by the way.

"I myself never cared for old people. My father was

poor and a failure, and his situation made me so bitter that I made up my mind to become rich. That's the whole secret of my success—no big ideas, not even overwhelming skill, nothing but envy and fear of poverty. Old people had no value for me at all; on the contrary, they were in my way. I had to exploit their weaknesses so I could shove them aside. Yes, their weaknesses. And that's what I did. That's the sum total of my achievement. The article mentions none of that.

"Fine, let's assume that I am an old man. Do you want to know what an old man thinks when he goes for lonely walks in a resort and all the waiters and desk clerks bow deeply and say, 'Certainly, sir'? Well, I can only speak for myself; I don't know what other chairmen of other boards think. But I—suddenly, as I promenaded up and down Berchtesgaden, I thought that some poor sixteen-year-old kid was watching me, hidden behind a hedge or looking up from his work, just as I had watched more than fifty years ago. Filled with envy and hate, he thinks, There goes a rich man, and I want to be like him.

"Fine, you'll say, that's how it always is. But me—what about me? Shall I tell the boy that it's not worth it? First of all it isn't true, and secondly he won't believe me. He'll believe the idiotic article. And perhaps he'll also talk about his duty to the community, like my son. No matter, I'm speaking only about myself now and about the impossibility of communicating.

"So, if it were up to me, I'd be more inclined to say that we are quite lacking in young people. And it must be added that I hardly have the right to complain, since in that sense I've never been young myself. Competent, yes—but young? No! I'd never have had the courage to formulate as simple a sentence as you had your character say—'We're entirely lacking in old people.'

"I can't judge whether you can dissociate yourself from your books or whether you even have the right to do so. You must forgive me for speaking about it once more. As far as I'm concerned, I must not instigate confusion. I can't even let it be seen that I'm aware of my total powerlessness. As an old and rich man, I can afford a number of pursuits. For example, I can play the Maecenas or organize endowments for the general welfare or take up religion. I'd be praised for any and all of these, and everyone would believe in my sincerity. Such activities would suit their image of me, would be a credit to a chairman of the board. And if you, for example, were to repeat what I'm telling you now, you'd be told, 'There is no such chairman of the board.' And that is because there must not be such a chairman, though if there should be, he would have to be declared incompetent.

"That, more or less, is the reason for my visit. You see, Herr Möncken, that there is no reason to expect anything from old people. Of course it was a heavy blow to me when I had to come to the sudden realization that the younger generation is just as uncertain of its affairs as I am—this younger generation for whose sake I had just decided to renounce being something quite different from what I was expected to be.

"I told myself that it would be fitting to end my little recuperative trip by seeing two people who were living their lives in a way quite different from the routine. And perhaps a better way. But you won't believe me when I tell you that—no, let me finish, my child. In the old days I didn't spend much time thinking about you. I thought yours was a marriage like every other marriage around us, no better and no worse, and advantageous to all parties. It never occurred to me that it must be difficult to live with people like ourselves. Today I understand, though I can't change the facts. Of course it makes me sad, that's true; but on the other hand, I'm impressed that someone has found the courage to live outside this . . . this achievement. This 'outside' is a world that's closed to me."

"But you mustn't leave now, Papa," I called as he rose and prepared to go.

"I've talked about myself long enough." He smiled. "Yes, and I didn't even bring you flowers or a box of candy for fear of creating a false impression."

"But that wasn't necessary. We know—"

"All right, then . . . ."

"We have nothing to offer you, Papa. Would you like Berthold to run out for something?"

Berthold got up at once, preparing to go out.

"What would you have been doing if I hadn't come?" my father-in-law asked.

"Us? Nothing special. Perhaps we would have gone to the movies. We go to the movies quite a lot, just to relax. Berthold was about to make coffee. But both of us are glad you came. We're mostly by ourselves."

"And what will you do after I leave?"

"Oh, nothing different. Berthold will get back to work . . . . Where are you going?" I asked.

"I just want to get the coffee. And some cigarettes," Berthold explained.

"You'll be back in a minute?"

"Yes, of course, what did you think?"

"We could all go out for coffee," my father-in-law suggested.

I looked at Berthold, but he turned away without speaking.

"Or how about having supper at my hotel?"

Berthold shrugged. "If Marion would like to."

"No, you say what you'd like. It depends on your work."

"Just say yes if you'd enjoy it," Berthold said.

"Wouldn't you rather work?"

"There's no hurry now."

"But you'll lose the whole evening."

158

Irresolute, he stood by the door and stared at the floor.

"All right, let's forget it," my father-in-law said.

"No, Herr Helldegen," Berthold replied. "You really cannot leave now. And if I've behaved badly . . . ." He gestured. "You and Marion decide. I'll run to the store. Yes, please. Anything is all right with me."

"Berthold," I called as he was already halfway out the door.

"Yes?"

"Be careful."

He smiled at my father-in-law. Then he left. I listened for the slam of the apartment door.

And then I told my father-in-law the whole story. There was no sense in trying to keep secrets from him.

I began to talk immediately; I didn't want my father-in-law to speak first, nor did I want him to remain silent. Nevertheless, at first I tried to talk about something else; but it always amounted to the same thing. I tried to apologize for telling Berthold that he should be careful, talking to him the way you talk to a child. I didn't want my father-in-law to think that I treated Berthold like a child. That's how it always was, I said, and I mentioned that Berthold thought of himself as invulnerable. But of course my father-in-law did not understand me, and I had to explain to him at once that Berthold had explained to me that he wasn't worth fate's taking an interest in him, and therefore he was invulnerable.

"You could take everything away from him, and he'd never miss it," I said. But again that was something I hadn't wanted to say, and to distract my father-in-law, I talked about the train wreck Frau Viereck had mentioned and about the many traffic accidents that happened every day. I said that it was always the same when Berthold went out as he had done just now, always as if he hadn't been here at all and had already forgotten the whole episode. That was why I was always

159

afraid that he wouldn't come back. No, not that he would abandon me—he'd never do that—but that one day they'd bring him home to me. Why, the other day that had almost happened. No, it was only my imagination, but . . . .

"I was standing at the window waiting for him, just like this time; he had only gone on a simple errand. That's when I saw him across the street, slumped against the wall of a house. They had laid him there, his face to the ground. People, children surrounded him. I can't tell you how I felt. One of the men leaned down to ask him something, but from up here I couldn't hear what he said. And I saw him trying to raise his head—in vain. How terrible it was! Why didn't someone go for the police? I wanted to shout to them, but I had no voice. Can you imagine?

"Yes, and then I saw Berthold walking along the street. He crossed the pavement to the slumping man. He helped him sit up and leaned him against the wall, and at that moment the policeman arrived. It hadn't been Berthold at all but some man who'd had a seizure. They were wearing the same kind of raincoat, that's all. You mustn't think I'm hysterical, Papa."

My father-in-law didn't answer, didn't even look at me; he stared past me at the window. I didn't know what to think, but I was terribly afraid that he might speak, and that would be the end of everything.

"It wasn't even a dream," I continued. "Berthold made fun of me. Yet, he's firmly convinced that nothing can happen to him. And yet he has such awful dreams. He moans in his sleep, and I have to wake him, but most of the time he only says he's sorry and won't tell me anything. He claims it's something he's eaten or the weather, but he only says that so as not to have to talk about it. I don't know anything about him, really. I know nothing of that other world that torments and destroys him. All his work, his writing—it's only a pre-

160

text, he says. First I thought he only said that because I was curious and he wanted to keep me away from it.

"The other day he almost fell out of bed. Please don't laugh, Papa; of course it's funny, I know, but if you'd been there . . . . He tried to throw himself out of bed to save himself. I had to hold him down, and he said, 'Thanks!' But he was out of breath. When I turned on the light, he was lying still, and then he smiled and said, 'If only one could paint that—the old brick house, the dead red. And the cunning grin of the sculptor standing on the front steps watching.' Berthold even told me the sculptor's name, but I've forgotten it. Berthold must have known him at one time. 'I never could stand his mouth,' he said, 'so smudgy and wary. And when you see these things, where does the light come from? There's no sun and no moon, you can't tell if it's day or night, and yet all the colors are much brighter than usual.

" 'I was lying on the tracks. Was the red building a railway station? I don't remember, but I'd been inside it and it's where I was coming from. I'd been there . . . yes, the ashen sculptor had told me that nothing could happen to me, since I'd already been murdered. With a knife, I think. And I didn't mind, I thought it was interesting. Why I was suddenly lying on the tracks—I don't remember that part. Perhaps I'd stumbled and that's why I was lying there, not across the tracks but parallel to them, on the ties. My head was hanging down over one, and I wanted to raise it because the gravel was hurting me, but it was heavy.

" 'There were three tracks, and I was lying on the middle one. And then there were trains on the tracks to the right and left of me. But such strange trains! The locomotives seemed a hundred years old, with funnel-shaped stacks and a very self-important cloud of smoke. And then the cars, so colorful, like toy trains, with tin wheels that were much too thin and light, blue and green wheels only loosely attached, rattling and rattling; the trains might jump the track at any second. Everything went well, the trains rushed past, but I still worried. I thought a train would soon come along my track, and that's why I tried to toss myself sideways, although I knew all the time that nothing could happen to me even if the train were to run over me, because I was already dead. But such colors!' "

Then my father-in-law said, "Let's not talk about dreams now. We don't have time."

"Yes, Papa. I'm sorry."

"Because he went out to give us a chance to have a talk alone."

"Of course, about supper. Yes."

"Don't, my child. He'll be back any minute, and we'll have gotten no further. Will you answer one question for me?"

"Yes. What is it?"

"A very banal question. But you mustn't get angry."

"What is it?"

"Does it have anything to do with money?"

"Oh, money!"

"Surely the two of us can talk sensibly about it."

"We have enough money," I said. I think there was more than two thousand marks left in the closet, and we didn't need much, after all. And now and then some money came in from magazines and so on, even if it wasn't a lot. When Berthold took me out, he took some of the money; he didn't count, and I too could take whatever was needed. He paid no attention to it whatever, leaving it to me. We could manage very well on what we had until November—even longer, if we continued our present way of life—and by that time Berthold was expecting more money for his work. We didn't scrimp either; we ate well, I saw to that.

I told all that to my father-in-law. "No, it's not

money." I had a feeling that our relationship might have been easier if it had been money, if we'd had none at all; but I didn't say so.

"That's all right," my father-in-law said. "It was just a question. The annoying thing is that I don't know any other way to help you. All I can offer is money, and that's not your problem . . . . You mustn't think that I hold anything against him because . . . well, because you went away with him. I like him very much, in fact . . . only . . . it's all so foreign to me. I don't dare to meddle. I don't want to be destructive. It was probably a mistake to come here."

"No, on the contrary, Papa. Your letter was a sign to me."

"A sign?"

"There's no one I can talk to. I have to figure everything out for myself. Can't you give me some advice, Papa?"

"No, I can't do that."

"Yes, you can, Papa. Who else is there?" And then I told him that I had thought about getting a job in the dress shop, not because of the money, but to give Berthold a chance for some peace and quiet.

"Do you think it's right to give him peace and quiet?" my father-in-law asked.

"But does he need me? You're older than I am, Papa, and much wiser. I'm so confused that I can't see clearly anymore. Can't you tell me whether he needs me? Sometimes I think he does, and then again I think he doesn't. Sometimes I think I only bother him and he doesn't need me at all. He doesn't need other human beings—they're nothing but a nuisance to him. He doesn't need me to eat and sleep and sew on his buttons. I have no idea what I'm here for. It's worse than being married. It's worse than being dead. How was I to know that there are such people, people who don't need anything? At first it seemed as if he needed me, no doubt about it. And now . . . a person could freeze to death.

"Guess what I asked him the other day. But you mustn't be angry at me, Papa—I only asked because I couldn't stand it anymore and because I felt so sorry for him. I asked him if he'd like to have a baby. I don't know what I thought I was doing; probably I didn't think at all. I just couldn't bear to see it anymore—I mean the insecurity. I wanted . . . oh, what's the point of talking about it?"

"Yes?"

"I should never have asked. My question frightened him so much, you should have seen his face . . . . And if he should need me after all? Perhaps it's all my fault. I can't picture him living alone again, Papa. Here in this room. He might need me again suddenly, the way he did before, and I wouldn't be there. What then, Papa?"

But he said nothing; he only sighed. Then I was ashamed that I'd told him all that and troubled him with my sorrow.

"Before, before you came, I'd made up my mind," I said.

"And now?"

"I even got dressed. Berthold has no idea why I put on the suit."

"You don't think so?"

"He cares about his work, that's all."

My father-in-law shook his head. "No, you're very much mistaken. He realizes very clearly that you're thinking of leaving him. I could tell by looking at him as he was standing in the doorway. Perhaps he thinks it will come out all right again—we all think that way—but he knows for certain that he cannot change things, and he's leaving the decision to you. No, don't interrupt me; we don't have much time. I don't want the three of us to sit around later on and not dare to open our

164

mouths for fear of saying the wrong thing. Besides, I didn't come here with the intention of giving advice. What would entitle me to do that? I'm a bad advisor in such matters. What would a businessman know about them?

"But perhaps your Berthold is right. I suspect that he's every bit as realistic as I am. What I mean is, when he claims to be invulnerable, as he puts it. In any case he is less vulnerable than you are. Yes, I'm right. Let me finish, please. This is the only fact I want to refer to. And if I'm to give you advice at all, I first need to know whether you have a plan; then I might possibly be able to say whether it's realizable or not. Go ahead."

He waited patiently for my answer. I no longer had a way out. "Couldn't we live together somewhere?" I finally asked, although the idea had never occurred to me before.

"Who do you mean—we?"

"You and I, Papa. I'd never leave you."

"No, that won't do."

"You mean because I've already failed twice—"

"No, that's not why. I'm grateful to you for the suggestion. Really—very grateful. But it won't do; I've made a different decision for myself, as I tried to explain earlier. But leaving me aside, I don't believe it would be the right solution for you."

"There is no right solution for me."

"In that case you have to do what's still possible. We don't want to blow the situation out of proportion, Marianne; there's no point in that. We both took a step outside the order of things, by accident or for some other reason, and we've learned that we are not suited to it. It's a very bitter lesson, yes, but . . . yes, at least that's how I see it. Of course it's very much easier for me to say something like that and make my peace with it. All I have to do is keep quiet for a couple more years and not bother the others; that's all that's expected of me. But you, on the other hand, still have so many choices. Yes, you do . . . . All right, then, you want to leave with me?"

"Where to?"

"You know exactly what I mean. Why do you bother asking?"

"No, it's impossible."

"Why should it be impossible? I'm firmly convinced that you've already considered it."

"No. There's no going back."

"My child, what's the use of grandiose statements?"

"No, Papa, I couldn't bear it."

"That's easy to say. We can bear much more than we think."

"No, it's impossible. And it would be mean. I'd rather . . . no, that sort of action is impossible for a woman. You cannot understand."

"Fine, let's drop it," he said, explaining that he'd meant it only as a suggestion. And that left him with only one other suggestion—that he give me money for as long as I needed it. That is, until I got my bearings. He himself, he pointed out, had gone to Berchtesgaden to get his bearings and gain a little distance. He would be the last person to criticize me. For him, too, there had been days when he believed everything was pointless, and that was much more shameful at his age than at mine. On such occasions people are apt to say, "Life goes on." Hearing that, you think, What a phrase—it's easy for them to talk. And yet it's true. You need only look at the street. Of course, when you've had a stroke of bad luck, you shout, "What do I care about this sort of life! It doesn't interest me!" All the same, it's there.

"But let's drop the fine phrases and talk very factually." There was Günther, for example. No, please, he must insist that I let him finish. He did not wish to pretend that Günther needed me. In fact, he believed

166

that the boy would grow up without me just as well—
I could see what an unsentimental view he took. He
himself had never had a proper childhood, and Max
had had to grow up without a mother too. So that wasn't
the main issue. Nor was it a matter of whether the other
way—having a mother—was better, as people always
insisted. Really, it had less to do with Günther than
with me. Yes, that was so, and I really should not make
it harder for him to talk about these things by sulking.
It was more or less acquired knowledge; he had accepted
it, since it did not affect him directly. Or at any rate . . . .

"All right, then, let's stick to the point." He had
always supposed that a child meant more to a woman
than, for example, the factory meant to him. As a man,
that was how he imagined it—at least she has something
when you don't know how to go on, something that
isn't a lie. But as he'd already said, that could just be
one of those age-old male prejudices, and he was only
parroting what he'd heard. His own experiences did
seem to contradict the received opinion, but how could
he possibly know what a woman really thought on the
subject?

One thing I must surely have noticed: he wasn't
talking about duty and other grandiose matters of the
kind that so handsomely embellished business reports.
He himself had never considered duty in his business
dealings; he'd had no time. Thinking about success kept
him busy, and what people called duty had been a by-
product. But no one needed to know about that; no one
would believe him, either. "Yes, what are we going to
do with you?"

Suddenly he changed the subject. "What surprises
me about Möncken is that he seems to care nothing for
his work. He constantly dismisses it. A pretext, he said?
A pretext for what? How is it possible to live like that?
I can understand everything else—I mean, that he
doesn't care about ordinary matters and doesn't want

them to tie him down. I even envy him that attitude. But . . . yes, I noticed the same thing when I was reading his books."

"Do you mean he has no talent?"

"How am I to judge that? Perhaps he's more talented than others, though that's not my business. But sometimes I have the feeling that he does not say what he should say and that he knows a great deal more than he tells. At times there's a resonance, and you think that now it's going to come—but then he quickly wipes it away again. If one wants to live the way he does, one must tell what one knows, whether or not anyone wants to hear it or whether or not it's upsetting. After all, that's the advantage he has over the rest of us. Or is it too dangerous to him too? Whatever the reason, he keeps secrets from us."

"It's because of his childhood, Papa," I said.

"I see. Yes, I don't know anything about that." My father-in-law looked at his watch. "All right, about Max: I never spoke with him about this; we avoid all personal conversations. But this is the practical situation—he's counting on your returning. That always surprised me a little; for my part, I never counted on it. But Max is different— more primitive, if you will.

"Never mind, it doesn't matter now whether we like his motives or even whether it's only that it suits his own business aims better. Forgive me for putting it this way. Yes, perhaps he is acting only from business considerations: you're a kind of investment for him; at the moment it's on a downswing, but with a little patience, if you simply leave it in your portfolio, one day it may begin to show a profit again. That's a common business experience.

"However that may be, I have no right to criticize Max. From the outset he has insisted that your absence was only temporary—to the rest of the world, at any rate. The word was put out that you'd gone for a rest

168

cure. That's what Max tells everyone. What choice do they have but to believe him? They want to go on doing business with Helldegen. So there's no problem there. Or we could just say that you joined me in Berchtesgaden or that we met up there. No one will check."

I felt so humiliated that I could not speak.

Perhaps my father-in-law didn't expect me to. He reflected for a while before continuing. "The only problem is you. I don't know whether you could bear it, and that's why I do not dare to suggest it to you. Yes, the material circumstances would be easier than the situation here, but that was always true, even before.

"No, please, don't take your bearings from me," he suddenly said, his voice very concerned. "It's unfair of me to take such a cold, businesslike view of the matter. That's all right for my own life, but it doesn't apply to you. Forget everything I've said."

"No, you're quite right, Papa. It's the only thing that's right." I would have liked to add that I wasn't worth giving so much thought to, but I didn't. It was too silly, it was self-evident. "When does your train leave?" I asked instead.

"We could take the night train," he suggested.

"Yes, if . . . then the sooner the better."

"It leaves just before eleven. I'm sure we could still get sleeping-car accommodations. I could call home to have someone meet us at the station."

"No, don't do that."

"I'm only suggesting it in case you should decide that way."

"I won't be able to bear it, Papa."

"Yes, that's the danger."

"I don't care about danger, Papa, I care about happiness. They'll notice that I've been happy, even though the happiness turned into unhappiness. Max will notice, everybody. Even Günther. When I laugh, they won't trust me, and they'll look at me with hurt expressions. No matter how hard I try, it will stand by my side always, and I'll look around at it. Even if I was never genuinely happy, still there was a hint of it—how can I forget it? No, no—even if it failed, Papa, that doesn't count. A person can go mad from it. Nobody is that good at pretending. No woman is, Papa. Things are different for women."

"Yes, I know."

"No, there's no way you can know. Why did your wife leave you?"

Not until the words had escaped me did I realize that I should not have asked. "Forgive me, Papa. My God, I've grown so inconsiderate."

"Why? There's no reason you shouldn't ask."

"No, I don't have the right, and it's none of my business."

"I thought you knew all about it."

"It just slipped out, Papa. Please don't be angry. Perhaps because . . . well, because I would never have left you."

"Oh, yes, in all probability you would have left me the same way as . . . . The doctors said she had the predisposition; after all, she died eighteen months later in the hospital. There's a medical explanation for everything, and if you want to, you can accept it."

"Please don't talk about it, Papa."

"I too accepted it; I wrote my wife off as a bad investment, just as we do in business—and the quicker you do it, the slighter the loss. Then you can turn your mind to more profitable efforts. Remembering that she left me would only have tied my hands. I wasn't a whit different from Max, at least not at the time.

"I refused to understand her farewell note; I considered her sick even then, even without a medical certificate. She wrote me . . . someday I'll show you the letter, if you like. I believe I kept it so as to have some proof against her. Yes, she wrote that she felt infinitely sorry for me because . . . I don't remember her exact words . . . but in short, because I wasn't alive at all, as she put it. And then she wrote that she felt too weak to help me, even blaming herself for her weakness, but that she wanted to avoid coming to despise and hate me . . . something like that. It came as a total surprise to me, but I made it easy for myself: I told myself she was a hysteric.

"I had married her out of ambition; I was a social climber with some money, and it was advantageous for me. She came from an old academic family. Sometimes these things work out—why not in my case? I was so convinced of myself and my abilities that I never doubted it would. Besides, I was more successful by the day, so I could see no reason for my wife to be unhappy. When I noticed that she was, I bought her presents, things money could buy. When I noticed that she hated the factory and the methods that are necessary in business, I made fun of her. 'Why cut off your nose to spite your face?' I said to her. I didn't take her seriously.

"Finally she was disgusted by me. She said that I had no manners, that I had never learned them at home, and when I relaxed, I relapsed. She was disgusted by my eating habits and could no longer sit at a table with me. When I chewed, she said, my jawbone cracked; perhaps it was because I put too much food in my mouth at one time. I'd never given it much thought, but then I began to be self-conscious and hardly dared to chew at all. But I didn't take even that too seriously; I thought, It's all right, this is the sort of thing that probably happens in every marriage as time passes. And for the rest, I always had my work.

"Sick or not sick, that's not the issue. The fact that she left me—that surprised me more than it troubled me. I sent Max to a boarding school, and our business took such an upturn that . . . . I'm not trying to blame myself; that's a cowardly method of justifying oneself retrospectively.

"But to get back to Max—he'll never throw it up to you, I can vouch for that. It's not his way. Yes, and about the other thing, the issue you probably have in mind . . . he won't bother you—as a man, I mean. No, let me talk about it. It's true I don't understand much, and I made it too easy for myself. But . . . surely it wouldn't be hard to keep him away from you. You know what? We may be a little crude, and besides we've been told that's what women like, but basically we're shy. But enough of that. I only want to relieve your misgivings."

"I have to discuss it with Berthold," I said.

"Yes, you do."

"You must understand, Papa."

"I do understand."

"Something like this—you can't just pretend it never happened. And what's to become of Berthold? Oh, if I were the only person involved! I'm a failure, that's all. And if I'm to stand it at all, then it's only because of you, Papa, only because you'll be there and because . . . no, it won't work. Not even if I grit my teeth. It's . . . . Can't you tell me what to do, Papa? I'm prepared for anything, I'm ready to pay. I've already given up everything other people value. Can they punish you for that?"

Then there was a knock on the door, and I called, "Come in." It was Berthold who had knocked—at the door of his own room. He had knocked because he didn't want to take us by surprise. As if already he had stopped being a part of it. And then he stood in the doorway, a few feet from us and yet so far away, with a whole room between us, an empty room, without any immediacy, so that we need pay no attention to him if we preferred not to, and he would make no further trouble if we wanted to send him away again. He himself was only half there, just stopping by, and please, his arrival shouldn't embarrass us, he had only come by to bring the coffee—where would we like him to put it? . . .

Yes, he was holding the jar in a brown paper bag, and he proffered it to us so that we would see it at once and say, "Oh, the coffee. Isn't it great that you could find some . . . ."

That was how he stood there, and I saw at once that he knew what we had talked about, that he knew precisely why I had put on the suit, knew that I was determined to . . .

When I think back on the moment now, I also knew clearly that it was quite impossible for me to leave him. It would be a betrayal such as nothing in the world could rectify. If I belonged anywhere at all, I belonged with him.

Yes, he stood there just as he had stood at the award ceremony, on the dais and later in the room among all the people, so alone that one couldn't stand it. And no matter what people preach because they won't admit the truth or they're afraid, he need have spoken only one word . . . oh, not even that, just made a tiny motion, even a twitch of his eye would have been enough, for we knew each other and had no need of words, that's how well we knew each other . . . and I would have run to him, and perhaps we would have died together and been released from all our agony.

Instead I stayed in my chair, paralyzed, unable to do what I should have done. I waited; I had been made so weary by all that had happened that I could only wait. Or it may have been that I was ashamed in front of my father-in-law— I don't remember now. I can't understand anymore why I didn't do something so simple. That was all that was left, and I frittered it away. I must have lost every ounce of good sense I ever had.

I let my father-in-law get up first, and I'm sure he did so only because I made no move; he gave me plenty of time to decide. I think that he was just as aware of the situation as I was and knew that there was really nothing left to decide and that everything else was hopeless. He probably thought my sitting still was my decision.

He went to Berthold and held out his hand in farewell. Not until then did I call out, "Surely you're not leaving already, Papa?"

Perhaps it came out wrong, perhaps it really sounded as if I intended to go with him and had decided in his favor. In this way everything came out differently from how it should have been.

"I'm going to my hotel now," my father-in-law said. "You can call me if there's any need."

And in his hasty way Berthold said, "You'll find a cabstand right downstairs, at the next corner to the right."

"Yes, thank you. I don't know if we'll meet again, Herr Möncken."

"It doesn't matter. Meeting again never matters. I'm sorry if I offended you."

"You didn't—"

"Yes, I did. Or perhaps—I disappointed you. I disappoint everyone. My desires are boundless, that's the trouble. That's why I don't even try the usual things— they're insufficient; they have too little reality. I wish I were as wise as you."

"Wise?" my father-in-law sounded astonished.

"Don't be offended by the word. Yes, 'wise' is old-fashioned; perhaps I mean 'beyond desiring.' No, that's not it either—it doesn't matter. I thought about you while I was out. I've lost the ability to talk, and in ten years I'll probably have stopped talking altogether. Why bother? What's the point of making oneself understood? Words only turn into lies.

174

"Yes, I thought about you. There's no way of helping you—I can help you least of all, so just stay away from me. Do you realize that there's nothing more positive than when someone has gone so far that no one can help him anymore? Yes, it's true. People used to think differently, I admit, but nowadays . . . . Yes, I'd like to be as far along as you are, but sometimes I'm still overcome by longing, that's the problem. But why talk about it? Please don't let me keep you."

Berthold said the final sentence as if he couldn't wait to be rid of my father-in-law. As he spoke, he looked at me for the first time since he had come back into the room. His look was cold as ice; he even raised one eyebrow in astonishment, as if to say, My, my, who else have we here? Oh, of course, it's her. My God, can't she leave me in peace at last? Surely it's too much to bear. One cannot be alone for a single minute.

I don't know if my father-in-law noticed. I think he did, because he turned toward me quickly. Then he said, "I don't want to keep any secrets from you, Herr Möncken. My visit turned out somewhat differently than I had expected. Perhaps I shouldn't have given in to my urge to come here. But what has happened has happened. Marianne and I discussed a number of matters. We reached no conclusions. As far as I'm concerned, I don't dare give her any advice—and you even less, of course.

"Please don't be angry with me for knowing how the situation stands. And please don't be angry at Marianne, either. Possibly it may help both of you that she talked to me; that's how it works sometimes. Yes, that's why I said that you and I might never meet again. There are many fine phrases for occasions like this, but I think we'd rather dispense with them, wouldn't we? All of us are much too serious. All right, then."

He nodded to me and left. Berthold walked to the apartment door with him. Should I jump up and run after him? Papa, take me with you! I'll only be a few minutes. I'm almost ready. And if you're with me . . . .

Yes, then I would not have had to talk to Berthold. I would have packed my suitcase and shaken hands with him like any visitor, and then I would have walked away at my father-in-law's side.

My chest ached terribly. I stood up, but I only made it as far as the closet. When I opened it to take out my odds and ends, Berthold had already returned to the room.

What was left to talk about? And who was to begin? We did not look at each other; it wasn't necessary. We already knew that both of us were still there. I took my underclothes from the drawer and laid them across the bed. I walked back and forth, trying to keep busy. Berthold sat down in the chair by his typewriter and read what he had written. He even rolled back the page in the machine so as to be able to read better.

I didn't want to make any mistakes. I told myself, You'll have to speak to him very coolly, very naturally. All right, so we spent some time together; all right, so now it's probably high time for us to separate; otherwise we're only in each other's way, and that's how it will always be; all right, so let's think kindly of each other; and so on. But I was afraid that it would come out all wrong and that when I heard my own voice speaking differently than I'd planned, I wouldn't be able to stand it and would run to him.

Then he would think that he could not leave me and that I could not live without him, and he would feel obligated to stay with me. Perhaps—more dangerous still—we would love each other; for that can happen quite against your will when you embrace out of grief.

People must not touch each other when they're sad. It may be enough for an hour or two, or even for a night—it gains you a little weariness. But when dawn breaks and you can hear the first steps in the street,

176

you're poorer than before; you've paid out even your grief, and nothing is left. That's why I concentrated on packing my suitcase.

Suddenly there was a screech as Berthold tore the piece of paper from the typewriter, and then I heard him crumple it. The sounds startled me so much that I came to a stop.

"Paper!" he said, standing up. "I'm sorry, it could have waited until later. Shall I help you pack?"

"Thanks. There's not much," I said. He pulled my overnight case from the top shelf anyway and slapped his handerchief at the dust it had collected.

"Don't forget your nightgown."

"I won't."

"It's so easy to forget that it's always best to pack it first. Funny, they always put it under the pillow, even in the hotels. At home it was always placed at the foot of the bed . . . . Would you prefer being alone to pack? Shall I go out for a while?"

"No, stay. Please."

"All right. But take your time. Don't leave anything behind. Or . . . . Of course I could send it to you. But . . . is there anything else we should talk about? Anything practical, I mean?"

"Not that I can think of."

"All right."

"The money is in the closet," I said.

"What? What did you say?"

"The money. Better put it in your pocket, or it will disappear."

"Who would take it? Frau Viereck?"

"No, of course not. But at least lock it away."

"All right, I'll lock it away. How do you figure it, actually?"

"What?"

"All this."

"Oh, Berthold."

"A splendid man, your father-in-law."

"I beg your pardon?"

"I mean it. He makes one feel a bit ashamed. We have our little problems, no worse than anybody else, and he . . . I came close to inviting him to stay with us. But we have nothing to offer him. And it wouldn't work out. Day and night with the awareness of being superfluous, an empty shell that can be blown away—no, that wouldn't work. But why talk about it? You're leaving in the morning?"

"Perhaps on the night train. There is one."

"Hm, yes, that's even better. For you, I mean. There's no point in postponing these things. Perhaps afterward I'll go to a movie. To the late-night showing."

"Yes, why don't you."

"Where can we have put the newspaper with the movie schedule? You can never find it when you need it."

"Isn't it in the pile with your letters?"

"My . . . oh, it doesn't matter. Maybe Frau Viereck has a newspaper."

"What are you going to tell her?"

"Who?"

"Frau Viereck. I don't want to say goodbye to her."

"But that doesn't matter. What do we care about Frau Viereck?"

"She's a nice woman."

"I'll tell her that you had to leave in a hurry. Because of your father-in-law. Or because somebody is ill. It doesn't matter. None of that is important. Come on, I'll help you."

He bent down and pulled a pair of my shoes from the closet floor, where they stood next to Berthold's shoes because there wasn't much room. One shoe had slipped way to the back, probably during sweeping or dusting.

Berthold weighed the shoe in his hand and smiled. "How light it is."

"Yes, they're pretty shoes," I said.

"They look good on you too. I was always proud when you . . . don't you want to wear them?"

"No, they're not right for traveling." I took the shoe from him and slipped it inside a stocking. Berthold watched me.

"Isn't that going to make a run?"

"They're old stockings."

"How practical you are."

"I get it from my mother, though she thought I was impractical. She always scolded me. She thought I was a spendthrift."

I remembered that once before, Berthold had stood by while I packed—that other time, in my room at home. But that occasion had been utterly different. It had been almost dark in the room, with only the night stand lamp and the lights on my dressing table turned on. And then in Hanover, many years ago—I think the hotel was called Luisenhof. A fancy hotel. Arnim was all in favor of such establishments. I didn't have much to pack, not much more than a briefcase. I had made up my mind to marry Max.

Always I ended up packing my things and leaving. Always everything was in vain.

Berthold had guessed my thoughts. "You mustn't think that I haven't thought about everything."

"And where does it lead you?" I asked quickly, pointing to the typewriter.

"What? Oh, I see. That isn't important. We don't need to waste any words on that."

"But I'd love to think that at least . . . . Is it because of me?"

"What?"

"That you tore it up."

"That has nothing to do with you. No, it's a piece of paper, nothing more."

"So everything was to no purpose?"

"No, why do you say that? That doesn't mean anything. Paper—that's just an expression we use. Paper language. Paper problems. That's what we call it. It's nothing special; it happens to everybody, and you have to be prepared for it. Don't worry. Really, the only way to start is to be prepared from the outset to accept that it will come to nothing. I guess I felt a little too sure of myself—that damned prize, yes, and the routine. But if you realize in time, there's no harm done."

"You won't finish it?"

"That piece of junk?"

"And there won't be an opening night in the fall?"

"What? But why not? I can write something else. A play can be written in a week if you're lucky. It doesn't have anything to do with time. Besides, that part doesn't matter; success isn't important, and it isn't important whether anybody wants to see it or read it. That has nothing whatever to do with it. I'm very grateful to your father-in-law, I mean for his coming here. I realized that earlier, when I was out buying the coffee. Shall I make you some? I think I'll make myself a cup.

"It's best if I start on something new right away, without a lot of dillydallying. If those scientists could just manage to build their space vessel, I'd volunteer. I've given it a lot of thought. Of course they're going to need volunteers for the first trip because it's probably going to be a total washout. Still, what a pleasure to have one single second out there, to see it all!

"But those incompetents can't manage to get the machine going. They've been dragging their heels for forty years. One day I'll be too old—because I'm certain that first they'll check out your heart and all that stuff. Well, for the time being I'm still hale and hearty—much

too hale and hearty! What's someone like me supposed
to do with so much health?"

"Will they take women too?"

"What?"

"In the rocket."

"That's no place for a woman. Besides, it's all nonsense. Have you finished packing?"

"No. I mean—"

"You mustn't think that I keep secrets from you,
Marion."

"I never thought that."

"Yes, you did. Everybody does. But I don't have
any secrets, I've never had any. It's just that I can't talk
about anything, so people think I do. When you're
gone . . . ."

"Yes, what happens then?"

"Nothing! I'll write something—anything at all. I
don't even know what yet. I have all sorts of ideas, but
that's not what counts. The ideas are unimportant, the
plot is unimportant—all those elements are secondary.
Basically it doesn't matter at all what I write about. It
could be this or that, but the main thing is . . . my God,
it's no big deal to think up some sad story or other and
write it down; anybody can do that. It doesn't require
going through all this. The main thing is . . . . Oh, well,
let's drop it. There's no way of saying it. I only mention
it so that you won't think I have some big secret. On
the contrary, writing is the easiest thing in the world,
and when it works out, it lasts a little while. Do you
realize that I'm going to long for you very much?"

"But don't write about me, Berthold."

"Why not, though?"

"I don't want to turn into paper."

"Don't pay any attention to me. What happens to
me doesn't matter anyway. I shall miss you because
with you I could sometimes forget that I exist. That's
a very rare thing. Sometimes when I looked at you, I

knew that I was nothing— that you were everything and I nothing. I didn't have to try to be something. And you knew it too, and you were satisfied. I'll miss that very much. But . . . during the day it doesn't work because you start to hate yourself, and you hate the other person for knowing. I'm telling you this only so that you won't think I'm hard. I understand it all."

"But I never thought that."

"I guess I'm not fully developed, that's what it is. I only act as if I were, but some people notice. Let's not talk about it. I'm embarrassed with other men. I'll never be like your father-in-law. Is he waiting for you?"

"Yes, at the hotel. And if I don't come, we should call him."

"Hm, yes. I'm glad that you have him, at least. Don't keep him waiting."

"I still have to pack my toilet things."

"Don't you want me to help you?"

"There's nothing to do."

"There, your washcloth on the towel rack."

"Thank you, yes."

"Take the soap with you, too. Please. The scent is too strong."

"All right, hand it to me." I grabbed the soap from his fingers. We had bought it together. Berthold had spent a long time searching in the shop until he found just the right cake. I closed the suitcase. "There, I think I have everything. And it's time."

"Is he really waiting for you?"

"What else should he be doing?"

"We could telephone him."

"But what for?"

"I could take you to the hotel in the morning in plenty of time. Or directly to the train. I only thought of it because your father-in-law already has a ticket for the morning train, and then he wouldn't have to bother to exchange it. But whatever you prefer, I don't care."

182

"It won't work, Berthold."

"All right. Let's not talk about it anymore."

"You mustn't think that I'm hard."

"I don't think that. It was only a suggestion."

"It really wouldn't work. I'd like to stay with you, but—"

"What for? We've talked everything out."

"I'm too much of a coward. It's probably true that I'm nothing but a fine lady, as you always said."

"Oh, what nonsense. Do you have any money?"

"Money? Yes, I think so . . . . My God, the heat. My suit is much too warm."

"Let me see." He took my purse from me and checked to see if I had money. "You better take some more. You'll need something for the taxi and then—"

"There's enough for the taxi. And afterward . . . Papa has money."

"No, no, you better take some. Just in case. It only lies around here—I have no use for it. And perhaps you'll think of something. One should never be out of money."

"But Berthold, that's silly. We're just making it hard on ourselves. I won't change my mind. I've thought it all over."

"All right, then. Let's not talk about it anymore. I hate goodbyes—they're for the movies."

"Will you go to the movies?"

"Me? Oh, I guess so. Maybe. Maybe not. No, probably not. It's just a waste of time. I'll make a cup of coffee, and then I'll lie down for a while. Now I can sleep when I feel like it, and I can stay up all night and work if I want to."

"Remember the other boarders."

"I don't have to type. Writing by hand works just as well. And what about you? What will you do?"

At that instant the phone in the hall rang. Both of us started up and froze. When I think back to that ringing telephone now, I feel as though it had given me the worst fright of my life. We didn't dare move. All ears, we heard Frau Viereck's bedroom slippers shuffle along and we heard her pick up the receiver. I clenched my teeth.

But the call was not for us; there was no one who would call. No one had called us the whole time we'd been here. The call was for Frau Viereck, just a short conversation. Or maybe the call was for another boarder and Frau Viereck said he wasn't home. One of the boarders got a lot of calls; he was a traveling salesman.

Even after Frau Viereck had hung up the phone and returned to the kitchen, Berthold and I stood there like two thieves for quite a while longer, not moving. I don't know how he felt, but I feared nothing more than that the phone would ring again. That's what often happens: all day nobody calls, and suddenly someone thinks of telephoning, and as if it were a conspiracy, a second and a third person call right afterward and even complain about your long conversations, about the line being busy for so long.

"I'd better go now," I whispered to Berthold. As if someone were listening at the keyhole! Yet I could safely have spoken out loud; the window was open, and the noise from the street was considerable. "I want to go now, Berthold. I . . . yes, I'm afraid."

Silently he reached for my suitcase.

"No, let me have it. Leave it to me . . . it isn't heavy. Yes, and give my regards to Frau Viereck. There's no need for her to know anything. All right, Berthold."

I'd taken the suitcase from him. Carrying my fur coat over my arm, I stood at the door. I meant to use my elbow to push down the handle.

"Don't you want me to take you to the taxi, at least?" he asked, his voice just as low as mine.

"No, please don't. All right, as far as the front door,

184

but close it softly behind me so no one will hear. But not to the stairs—we might bump into somebody. And please don't watch me—from the window, I mean. I won't turn around either. All right. Oh, one more thing."

"Yes?"

"Don't write me. Please! Never write to me. Promise. Or I'll go mad."

"But what could I write to you?"

"No, please, promise."

Berthold nodded almost imperceptibly and opened the door for me slowly, without making a sound. I had to step aside. After looking out into the corridor, he waved to me and whispered, "Hurry."

He walked ahead, and I followed; both of us were on tiptoe. At the back of the hall the kitchen door stood open, the yellow light of the evening sun streaming out. Frau Viereck was rummaging in the pantry; there was the clatter of dishes, and a fork or a cooking spoon dropped. She muttered to herself.

Berthold managed to open the front door silently too. He opened it only a crack, just wide enough for me and my suitcase to squeeze through sideways without bumping into it. Berthold held on to the handle to keep the door from squeaking.

Neither of my hands was free to press the button for the stair light. The staircase was dark, but there was just the one flight. I did not even notice that Berthold had closed the door behind me—he was very quiet.

The street was even warmer than the room had been, the building walls radiating the heat of the day. My feet moved as if by themselves, without my having to make an effort—as if someone had given me a push and now I had to go forward whether I wanted to or not. And that was the way it should be.

Or as if the street were downhill. But it wasn't downhill, it was absolutely flat. I stayed on our side so that Berthold couldn't see me from the window—unless he leaned far out, that is; but he wouldn't do that.

At first I was afraid that he might call me back because I'd left something in the room, or that he'd come running after me to bring it to me.

That was why I quickened my steps almost without thinking. But what could I have forgotten? It couldn't be anything of importance.

I even crossed the street at a run, and I only began to feel a little bit secure when I was on the other side. I immediately spied a taxi, waved my coat, and said to the driver, "Hotel Europe, please."

3

Somewhere—on a calendar or in a newspaper supplement—I read that if you admit your mistake, it ceases to be a mistake.

I don't know who said it, and perhaps I misunderstood. Nor am I trying to justify myself; I admit everything.

Only . . .

I almost brought it off—the business about the mistake, I mean. I'm sure I would have brought it off, I'm certain of it. Only three days—three days, that's all!

Yes, if Max had taken me to Milan on the previous Friday instead of on Tuesday, everything would have come out differently. But the conference he had with the Italian industrialists was set for the Thursday of the following week. That wasn't my fault, and it wasn't Max's fault either. Everything depends on petty details, you can't plan these things in advance. You think about all the important matters, and you prepare for them so they won't take you by surprise. But the little things . . . .

I'd even looked forward to the trip. I was always glad to be away from home; at those times I didn't have to brood. Max thought I was pleased about going away with him, and I let him think so; it was right for him to feel that way. But that wasn't the real reason. I felt safer when I was away.

At home it could come over me at any time, from some forgotten corner. It might be the window curtains billowing a little because the window wasn't shut tightly that made me start up in fright. Or the radio. I didn't even turn it on anymore. Either they broadcast something that doesn't concern you, making you feel sad because the whole world thinks it's the right way and doesn't want it otherwise. Or you suddenly hear a sentence, or just a word that may not even have been meant that way, that seems so familiar; that's even more unbearable, because it comes from the radio and there's no real person there saying it.

Only when I was with others did I have any control over myself; say what they might, no one could detect anything by looking at me. But as soon as I was alone, when I was tired and thought I could let myself go, the danger set in.

Funny as it may sound, sometimes when I was in my room changing my clothes, or even when I was having a bath, something inside me would ask without my willing it, What's the point of all this? For whom are you doing it?

Then I had to get very busy to chase away the thought. I would talk out loud to myself merely to guard against it, without even being aware of it. Only when Günther, playing in my bedroom, would ask "What did you say, Mama?" did I become frightened.

It was like a poison that might course through me at any time. Yes, really—like a poison. I noticed it in my knees and my armpits and my fingertips—a strange sensation, soft and paralyzing, that made my movements imprecise, as if I had no control over them. Sometimes it went so far that I myself believed the lie they told about me: that I'd been to a rest home, where they'd made me well. But not quite well—I still needed to take it easy. Though the disorder had been contained, so that people were no longer aware of it, it still lurked in some dark recess, lying in wait day and night. I was the only one who knew that; no one else did.

Max least of all. I was always ready for anything, and I was cheerful when they wanted me to be. I went along with everything, I never said no. I owed Max that much. I wanted to be what he needed me to be for his house, for his business, for his social obligations. And he was extremely pleased with me. Just let everybody think I'd gotten over the illness—it was a help to me, too, to have them think so. I mean, that way I really would have gotten over it by and by, out of sheer habit.

Occasionally I had a feeling that I was speaking more softly than I used to, and then the fear started. Did they notice? I think I really was speaking more softly, out of caution and also in order not to miss anything, as if I were listening for something. Then I would immediately try to raise my voice or laugh. They probably never noticed, not even my father-in-law. And we were rarely alone together.

That was something we avoided from the outset, without discussing it. I didn't want him to so much as look at me questioningly. I didn't ask him about his life either, or about whether he found it hard to do without and to exist only as a figurehead. I don't know what he was up to. He walked silently up and down the stairs. When we encountered each other, we exchanged a cordial smile, like neighbors on the staircase of an apartment house.

Sometimes he took Günther for a walk. At night, at supper, there were enough topics of conversation between him and Max. I believe that my father-in-law also avoided being alone with me so that Max wouldn't suspect some kind of complicity.

Or might my father-in-law know how I felt after all? Perhaps it would have been better if I'd talked to him. Better for both of us; we belonged together. Sometimes when I heard him taking his coat from the hanger in the vestibule downstairs, I was on the point of calling out to invite him up to my room for a little while. But then I heard the front door open, and I kept silent.

I don't even know whether I would have talked to him about Berthold; I'm sure I would have been ashamed to bring the name up myself, but everything else we might have talked about would really have been about Berthold at bottom. Possibly he might have raised the subject.

Perhaps he would have asked me if I'd heard from Berthold. During the first few weeks I was terribly afraid that a letter would arrive, in spite of Berthold's promise. When I saw the mail lying in the front hall on the silver tray, I hardly dared look through it. What would I have done with a letter from Berthold? Would I have opened it?

But no letter came. So much the better! Gradually I began to lose at least this fear, even if not entirely.

Why should he write to me anyway? He had his work, and perhaps he'd long since found consolation. He was fully entitled to it. He did not need me; I had left him of my own free will because I was too much of a coward to endure life with him. Yes, he was fully entitled to despise me. I overestimated myself, that was it.

I would have liked to talk to my father-in-law about whether the whole thing had simply been my imagination, whether I'd read something into Berthold that really wasn't there. The first time I met him, at the award ceremony, I was tired and discontented, and Berthold was so entirely different from Max and all the people we were used to seeing. Perhaps I had let myself be tricked. Perhaps it had nothing to do with Berthold at all.

Often I tried to summon up how it had been, but I couldn't. I'm sure there's no way of remembering bliss.

There's an empty space of which you know only that it must have been then when you were happy. When you try to fill it with images, nothing fits, and you begin to doubt that it ever happened. But the empty space remains.

My father-in-law could have explained everything to me very clearly—whether it had been right for me to return here or whether Berthold might not need me after all and was missing me. Yes, perhaps all my doubt was caused only by the fact that he thought about me a lot. I always felt that he wasn't far away from me at all, no farther than the next room or around the next corner, and that all I had to do was call his name.

When I was downtown and glimpsed a man of Berthold's height wearing the same kind of raincoat— the raincoat with the greasy collar and the frayed sleeves, which Berthold refused to have cleaned—then I clenched my teeth in fear and was unable to walk on. Of course, there are a lot of men Berthold's size, and even his raincoat was nothing special.

If it really had been Berthold, all my efforts would have been in vain. I would have had no way to resist. I could not even have spoken. But how could I ask my father-in-law about such things? I would have hurt him, because he had faith in my strength. He could only have told me that I belonged with Günther and Max, not with Berthold. Anybody would have given me the same answer, and I told myself as much all the time.

There is no justification.

Everything else was very easy. From the first moment it came all by itself. Max was admirable, as he is to this day. What other man would have been like him? Yes, I was deeply in his debt. I had a lot of unfairness to make up to him.

He met us at the train—my father-in-law had talked to him on the phone—and he brought Günther. Max was holding the boy's hand as the train came in, and Günther was waving. As soon as we were on the platform and I could pick Günther up, everything was as if I had come back from a vacation trip. Max asked whether the train ride had been tiring, and he told his father that he looked well and rested. The car was parked outside the station. Gertig raised his cap, and I shook hands with him. Then the four of us drove home, chatting with Günther.

At home breakfast was waiting for us. Fräulein Gerda was there, as chatty as ever, babbling away about Günther and about how he had asked about me constantly and about how glad they were that I was back. Everything was as it should be.

I hadn't brought Günther a present—I hadn't had time—but on the train my father-in-law had offered me a couple of toys he had bought in Berchtesgaden or Munich, and these I gave to the boy. Max had changed a couple of appointments, and on this day he left for work later than usual.

Upstairs in my room, in my closets and drawers, nothing was changed. It was as if I'd never been away. And in fact I'd been gone only a little more than two months. All I had to do was start to live in the room again; it required no effort.

I think that they were honestly pleased to have me back. They weren't just pretending. Yes, it's true: each in his own way was genuinely glad. As if they'd missed me. How could I possibly help them?

When I saw my room again, I immediately made up my mind to do a lot of reading and in general concern myself with serious matters. Because who was I?

In other ways, too, it was good timing that I came back just then. A week later the schools closed for the summer and all our friends went away, so I did not have to see a lot of people and tell them a lot of lies. The few I did see were much too preoccupied with

192

preparations for their trips to have time to think about me. Even if they had their suspicions, they didn't care at the moment.

A week later everyone had left, and I too went away with Günther for four weeks at the North Sea. It was Max's suggestion and very tactful of him; a supplementary rest at the seashore, he called it. And how he trusted me! I said that it would be nice if he came along, and he said that he'd see if he could join us for a long weekend. During this time Fräulein Gerda also took her vacation.

In Kampen I was totally among strangers; during the day we went to the beach with the children, and at night the grown-ups sat together for a while. Everything was the way it always is at a resort. I deliberately spent time with the strangers, though I would have preferred being alone. I wanted to introduce Max to these people when he came to visit, because I didn't want him to think that I was avoiding company and wished I were elsewhere.

Max did come to see us, and he stayed a whole week. He was very pleased with me. I introduced him to a bank president whose wife was seated at the adjoining table, and Max spent a good deal of time with him.

We also had a night out at a nearby casino, and I won a couple of hundred marks. Max himself did not gamble—I don't know whether he really didn't like games of chance or was just reluctant to let me see him betting—but he urged me to have a fling. He gave me money and explained to me how to go about it, for I had no idea. I did the wrong thing right away, and Max was thoroughly annoyed with me. But I won all the same. How pleased Max was then! Not because of the money, but because he didn't like to lose. I think he would have been immeasurably enraged; he would have felt ashamed.

I tried to give him the money I'd won, but he refused to take it. He insisted that I keep it because I'd earned it myself. So in fun I invited him to dinner in the casino, and I ordered champagne. That was an enormous pleasure for him—he tells all his friends the story to this day.

But it made me sad. The clatter of dishes and silver, the conversation of the people around us, the music, the headwaiter's alertness as he stood by the little serving table ready to refill our plates—all these made me nervous. Everything was so unreal, as was the money I'd won; and my inviting Max—it was like the movies, but it was hard for me to play out my part to the end.

When I looked out the window, there was the surf, one wave after the other, never flagging; you could hear the roar. That made everything even more unreal. I would have liked to be alone on the other side of the island, where it was more quiet.

I told Max that I was tired, and we went back to our hotel.

When the holidays were over and everyone was back home, they all talked about nothing but their trips—where they had gone and how the hotel was and the quality of the meals and how much it had cost and the weather and the side trips they'd taken. And of course they showed their photographs. The usual. They said to me, "How rested you look," and I said the same to them. Everything else had long since been forgotten. It was as if it had never happened. No one gave it a thought.

I don't know what Fräulein Gerda was really thinking. Even if she made a nuisance of herself with her incessant chatter, she was a good soul, and Günther was very attached to her. Nevertheless, it troubled me that she was still in the house, and I would have liked to dismiss her; she must have known that I had left with

Berthold that night. Even if she wasn't too bright, she could hardly believe that it had simply been a coincidence and that I had really left for a rest cure. She also knew that I'd taken very few things with me. She was a woman, after all.

Perhaps Max had so intimidated her that she didn't dare to believe otherwise. In any case, she always acted as though nothing had happened, to my great annoyance, although she was the last person with whom I would have discussed my affairs. Sometimes it seemed as if she really did treat me like a sick person and had been hired to watch over me and and do everything for me so that I wouldn't have to exert myself, much in the way she used to watch over my father-in-law. I even harbored the suspicion that Max kept her on only because he didn't trust me, but it was unfair of me to assume any such thing. I was feeling unsure of myself and thought everybody could tell by looking at me that I did not entirely belong to him, and that was what made me suspicious.

Finally one night I told Max that we didn't need Fräulein Gerda anymore and could safely let her go. At that he raised his eyebrows, and I realized that he thought I had an ulterior motive for making the suggestion. I immediately added in explanation that I could look after Günther myself; it would keep me from feeling quite useless. Max could see my point—he probably approved of it, too—but he said it would be ungrateful of us to dismiss Fräulein Gerda just then. In a couple of months she'd be leaving of her own accord, since her fiancé was about to take his final exams and would be marrying her right after he passed them; we would have to keep her until then. I couldn't argue with his reasoning, and so she stayed. I gave her some of my things; she and I had almost the same figure.

Blanck, too, was still around; of course. He was at the house even more frequently than before. The business was growing by leaps and bounds, and I could tell from their conversations that Max was hatching some great plan. He succeeded at everything he undertook.

But I had no dealings with Blanck. I saw him only in passing. I knew when he was in Max's study, and when I ran into him, I shook hands with him politely. "Hello, Herr Blanck. How are you? And Frau Blanck?"

And he bowed correctly. "Fine, thank you, Frau Helldegen."

He was only too happy, I sensed, when I immediately added, "Please don't let me interrupt you."

He still wore the same dark suits with the narrow pinstripes and sharp creases, and the large birthmark on his left temple near his glasses was still in place.

A couple of times I went to the factory to pick Max up. The employees were very excited and held open the doors for me. All this I did to please Max.

When the new lunchroom was opened, I went to the dedication ceremony. Max was very proud of the canteen and of all he did for his people. I was asked to admire the murals: a woman holding a sheaf of wheat, a man with a scythe; on the opposite wall a mill and a brook; and on the short wall an old baking oven and a board with several loaves of bread. This because we were a food-processing plant.

The pictures were pale and boring, but of course I didn't say so; they had cost a lot of money, and they had been photographed for the newspapers. In general, the name Helldegen appeared frequently in the papers. Max, who had cut the workers in on the profits, was referred to as "one of our most forward-looking industrial leaders."

Now and again I went along when Max had to go away on business. Usually the cities we visited were quite dull, and since Max was in conferences all day long, I had nothing to do. But he enjoyed having me with him, and each time he asked me beforehand whether I'd like to come. Perhaps, too, he was trying to show me that he wasn't taking a secretary along and that he preferred my company. At night there were dinners with the other men and their wives. Max was proud because I dressed well and cut a fine figure. Everyone thought of us as a very happy couple.

Once I almost gave myself away. That was on the highway, near one of the exits, when I hadn't been paying any attention to the road. Gertig was driving, and Max and I were in the back seat. I think Max was looking through some papers to get ready for the conference. Suddenly I saw a large yellow sign indicating the turnoff to the city where I had lived with Berthold. And the town name was followed by the distance—178 kilometers.

I began to shake. It was only a three-hour drive, not much more.

Already we had sped past the sign. Gertig was driving straight ahead.

The shaking came so unexpectedly that I couldn't hide it from Max. He had not seen the sign, and when he asked me what was the matter, I said, "Nothing! Perhaps I'm not up to the drive." We were already a long way past the turnoff. Even so, Max would probably not have given a thought to the sign and the name of the town. He had Gertig stop at the next rest area, where we stayed for ten minutes. Then everything was back to normal.

I didn't even know whether Berthold was still living in that town.

And then it was fall. There were a lot of parties and dinner invitations. Everything was the way it was supposed to be. I was tired; I was always tired from all these distractions, but I made an effort. Max was delighted with me.

And he left me alone in other ways. Of course I

would not have refused him; that would have been wrong of me. I owed it to him to play my role very realistically. But it was good that he asked nothing of me. Perhaps my father-in-law had had a talk with him? But no, that was impossible; the two of them never talked about such matters. So Max had made the decision for himself. I was extremely grateful to him.

But every night when we went our separate ways, I was afraid that the situation might change. I wanted to prove my gratitude; often I thought that I should be more cordial to him, and I wondered how to take the first step. I never managed it, though; at the last minute I always got cold feet, and things stayed the same.

I hoped that, as time passed, I would mind less. Each day that went by was a day gained. At heart I knew very well that other people thought we were a couple just like themselves—and it's possible that the situation in other houses really was the same. There's no way to tell from the outside.

But there was one difference. Never mind the husbands, they had their work and that was all they needed. It was unthinkable that they should care whether everything at home was as it should be. For them it was only a thing apart, a kind of luxury. When I considered the wives, however, it seemed to me that they accepted everything much more lightly than I did, as a matter of course, and that they didn't care if both parties lived for themselves. It did not rob them of any aspect of their safety. Most of them were very ambitious and cared only for their position, and of course for their children, who were part of their position.

The difference was that they were content, while I could not come to terms with such a life. But what did I know about them really? Perhaps they felt exactly as I felt, except that they were more clever. And some may just have been superficial—they were the lucky ones.

I felt like I was being punished, like I was living in

exile and had difficulty speaking the language of the country. Everyone was pleasant to me, and all were careful not to make me feel a stranger among them. They made it so easy for me to acclimate myself: all I needed to do was forget what was in my past. That I could not bring it off was my fault alone.

They were gentle with me, they praised me as a hostess, they praised my dress, they praised everything. Perhaps they did so only because Max was standing by and they wanted him to hear; all their behavior seemed rehearsed. They can't help but notice, I thought, that I just happen to be here quite by accident and that I say only what it is proper to say. And that was why it was all so exhausting for me.

When we got home at night, I was worn out and had trouble falling asleep. Did I do it right? I asked myself, inwardly repeating everything that had been said and reciting all my replies. Or had I given myself away somehow? Didn't Frau X have an astonished expression when I said . . . .

And then again I told myself that it hadn't been so very different before; even then I'd never really belonged. I just went along because I was married to Max, and how often had he complained that I didn't treat other people the way I should?

He never complained anymore, and to that extent my life was better, but there was nevertheless a big difference between now and the earlier days. At that time I thought things had to be as they were; I had never yet been outside, and I didn't know that there was another way. I blamed myself just as my mother blamed me.

How different my parents' life was! Even if they weren't happy, they never doubted that the way they lived was right; being happy wasn't important to them. Now I had learned that there was more to life, even if I hadn't been able to endure it, and sometimes I began

199

to hurt as soon as someone approached to shake my hand, almost as if they were trying to injure me—that's how vulnerable I was and how unprotected.

When I heard them laughing down at the other end of the table, it was like a shock. They lived in denser air, air that surrounded them like a shell, and that was why nothing was able to touch them. When they came into the house, they brought their air shell with them; you noticed while you were still some distance from them—that's when you bumped into the shell. But I myself was clothed only in a very thin veil of air, I felt much too light when I was with them. Some wind or other could have blown me away. That's what I was afraid of, and that's why I often held on to chair backs or to the banister—just to grasp something solid.

What was it I wanted? Everyone was nice to me, I was carefully tended and secure, and still I complained. Yet when I went outside, I ran back because I was afraid the outside would be the death of me. I was quite worthless.

Often I sat before the mirror in my room and forgot my surroundings altogether. I stared at myself, and not out of vanity or to put on my makeup. I just sat without moving. I saw myself in the mirror, and at the same time I did not see myself. The person sitting there was me—I knew that, but I did not care. I wanted to see myself as Berthold had seen me when he looked at me in astonishment—often for hours, it had seemed to me. I wanted to find out how I was and then be that way forever; in those few hours I must surely have been who I really was; otherwise I wouldn't have been so happy.

But you can't see yourself, not with your own eyes; there's no point in trying. You can only see yourself in the eyes of another, and then you become the way he sees you and you want nothing else.

All I did was wear myself out—and all for nothing. I was glad when there was a noise in the hall or the room next door. Then I quickly ran out and played with Günther.

We had adopted a little kitten, just a couple of weeks old. Its mother had abandoned it or had been run over. We had found it in the bushes at the edge of our garden. It still had very blue, very astonished baby eyes. Fräulein Gerda and I fed it with a pacifier and an eyedropper while Günther stood by and wiped the kitten's whiskers when they became smeared with milk. We had to be very careful not to step on it when it stumbled through the room. What it liked best was to sleep on a pile of dirty laundry.

But that's not what I meant to talk about. It's not important. I wanted to say that sometimes I thought of Berthold when I was holding Günther. I was very ashamed whenever I realized what I was doing, and I'm even ashamed to mention it.

But I never cried. All those months I did not cry. No.

All the same, I'm sure it would have worked; after all, it was what I wanted—to get used to it. If I had read in the newspaper that Berthold's play had been a hit in some other town, I would have been pleased, and at the same time he would have been a little further removed from me. I would have been pleased for him— his success had nothing to do with me.

But I didn't read his name a single time. He could just as easily have ceased to exist, or the whole thing could have been something I dreamed; that was what made me uneasy. If someone had told me that he'd gotten married, it might have made me sad, but it would also have freed me of the misery of thinking about him and longing for him in a void.

But there was no one to bring me such news.

Once, at some party or other, the Riebow woman said to me, "Have you heard anything from Möncken?"

There was a wary undertone in her voice, at least

so I thought, but I was on my guard against her, and there was nothing she could do to me. "No," I said. "Has he published another book?"

She didn't know, nor did she care. I asked her husband the same question, but he didn't know anything either. When I began to talk to her husband, the Riebow woman turned away. He was a likable man who kept himself in the background.

"Do you consider Möncken a major writer?" I asked him.

"Major? How can one make such a judgment, my dear lady? He has a particular voice—a slightly disconcerting one, I might add—and nowadays that's quite a lot."

I would have loved to listen to him expound on the subject of Berthold, but I did not dare involve myself too deeply.

Even at the very end it would have worked out, if only Max had made up his mind to advance the trip to Italy by a few days. But unfortunately the decision wasn't his alone. I did all I could to talk him into it.

Of course I could not tell him the real reason, so I used the pretext that it wasn't a good idea to go away so soon before Christmas; I still had a lot of shopping to do, and with his schedule, too much would be crowded into the last few days before the holiday. Seeing the wisdom of my argument, Max paged through his appointment book and even consulted Blanck as to whether the change could be made. But there was really no way to arrange it, and I could do nothing more.

I had no one whose advice I could seek, no one who could help me wait. It's a miracle that I didn't become ill. My heart ached with fear and excitement, and the closer the day came, the worse it grew. Often I thought I couldn't stand it another minute. Any moment the decision could be made, and I did not know what the decision would be. It did not depend on me.

202

My vigil lasted an endless three weeks. Then, early in November, I ran across a tiny notice in the entertainment column of the newspaper saying that Berthold's play was to have its world premiere in our city on the twenty-third. The title was *Appeal Denied*, which surprised me very much, for it did not suit what I'd seen in his typewriter. Of course it was possible that he'd written a different play altogether, since he wasn't getting anywhere with the first one.

Why was he having the premiere in our city, of all places? Was it intentional on his part? Perhaps because of me? When I begged him not to write to me, I meant that he should not try to get in touch with me because I wouldn't be able to bear it. Surely he must know that it might be embarrassing and upsetting to me for the first performance to take place here. He would not have agreed to it if he had any consideration for me. Didn't he have any inkling that it might destroy me? And after all the torment and grief . . . .

Perhaps I was being unfair. He was probably not responsible; no doubt his publisher or the theater management had arranged the whole thing. I don't understand how such matters are decided, but somebody probably chose this town because it was best for Berthold; since this was where he had been given the prize, he was known locally and his success was more assured.

I read the item one evening after supper, after I'd put Günther to bed. Max was sitting across the room in his armchair reading the political and financial sections. He had handed me the feature pages since such things didn't interest him. He did not seem to notice, but as a precaution I took the section to my room with me later. Max laughed and said, "You must need the serial to put you to sleep." I still remember it clearly, because for a split second I suspected him of making the remark because of the item. But he really knew nothing about it; he was only trying to make a joke.

Usually we left the paper downstairs, and the help took it; that was why I wanted to remove the page with the notice. My father-in-law had a subscription of his own, but that wasn't so bad, for I was sure he would never say anything to Max without speaking to me first. But he might leave the paper lying around, and Fräulein Gerda . . . oh, how she would have chattered away on the subject, without any evil intent.

She read every last word in the newspapers, including the wedding announcements and the personals from young men trying to get a date with a girl they'd seen somewhere. She was precisely informed about lost dogs and missing sable stoles and the amount of the reward offered for each. She was also in the habit of reading everything about actors and actresses—what roles they had signed for and whether they were getting divorced and how many marriages they had had. But this particular item was hard to find. It appeared quite inconspicuously between a professor who had been given a medal and a foreign painter who was celebrating his seventy-fifth birthday.

Occasionally, when he was in a good mood, Max asked Fräulein Gerda about all these ridiculous items, and she never even realized that he was teasing her. He made fun of her the same way my father-in-law had made fun of Blanck in times gone by.

Yes, and how about Blanck, that snoop?

I trusted no one. It was entirely possible that they had agreed among themselves not to speak of the notice because they thought that I had not read it. Or perhaps they were testing me, trying to find out if I cared. I watched them all, I couldn't figure them out; nothing in their demeanor changed. No, they really had not read the item; such things were too insignificant for them.

Life in our house continued as before. But instead of pleasing me, it was precisely this sameness that was so hard on me. It would have been a relief if someone had spoken of the notice—then I could have adjusted. But I couldn't possibly be the first to raise the subject.

And Berthold? When I tried to think what he might do, it made me fearful. Anything was possible, and everything was beyond my power to prevent. If I wrote him now, it might be precisely the wrong thing to do; possibly he had already stopped thinking about me altogether. Or he might suddenly send tickets here to the house for the opening night—what would I do then?

He had always wanted me to be there. He had even talked about what dress I would wear. The way he was, he never gave a thought to what other people might say. He was quite capable of including a ticket for Max. Throughout our time together he talked about Max as if he were some casual acquaintance of mine. Berthold took no account of the fact that I was married to Max.

And the day of the opening? Would Berthold be coming to see the performance? Or was he arriving in time to watch rehearsals? What would I do?

Day after day I searched the papers for some new announcement, but the play was never mentioned again. And so my uncertainty grew and grew.

Just to make sure, I finally went to the box office to ask if the performance was still scheduled. When they told me it was, I had no choice but to buy two tickets. I asked for the first two seats in the fourth row, right by the side exit. Just in case. I did not want to sit too near the front because I didn't want to be visible from the stage or stand out in the audience. The local theater had only six hundred seats, and when there was a premiere, it sold out, so that one had to reserve seats way in advance. I planned to return the tickets Berthold might send me at once, and then, if necessary, to sit in quite a different location so that he would not be able to find me. If worst came to worst, I could always leave covertly before the houselights came back on.

All these were only precautionary measures. I still

hoped that Max would push our trip forward—I hoped to the bitter end. It was only a matter of three days. Besides, Max and I rarely went to the theater; he was usually too tired, he said. And I could hardly ask him to attend a play by Berthold, of all people. How silly of me.

And how ill at ease I was. The man in the box office didn't even know me. How could he know that I'd been with Berthold? But as he talked to me through the window, all the while leafing through a bundle of tickets, I felt that he was thinking, You can't fool me, my pretty. We know all about why you want so much information about this particular play.

Oh, it was ridiculous! But I had become so nervous from the whole thing—yes, of course I was afraid that Berthold might suddenly appear in the lobby, perhaps to smoke a cigarette while the rehearsal continued inside—that I had to go to a café to gather my wits. There I took the tickets from my purse and examined them carefully, studying the date and the seat numbers as if they were a miracle. And then I looked around to see if the waitress might be watching me. I wondered whether to make a little tear in the lining of my purse and conceal the tickets there. For if I happened to leave my purse lying around, not thinking . . . .

But how could I stop thinking about it? During those weeks I was doing a lot of early Christmas shopping. I'd bought most of what was needed. Every evening I discussed my purchases with Max, and we talked about what we were going to give Günther; Max enjoyed the conversations. I had hidden most of the packages in my closet, and when I came home, I told Günther that I had met Santa Claus. Each time I returned—no, each time I unlocked the front door—I was afraid that someone would rush up to me. "Have you heard, Madam?" Or "Frau Helldegen." I couldn't look directly even at Günther, although of course the child had no idea.

I put the tickets in the top right-hand drawer of my dressing table, under a box of bath powder. Sometimes I took out the two bits of gray cardboard and looked at them. They were dusted with powder. I had to blow it away first.

A few days before the twenty-third—in the meantime posters announcing the repertory program appeared, with the title *Appeal Denied* printed in red, a little heavier than the other plays in the repertory, but Berthold's name was in such fine print that it did not stand out—a few days before the twenty-third there was another small newspaper announcement. It said that because of illness the author of the play was unfortunately prevented from participating in the world premiere. Three tiny lines, almost invisible to anyone not looking for them.

I breathed a sigh of relief. Now everything will be all right, I thought. Surely the illness was just a pretext on his part. He did not want to do it to me. Yes, I had to be very grateful to him for sparing me.

And yet I was sad. Yes, I was even annoyed. But what if he really was ill? Who was looking after him? Was he still living with Frau Viereck? Supposing it was a serious illness?

And what was I to do about the tickets? Of course I could simply tear them up into tiny bits. So what if the audience wondered about the two empty seats. What did I care? They didn't know my name. How absurd. No theater has ever telephoned a patron because he wasn't using his seats. "Hello, won't you rush right over, the curtain has already gone up." Something like that.

Oh, those three days! During the days just before, I'd almost stopped being afraid, I was willing to face whatever happened. But this time the others must have read the announcement as well, and that made it more horrible than before. Although it had been only a tiny notice in the outermost column of the newspaper, quite unimportant, yes, nevertheless . . . people wouldn't overlook something like that twice, you can't expect that. It never happens.

And yet everyone was pretending that nothing had occurred. Their behavior was quite incomprehensible to me. Surely their attitude was unfair. Why? Couldn't they trust me even a little bit? Hadn't I proven all these months that none of it mattered to me anymore and that I wanted to stay with them? What were they demanding of me? I just couldn't figure them out. They talked only about the usual things, and of course about the trip and about Christmas.

Blanck was there in the evenings, and I arranged things purposely so that I ran into him as he left. He too was unchanged; nothing could be read in his opaque brown eyes. He bowed as always and disappeared. Before that he had been in the study, and when Max went in to him, they had not whispered; the murmuring was as always when they discussed business.

I hated them all for their silence, especially Fräulein Gerda. I could hardly contain myself. If I'd had my way, I would have thrown her out. If only the silly goose would hurry up and get married.

And so two more days passed. Even though, thanks to the illness, I no longer had to fear that Berthold would put me in an embarrassing position, the tension was greater than before. I don't know what I was actually afraid of, but as I said, it grew worse hour by hour.

And then something happened that I might have foreseen. I thought of everything else, of quite impossible things—but not of something so obvious.

The evening before the opening, Berthold's picture

208

was in the paper—on the feature page, which Max handed to me as always. A fairly large picture, no way to miss it. Your eye fell on it even if you didn't bother reading the page. And under the picture it said that this was our town's own prizewinner, that the following day would see the world premiere of his play, *Appeal Denied*, and that illness prevented the author from attending. Of course the theater had sent the information to the paper to publicize the performance. That's how it's always done.

It was a very bad picture. It was Berthold, you could tell, but it wasn't the man I knew. It must have been several years old. Berthold didn't like having his picture taken. The man I knew could not be captured in a photograph.

Even if they had missed the previous announcements—now all of them knew. My father-in-law read his newspaper upstairs in his room; he rarely stayed with us after supper, for he wanted to leave us alone together. At the very moment, then, when I discovered the picture, he knew everything. And by tomorrow morning at the latest Fräulein Gerda would also know and come running to me with the paper. And Blanck as well, of course.

I'm convinced that Max had noticed the picture before he handed me the page. I'm sure he had also read the item that went with it. Perhaps he was satisfied with the news of Berthold's illness. Yes, it may well be that as far as he was concerned, the matter ended right there. He gave no sign.

I, too, let nothing show; I merely glanced at the picture indifferently and then folded the paper so that the photograph was on the back, facing Max, as if it were of no interest to me and I were reading about something else entirely. Even afterward I left the section lying on the sofa; I didn't want Max to think I cared about the picture.

209

After all, he always left the paper lying on the coffee table. Sometimes he used his penknife to cut something out, placing the clipping in his wallet so he could talk to Blanck about it the following day. But not very often; Max had an excellent memory.

This time the paper carried the obituary of an industrialist Max knew and had seen only a few weeks earlier. The man had died at the age of fifty-two. We talked about it, and I told Max to take good care of himself. It was all a lie; I thought myself very wicked.

Not a word about the picture or about Berthold. As if Berthold had never played a part in my life. I don't know what Max was thinking, but I couldn't sleep all night. I was at the end of my rope. I took a sleeping pill, but it didn't work. Only my body lay still, as though paralyzed or like some strange object. But my head kept on thinking, Tomorrow! Tomorrow! What will happen tomorrow?

What exactly was I afraid of? Everything would happen the way it must anyway, and there was nothing I could do about it. At least I should sleep now; perhaps there would be no time for sleep later. Besides, what was the point of all the excitement if the others weren't upset? And if Berthold was ill, none of it need trouble me. I wasn't interested in the play . . . . Of course I wanted it to be a success for him, but it had nothing to do with me and was of no great importance. What did I care about the play? Appeal denied?

But it was no use.

In the morning I came downstairs to keep Max company at breakfast as always, and of course the newspaper was no longer in the living room. Everything had been cleared away.

And Max was the same as always. No, he hadn't kept the newspaper, definitely not. What nonsense even to think so. Max was always very rushed at breakfast because he liked getting to the factory early. He used to say that the boss had to get there before the others and had to stay later, too, or everyone would start slacking off. In his day my father-in-law also used to be one of the first to arrive. And precisely because Max felt so rushed, he always made a special effort to be particularly calm and friendly so as not to show it. He was the same way today, the same as ever.

No, I couldn't possibly bring the subject up just then, when he had so many other things on his mind. Instead we talked about our trip; yes, silly as it may sound, we talked about how many shirts Max planned to take. It was my idea to get everything ready. Max told me not to give it a thought—if necessary, he could buy very good shirts in Italy. Or words to that effect.

We were always alone at breakfast. I only had a cup of coffee, mostly as a formality, for I couldn't eat that early in the day. So it didn't seem odd if this day too I just sat there with my cup. Max didn't like to have other people around him so early in the morning; it made him nervous. He even told me sometimes that it wasn't necessary for me to get up with him. Why didn't I get my beauty sleep? But I considered it my duty, and at heart he enjoyed my presence. It wasn't a real sacrifice to get up at seven o'clock. I could always go back to bed after breakfast if I felt like it.

When he lit a cigarette—it was always the same: he pulled one out, already holding the lighter in his other hand, and then he said, "I'm sorry," and offered me a cigarette, although I rarely smoked and certainly never at this time of day—that usually meant he was ready to push back his chair and jump to his feet. I walked with him to the coatroom, where he picked up his hat and coat, carefully arranged his muffler in front of the mirror while making faces at himself because his eyes burned from the smoke of the cigarette which he kept in the corner of his mouth. It was the same ritual every single morning.

Outside, Gertig had the car waiting. The front door closed. I stood in the hall and heard the car door slam, the motor start softly, and then the wheels crunch on the gravel.

What would happen? In the office they would tell Max about the opening night. Blanck would call his attention to it and then stand there expectantly. Perhaps Blanck would place the newspaper on Max's desk, with Berthold's picture circled in red. I had no idea how this sort of thing was done. And how would Max react?

If he turned around and drove right back home to have an open discussion with me, perhaps then we could start on our trip at once, in spite of everything— yes, that would be the best outcome. I would let him take the initiative; I no longer had a will of my own.

I would tell Max that there was no reason to get upset, especially not on my account, and for the rest, Herr Möncken was ill and wouldn't be coming to town, and if I had felt any uneasiness at all, it had been only because of Max, because perhaps he believed I had known all about it for a long time and was in touch with Herr Möncken. Something like that.

But I did not really believe that Max would come home to talk with me. In fact, that was the last thing he would do; it wasn't his way. He preferred to arrange matters without discussion; speaking about this kind of thing made him unsure of himself. Should I take the initiative and telephone, asking him to come home at once because there was something I had to talk to him about? Wouldn't that make it sound much too important? Besides, I could have broached the subject at breakfast; I didn't have to wait and then call him away from his work.

No. But I would talk to my father-in-law.

I went upstairs. My decision made me very happy.

Yes, this way was best. I would talk to my father-in-law, and I would ask him to drive to the factory on some pretext, it didn't matter what. After all, he sometimes went to the factory to do Max a favor and to let himself be seen there. Then he could talk to Max about business and quite casually mention tonight's premiere, as if it were nothing special.

That would be enough. He didn't have to ask Max to talk with me. What was the use of all that silly talking! It wasn't necessary, it only embarrassed all parties concerned. I would quite simply accommodate myself to whatever Max decided. Then I wouldn't have to make up my own mind anymore. I'd be rid of the whole thing.

Really, the idea cheered me tremendously. I even hummed to myself when I was in my room. The prospect of talking with my father-in-law didn't bother me; there was no need for many words, because he always understood at once what was involved. I need only wait in my room until I heard him go downstairs, which was usually around ten.

He breakfasted in his room and then went for a walk or did I don't know what. I think that at noon he dined in town, not in the factory canteen like Max did because he thought it was the right thing to do. I don't know whom my father-in-law saw during the day. I don't think he had any friends. It's possible that in the afternoon he went to the stock exchange. He certainly kept up with everything, as I realized from his remarks to Max at the supper table.

I did not lie down again; it would only have made me nervous. I poked among my things, I brushed my hair—I don't remember what else. I was very, very calm.

But the encounter never took place. It was Fräulein Gerda's fault. No, it was my fault; I could have talked to my father-in-law in spite of Fräulein Gerda. I don't want to exonerate myself.

When she brought Günther into my room so that he could say good morning to me, she burst out with it at once. "Did you see? They're putting on a play by Möncken today."

"Who?" I asked while I adjusted Günther's play-suit.

"Herr Möncken," she repeated in high excitement. "The one who was here that time, the one who got the prize."

"Oh, him," I said. I acted uninterested and talked to Günther about Christmas and Santa Claus.

Fräulein Gerda was tenacious. "And there's another picture of him in the paper."

"A picture? Whose picture?"

"Herr Möncken. Shall I get it for you?"

"Oh, for heaven's sake," I said, rising from the floor, where I had been kneeling with Günther. "Do you suppose he expects us to invite him here again? We don't have time right now."

"But he's ill; he's not coming."

"I'm sorry to hear it," I replied. "Well, and what's the name of the play?"

"Something about an appeal."

"Tonight, you said?"

"Yes, tonight is the first performance."

"What's today's date anyway? Is it the twenty-third? That reminds me of something. Wait, I'll check. I forgot all about it because of the trip. Where did I put the things anyway?" I went to my dressing table and opened a few drawers at random as if I were looking for something.

"Somebody sent us some tickets a while back. Probably the management. Could I have accidentally thrown them away? Oh, there they are. That's right, they're for tonight. Fourth row, orchestra. I have no idea how we came by them. And you said it was a play by this . . . this Möncken? Perhaps he told the theater to reserve

214

the seats for us because my husband advocated the prize so strongly. That must be it. What a lucky thing that you happened to notice it in the paper; otherwise the tickets would have gone to waste. They're covered with powder. Yes, but what shall we do now? I'm sure my husband won't want to go, and I . . . I have so many things to take care of for the trip. Would you and your fiancé like—"

"Me?"

"Why not? Surely no one cares who occupies the seats. And the tickets don't say 'Not Transferable.' Why don't you call up your fiancé and see if he'd like to go? Or can't you reach him by phone?"

Half an hour later she managed to get in touch with her fiancé. Everything worked out. Fräulein Gerda was quite beside herself with joy. She was much more excited than I was; she had never been to an opening night. And how proud she was of knowing the author! She asked whether she would have to wear a long gown, and I told her that it was hardly obligatory but . . . . And so we picked a dark dress for her from my closet. I wanted her to look decent, and it only required a few stitches to make the dress fit. I helped her and gave my expert opinion on every detail.

Fräulein Gerda was so agitated that she was good for nothing else. I was enjoying myself as well; the activity distracted me. I also gave her a stole that matched the dress. And I told her she could take the afternoon off and leave right after dinner if she wanted to spend the time with her fiancé. Or she could go to her sister's house. "I can look after Günther all by myself. Isn't that right, Günther?"

At the last minute she almost forgot the most important thing—the tickets. They were still on my dressing table.

Of course I heard my father-in-law leave. My door was ajar, and I could easily have called to him. But I didn't. Let him think that we were gossiping about clothes and similar women's concerns in my room. Why bother the old man? It was no longer necessary. The less said, the better.

But in the afternoon it came over me, more and more strongly. More strongly from minute to minute.

It began with the ring of the telephone in the living room. Fräulein Gerda had left a long time before, there was no one in the house but Günther and me and the kitchen staff. Günther was having his nap, I too was trying to nap, and then the telephone rang downstairs; I hadn't switched it to the extension in my room. That day the telephone rang more often than usual—or maybe it just seemed that way to me. It was unbearable. It rang as I lay on my bed and listened. After the third ring someone answered it, there was a short conversation, and then the receiver was replaced. It hadn't been for me.

I got Günther up. This was a time when he was always a little grumpy. He was supposed to drink his milk, and I said that Santa Claus would find out if he didn't. When the telephone rang again, I told Günther that it was Santa Claus calling to find out whether he had drunk all his milk.

The maid was standing in the doorway; I thought, Now she'll say that a Herr Möncken is calling and asking to speak to me. But it was the dressmaker who was making some alterations on a suit I was planning to wear on the trip. They asked if I could come in for a fitting, and I said yes, I'd stop by tomorrow.

Günther and I planned to cover a box with colored paper; it was to be Günther's Christmas present to his grandpa. I was so on edge that I botched everything. The strips of paper stuck to my fingers and became stained with glue. And it was supposed to look so pretty and neat.

216

When the telephone rang again, I went out on the landing to ask who the call was for. Once it was for Max, and the girl told the caller to try the office. Another time it was for Fräulein Gerda. Between calls the house was deathly quiet, as it had never been before. I waited for the next ring. When it came, it was the wrong number, as the maid reported. "The wrong number?" I asked. Yes, the man had misdialed, he had apologized.

Why today of all days? I thought. Was everyone in on the conspiracy? Or had it been Berthold, wanting to find out whether I would answer the phone and pretending he'd dialed a wrong number?

No, it couldn't have been Berthold, not yet. Or only if the call had been long-distance, but all the calls so far had been local ones.

Actually I should have taken Günther for a walk; the weather wasn't great, but he needed some fresh air. Yet I was reluctant to leave the house; I needed to know what was happening. If I went out for no more than half an hour, something could happen in that time, a call or something, and I wouldn't be there. I could have sent Günther out with one of the maids, but then I would have been all alone. Günther gave me strength.

Because I knew that Berthold would be coming after all. I felt it; something drew me. He was not here yet, but he was on his way; each minute brought him closer.

If you tell people about such feelings, they insist that there's no such thing, that it's only imagination. Nor can there be any proof. I felt it all the same. I felt him being on the way, and I thought for him, Only three more hours and I'll be there. Only two and three-quarters of an hour now. Two and a half hours! Oh, how slowly time passes. If only it would go more swiftly. Two and a quarter hours more, then I'll be there. I'll be with her.

Oh, how it drew me. I was so tempted to run away, run out of the house, toward him.

The telephone was ringing again already. This time it was the office—Blanck. The maid ran to the study because of some paper or other that was supposed to be there. Blanck had asked for it. Was that a pretext? Were they checking up on me?

Shortly before five o'clock the front door opened. It was my father-in-law. I told Günther, and he ran down the stairs to meet his grandpa. They came up together, and when they reached the landing, Günther ran ahead and barred the door to my room with outspread arms. "You can't come in, Grandpa. Santa Claus is here for you."

My father-in-law looked at me, and I nodded. I was sitting at the table with the scraps from the Christmas box. He looked at me from under his white eyebrows as always. Did he know? I mean, did he know that Berthold was on his way here? But how could he know? It wasn't his affair. I showed him my hands, smeared with glue, meaning by the gesture only that I could not shake hands. Perhaps he was thinking, So there she is, playing with Günther. Then everything's all right.

"I'm allowed to have supper downstairs tonight," Günther said.

"Is that right?"

"Fräulein Gerda went out. She went to the theater."

"She did? The Christmas show?" My father-in-law did not look at me as he spoke.

"When will you take me to the Christmas show, Grandpa?" Günther asked.

"When Mama is away on her trip. That is, if you're a good boy." My father-in-law ruffled the boy's hair. "Then we'll be alone tonight?" he asked me.

"Yes."

"That's fine," he said, walking on. As he climbed the stairs to the third floor, I watched his back. He walked very slowly, a little bent over. His left hand touched the banister.

218

And even as the old man was going up, Berthold was coming closer. By rights my father-in-law and I should have exchanged a wink; there was, after all, a kind of secret between us. We might even have laughed up our sleeves. What? What a surprise it will be! Imagine their faces. They think he's far away, ill, and suddenly . . . .

"Come, we'll have to dress," I said to Günther. "A young man cannot come to supper in his play-clothes."

I changed his outfit. I did it to pass the time, for of course he could have eaten with us in his ordinary clothes. But he enjoyed dressing up, and of course it was a matter of upbringing too.

And I enjoyed it as well. Why not make life a little festive? The others would be surprised, especially when nothing happened, but it gave the whole thing a certain prestige. And it added a degree of strength.

"All right, and now Mama wants to get dressed," I said. "You may come with me." Günther was always pleased when he was allowed to stay in my room with me, and that way I could keep an eye on him.

I wanted to put on the dress I had worn the first time Berthold saw me. It was still hanging in the closet; I had not worn it since. The skirt was a tiny bit wrinkled, and there was a crease at one shoulder; I must have packed it carelessly that time. And I had never taken it out of the closet, I had never wanted to see it again. I'd pushed the hanger along the rack to the very end, where I kept the clothes I did not need. That was where it had stayed.

I found the traveling iron and took it to the bathroom to press out the wrinkles. I had all the time in the world.

Günther stood by and watched. He asked, "Why do you touch the iron with your finger, Mama?" And

"Why are you using a damp cloth, Mama?" I explained everything.

When it was ready, I put the dress on. But then I was cold; the dress was very low-cut. I draped my broadtail cape across my shoulders, but it didn't help; I was still cold. So I picked up the intercom and asked the people in the kitchen whatever could they be thinking of to let the furnace go out. They promised to check it at once, and soon after, I heard them poking around in the heating system. But the radiators were not at all cool. The chill was in me.

I was worried that I looked my worst because of the sleepless night and the excitement, but you could tell nothing by looking at me. I was quite pleased with my face.

By now Berthold must have arrived. Probably he had gone straight to the theater for some final discussion. He would have little time to think of me. The phone had stopped ringing.

The performance was scheduled to begin at seven thirty. Unless we had special plans, we always ate supper at seven thirty. A great deal could still happen in the next couple of hours. I was very calm again.

Then I heard Max arrive. His manner of closing the front door did not reveal how matters stood.

"Come on," I said to Günther, taking his hand. "Let's go meet Papa. But let's walk slowly, and let's be very mannerly so that he'll be astonished to see you so handsome. You must walk to my left; the gentleman is always on the lady's left."

We really did go down the stairs very slowly, step by step. I hummed to establish the pace. Günther, with his little legs, made a great effort not to lose his balance.

Max was standing by the tray where the mail was always placed. He had his back to us, but when he heard us, he turned around. I smiled at him.

220

I think in that first instant he really was frightened. He was holding one of the letters, staring at us wordlessly. That was how I realized that he knew everything, at least everything about the opening night, and that they had talked about it in the office. After all, the mere fact that Günther and I had dressed up was hardly reason enough for him to be aghast. Perhaps he thought we had invited someone to supper without letting him know. I even had the feeling that his lips narrowed, as they always did when he was upset and was trying to swallow his feelings—but it may just have been a trick of the light.

I continued to smile. I was glad Günther and I had dressed; it gave me a great advantage.

"I'm allowed to eat with you," Günther called to him.

"Is that ri-i-ght?" he asked, just as his father had done but a little more slowly. That relaxed the tension.

"Fräulein Gerda went out. She went to the theater."

"My, that's wonderful." Max picked Günther up to hug him. He busied himself with the activity, avoiding my eyes.

"We got all dressed up," Günther pointed out.

"Then I'd better change, too." Max's statement was really a question directed at me.

"It's only a game. We're quite alone," I said.

It annoyed him that I was still smiling. He went back to the tray and pretended to look through the mail. "Really? Is it her day off?" he asked, but he must have realized that the question was foolish, since he never concerned himself with such matters. "Well, all the better. Isn't Father home?"

"Yes, he's upstairs. Why? Does he have other plans? He said nothing to me."

Max tore open another envelope and crumpled it. "Not to me, either. So, she went to the movies?" he asked casually, glancing through the letter.

"No, to the theater," Günther answered in my place.

And I added, "Yes, to the municipal playhouse. With her fiancé."

"If that ri-i-ght? Well, that's great."

"How about a drink while we wait for supper?" I suggested.

"Good idea," Max agreed. Having no choice but to play along with me, he went willingly to the cupboard. We very rarely drank before supper unless we had guests. Max didn't like the custom; he wasn't much of a drinker at the best of times. Of course he had to drink with business acquaintances and when he attended official dinners, but privately he stayed away from alcohol. It was his fear of gaining weight that made him practice moderation in all things.

"And what may I serve you?" he asked, like a head-waiter. All three of us were standing in front of the open cupboard. Max had opened the built-in refrigerator as well, and Günther, wide-eyed, was staring at the entire contraption.

"For the young gentleman, some orangeade, please, with a shot of soda water," I replied in the same spirit.

"Oh, yes," Günther exclaimed. "And in one of those little glasses!"

"And for me? . . . It doesn't matter. A sherry, please, perhaps with a drop of gin. What's that over there?" I pointed to a bottle that looked familiar, a tall bottle with silver foil around its neck.

"Pernod," Max said.

"Oh, then I'd prefer to have a Pernod."

"That poison?"

"What do you mean? Where did you get the bottle?"

"From Brodersen, more as a curiosity, just in case anybody should ask for it. You're better off with something else."

"No, I want Pernod."

"But it's served with water."

"Oh, just pour it. I'm sure we can do without the water just this once."

It was a strange coincidence that Max had a bottle of Pernod, almost providential. Because in Ludwigshof I had tasted Pernod for the first time in my life. The innkeeper had some; now and again someone brought a bottle across the border. Berthold couldn't stand the stuff either, but I enjoyed the taste.

Max poured a cognac for himself. We carried our glasses over to the little table. Max and I clinked glasses with Günther, very ceremoniously, as if he were an adult. Anyone watching us would never have suspected that anything was amiss; he would have thought, What a nice family! How charmingly they live together.

"Is Blanck coming?" I asked after we had taken our first sip.

"No. Why?" Max raised his eyebrows so high that I just about laughed in his face.

"Nothing. I was just asking."

"No, there's nothing important on the agenda," Max said.

Then my father-in-law came downstairs. He and Max shook hands, but they exchanged no looks of secret understanding. It did not seem that they had yet talked about me and the opening night.

At supper I had to bite my lips again so as not to laugh. Because they talked such a lot, more than usual and more than necessary; what they had to say could have been said in far fewer words. It was clear that they were going to great lengths to keep silence from setting in.

Of course Max talked about the business; he acted as if this time he had to explain things to his father in particular detail because of our trip, so that his father could run things while we were gone.

And my father-in-law went along with him, asking about this and that and how Max saw it and how Max wanted it handled. All the time I knew that my father-in-law couldn't have cared less, that he was bored. And Max knew that Blanck had already received instructions about everything and that my father-in-law's advice was to be sought merely as a formality. How funny men are. I think they were afraid of me. Even a man as old as my father-in-law was afraid.

Then, luckily, they found a still more fertile topic. They talked at endless length about some chairman of the board they knew, whose name I can't remember, a big wheel in some other business. Max worked himself up into a great outrage because the man had made a tactless remark at the public stockholders' meeting; the workers and the unions took umbrage, and there was danger of a major protest strike. At least that's how I understood it, but I was listening with only half an ear. Max said, "And now of all times. It hurts all of us. At night when he goes to bed, let him think what he wants, but in public . . . ." And my father-in-law said, "It's the idiotic arrogance of a fraternity man," to which Max replied, "True, I was a fraternity man myself, but . . . ."

I was tempted to interrupt them by shouting, "I spy, I spy," like in the children's game—the words were on the tip of my tongue. I would have loved to see their helpless faces. But I stopped myself because Günther was with us. Though I put in a word now and again, for the most part I chattered softly with the boy.

The clock in the living room chimed, making it unnecessary for me to consult my watch secretly under the table. The meal lasted much longer than usual. That too happened as if it had been prearranged, as if they were afraid to leave the table. Yes, what were they to talk about when they stood facing each other in the living room? They couldn't make fools of themselves. The kitchen help would be surprised, wondering what

224

took us so long. And no one remarked that it was past Günther's bedtime, not even me.

The situation suited me very well; it was important to kill time, so let them talk about business to their heart's content. They needn't worry that I would interfere. The performance, I had calculated, would probably last until nine thirty, no later than quarter to ten. Even if Fräulein Gerda came straight home from the theater, she could hardly get here before ten or ten thirty. And perhaps she and her fiancé would stop somewhere for a beer. Until then, the time would have to be passed somehow.

"Good heavens, it's eight thirty already," I exclaimed when we finally left the dining room.

And Max said, "What a blessing to be alone for once. Without that. . . ." He faltered and thought better of it. "Without strange faces." The emendation was for Günther's benefit.

"It's high time for Mama to put you to bed," I said to Günther. "Come on, say good-night."

"He can sleep late in the morning. Let's tell Fräulein Gerda not to get him up at the usual time."

"I have no idea when she'll get back from the theater."

"Oh, yes, that's right. Well, we'll leave a note for her."

Max had opened the paper and buried himself behind it. Go right ahead, look in the paper, I thought; today there won't be anything about Berthold. Tomorrow, yes; but by the time tomorrow comes . . . .

Günther said good-night to his grandfather and then went to Max. Max said to him, "If nothing comes up, we'll do this more often, right?"

"Do what?" I asked.

"Spend a cozy evening like this one."

"Are you in a crisis again?" I asked.

"What? What do you mean?"

225

"Because you said, 'if nothing comes up.' I thought maybe because of that chairman of the board."

"Oh, I see. No. That's got nothing to do with us; it doesn't concern us. On the contrary, I'm hoping that things will run smoothly and that I won't have to keep after everything myself. I mean, if nothing comes up."

The telephone rang. I started for it, but Max also rose. I was closest to the instrument and was about to pick up the receiver—it was an instinctive gesture—but then I motioned to Max that I wanted him to take it. My father-in-law stood a little to one side, looking at me intently.

Max promptly picked up the receiver. "Helldegen speaking. Oh, it's you. Yes? Yes? That's fine. Yes, thank you, it can wait until morning. Good night." And he hung up.

"Blanck?" I asked.

"Yes. Why?"

"It couldn't be anyone else."

"What is it you have against poor Blanck all the time?"

"Me? Nothing. Why should I? What could I possibly have against Blanck? He's never done me any harm. Is he at the theater?"

"At the . . . where? What makes you think that?"

"No special reason. Why shouldn't he go to the theater now and then?"

Max's laugh rang false. "I've never known Blanck to take an interest in the drama."

Go ahead and lie, I thought. I know perfectly well that Blanck is at the theater and that he called you from there. It doesn't matter how I know; I know, that's all.

"People like Blanck are indispensable," Max said. "You must understand. Yes, quite indispensable."

"Come, my darling, let's put you to bed," I said to Günther. "It's very late."

I took his hand. We walked to the stairs together,

leaving the two men behind. But then, before we had reached the first step, I thought of something else. We would sing as we went up the stairs, I decided. I never did that; I sang with Günther only when he was in bed, when we were alone. But this time . . . what a joke! What pathetic faces the men would make!

That's why I sang our lullaby, and Günther sang along. The words were happy: about a young man who left home to live with the neighbors in a happy place where they slaughtered a pig, drank wine, and made merry.

In this fashion Günther and I slowly proceeded up the stairs, marching to the beat, looking back not even once. I felt the living room behind me grow very still and empty. I felt their stares on my back, Max holding the paper, my father-in-law more covertly, looking up a little because of his bushy eyebrows—more like a dog.

Yes, like the dog we'd had at home when I was a child. If you put on your coat, he stayed in his corner, lying there as if he didn't care. But he observed everything carefully, every little movement. Then if you said, "How about it, want to come along?" he was at your side in a single bound. If you didn't say it, he must have been very sad, because he sighed.

And what were the two men thinking? Perhaps they thought, How can it be possible! There she goes, singing her way up the stairs, a woman with her child. There's nothing else on her mind, and she is happy. Could we have been mistaken?

I was tempted to turn around and look at them and stick out my tongue. But of course I didn't—on account of Günther. Let them stand in their living room, so small and such strangers, in a different world. Let them think what they wanted.

Happy? Does a person have to be happy to sing? How simple everything is for them. When I was younger, at home, everyone felt the same way about me. Except that in those days I didn't sing, I whistled. "Girls should not whistle," my mother called to me as I went out, "it's not proper." So that was another thing I did wrong.

I was reminded of Arnim; it must have been the song. Funny, lately I thought of him a lot, almost more than of Berthold. That time, too, I pretended to be cheerful when I felt particularly low and all I really wanted to do was sob my heart out. No one should know anything about me—that would have been the hardest to bear. Just let them leave me alone. My mother used to watch me, shaking her head, and I bet she said to my father, "I hope she'll come to her senses in the end." Poor Arnim, how fat he had grown.

"Come, my darling, hurry up and get into bed. Mama has to go back downstairs. Papa and Grandpa want to talk to her about something."

No, Mama will never come to her senses, Mama is just pretending. Mama is not cheerful, that's merely what those two downstairs believe. On the contrary, Mama is very, very sad. Because now they are talking about Mama down there, and they cannot figure her out. Mama has to help them, you have to understand, my darling. Otherwise they'll say something about Mama that isn't true, and we've had such a lovely evening, haven't we?

"You can't do that, young man. The suit has to be hung neatly over the back of the chair. Who is supposed to press out all the wrinkles if you're so careless with your things? And look at Jubi. He was so tired that he fell down on the floor with his arms and legs sticking up in the air. That's no way. And look how dirty he is. Tomorrow is Saturday. Tomorrow we'll toss him into the tub and give him a good scrubbing, very carefully,

228

with soapsuds. Just his fur. And afterward we'll blow
him dry with the hair dryer to keep him from catching
cold. You'll be surprised how clean he'll be. Where did
Fräulein Gerda put your washcloth?"

Poor Teddy!

Do you know what they're saying about Mama
downstairs? You're still too little, but when you're bigger, when you're grown up . . . you better ask Grandpa,
my darling, if you want to know. Grandpa can explain
it best. All the others will say bad things about Mama.
Yes, I'm sure they will. You can't understand that now.
Only Grandpa understands.

And suppose Grandpa has died by then?

Poor Grandpa!

"Now I know why Jubi is so dirty. Of course, he
secretly pads through the house on his white paws and
sticks his nose through the banister and eavesdrops on
what they say downstairs. And that's why he's so tired,
too. You really must be a little stricter with him."

But you must never ask Papa about it, my darling.
Under no circumstances must you ask Papa, for it would
make Papa angry. Papa loves Mama very much. Papa
has a big factory, so-o-o big, and he has to look out for
many, many people. The factory grows and grows, and
in the end it will be the biggest factory in the whole
world. And all of it is for you, only for you, my darling,
so that you'll have a good life. No, Papa has no time
for such things. You must understand.

Poor Papa!

"Stop. You're staying right here, you little scamp!
You've got to wash up properly. What would Fräulein
Gerda think if she found soap in your ears tomorrow?
Not to mention Santa Claus!"

229

Because one day you too will want to marry. That's what all the young men want. What will your wife think of you? She'll say that Mama didn't bring you up properly because Mama . . . . Everything always comes back to Mama. You better not discuss Mama with her, or she'll say bad things about Mama, and then you'll have a fight. And I don't want her to say bad things about Mama, and I don't want you to fight.

Poor little scamp!

"All right, and now your teeth. Must Mama always keep reminding you? From now on you'll have to think of it all by yourself. Papa brushes his teeth before he goes to bed, and so does Grandpa, without anybody standing over them. Mama can't always watch out for everything."

Papa and Grandpa are waiting downstairs for Mama to come back. They are waiting for Mama to tell them something they don't already know. And they really do want to know, otherwise they'll think the wrong things. They're already saying things that aren't true, my darling, just because you're dawdling and won't let Mama go downstairs. Mama could tell you down to the last word what they're saying down there, but if you ever repeat any of it, no one will believe you. No one believes your poor Mama.

"Forward, march. Hit the hay. And here's your Jubi. My, what a dirty little fellow he is!"

Or perhaps Mama should tell Jubi all about it. Jubi is smart, Jubi is the only one, Jubi believes every word Mama says. And then, later, Jubi can repeat it to you after you've gone to sleep, and even later than that. Well, go ahead, Jubi. Begin. "Max said . . . ." Max?

230

Max? What can Jubi be thinking of? His name is Papa, his name isn't Max.

"Can't we do without the song just this once? We've already sung it on the stairs. Oh, you little pest."

Mama would give a lot to be able to lie down and sleep like the two of you. But Mama has to stay up some more. Mama is expected downstairs.

All right, Jubi, start talking. Max said . . . what did Max say? Tell it your own way.

No, let's stop. It's a game. You have to tell the story the way it's going to be told one day. Nothing else counts. Just go to sleep, you two.

No one will remember whether it really happened that way, and no one will care. They'll believe what they're told. Perhaps they will have stopped caring as early as tomorrow morning.

You have to tell it the way it will be told to Günther when he asks one day, and when I won't be there to explain it to him. When I'm no longer sitting by his bed. When he has long since forgotten that I sat with him while they were perplexed about me downstairs.

It will actually be better for Günther if he forgets soon. For if one day he asks how it all was and they tell him and he thinks about it, then he will be very alone. I won't be able to help him, and by that time Jubi won't count anymore, either.

This is how they will tell him.

"Did she talk to you?" Max asked at once.

My father-in-law usually went to his room right after supper unless we were entertaining; he didn't want to be in the way. But tonight he stayed downstairs. Perhaps it was only coincidence, or perhaps as a favor to me and because there was something in the air.

"About what?" he asked with deliberate calm.

At that, Max's patience was at an end. He hit the newspaper with his hand. "About this mess here!"

My father-in-law said, "You mean the opening night? No, I didn't talk with her."

"How did she know that Blanck had gone to the theater?" Max's voice cracked. "He telephoned during the intermission. Who told her? The maid, do you think? She's got it coming to her. I myself only found out about the whole business this afternoon, by pure chance. I criticized Blanck severely. He claimed to have known nothing about it. Of course, he can't be expected to know everything about theaters and such nonsense, we must be fair. And where did the girl get the tickets?"

"Fräulein Gerda? I presume she bought them."

"Her, buy anything? You don't believe that yourself."

"Perhaps Marianne gave them to her."

"And nobody tells me anything about it?"

"I think, Max, that it would be best if you had a very frank talk with her."

"And who's frank with me? What am I told about what goes on in my own house?"

"To the best of my knowledge, nothing is going on at all."

"And how long have you known?"

"About the play? Two weeks ago I saw a notice. Maybe longer ago than that."

"And you did not consider it necessary to mention it to me?"

"No, why should I?"

"Why? Listen, Father . . . ."

My father-in-law shrugged his shoulders. "I don't consider myself privileged to interfere in your affairs."

"But in a case like this—"

"Especially in a case like this. Once before, I found myself involved quite against my will, and . . . and . . . . By the way, I think you're taking it far too seriously."

"Taking it too seriously? How? I ask you, Father. Quite aside from the fact that this character could have written about us—you never know when you're dealing with an unprincipled adventurer—and we simply cannot afford to . . . to . . . ."

"Well? What did Blanck have to report?"

"Blanck? Why Blanck?"

"But you sent Blanck there as an observer."

"The play? You mean the play. Some medieval claptrap. It's got nothing to do with us, thank God. But even so . . . I would have known how to put a stop to it. I know more about that fellow than is good for him. He has a political past. Ten or fifteen years ago he was active on the left-radical front, there's no doubt about it; there are documents to prove it. He was never granted a promotion during the war. You know the type. Too lazy to take up a proper profession. He was a factory worker for a long time, in spite of his background. In Ludwigshafen, I believe. You'll have to look at the papers sometime when we have time. Very illuminating. Presumably he was thrown out by his family. His own mother . . . yes, the detective agency even checked with his mother. She says . . . I have it in black and white . . . even his mother says she was in constant fear that he would come to a bad end. A very dubious character."

"Hm."

"But I don't care about any of that. Let them put on the play in any other city, as long as they don't perform it here. What, here of all places? The theater has a sizable subsidy, God knows how much. Let's face it, the Helldegens are among the city's major taxpayers. And if I'd been able to drop a hint to the mayor in time, I wonder whether that idiot of a producer wouldn't have had second thoughts. Wouldn't it be ridiculous if we didn't even have the right—"

"How vengeful you are."

"Vengeful? Now listen, Father. It's simple self-defense. And besides, I consider it my damned duty to protect the city and our business from such negative elements. Surely it would—"

Max was unable to complete his sentence. The telephone rang. He ran to it and tore the receiver from the cradle. "Helldegen speaking. What? Who? Oh, I beg your pardon, my dear lady. How are you? And your husband? What? Would you mind repeating that? Yes, of course my wife is at home. Why at the theater? Is there anything special going on? By whom? Is that right? No, this is the first I've heard of it. We're busy packing our bags, in a manner of speaking. Yes, on Tuesday. To Milan. I have business there. Naturally my wife is coming along. We plan to relax on the Riviera for a couple of days afterward. No, not longer. Because of Christmas, yes. What? Yes, it's true, far too rarely. But I'm sure your husband is kept just as busy. No, why? My wife has recuperated completely. You know how doctors are. She still has to take it a little easy. And the social whirl . . . . What? Monday? We're leaving on Tuesday. But that's my wife's department. I don't make these decisions. Would you like me to connect you with her? She's upstairs with Günther; the girl has the night off. Yes, yes, give my best to your husband." With that he rang through to the upstairs extension.

"Frau Kauer, from the refinery," he reported to his father. "A real gossip—they broke the mold when they made her. No way of stopping her. If it weren't for her husband . . . . Well? There you have it. What does she want, why is she telephoning tonight? What about her honey-sweet question whether we were at the theater— how about that? No, it has to stop, once and for all. There'll be some changes made. After our trip I will . . . . And Marianne really hasn't said a word to you about this stuff?"

"Not a word. I told you."

"Then how does she know about it?"

"Probably from the paper, just like us."

"Is she in touch with that character?"

"I've never talked to her about that, either. In fact, I make a point of avoiding the subject."

"But you spend more time at home than I do. You must know what goes on here."

"What should go on? It doesn't suit me to play the watchdog. But if you insist on hearing my opinion, I don't believe that she writes to him. It's not in character."

"Oh, women. We have to be prepared for the most impossible actions."

"There's one thing I don't understand, Max."

"Why? What don't you understand?" Max flared up.

"Why you don't talk to Marianne. That's the only way. And I have a hunch she's just waiting for you to start."

"Me? Why should I start? Why am I always the one? No, I don't want to give this . . . incident more importance than it deserves. Where would that lead us? And surely no one will be able to say that I didn't behave with enough magnanimity in the matter. But everything has its limits, and if I'm attacked . . . . In short, there has to be an end to this business or . . . . On the contrary, Father, I don't understand you."

"Me?"

"Excuse me for saying so. Yes, I'm infinitely grateful to you for talking her into coming home that time."

"I didn't talk her into it. It was her own decision."

"No matter. What else could she do, anyway? In any case, she came back with you. I don't want to know the details, they don't interest me in the least. And yet, in spite of everything, I have the constant impression that you're opposed to me in this affair. That's what it is."

My father-in-law did not reply at once. "I'm very sorry to hear it," he said finally. "I really don't know what to say to you."

"But surely it's in your own best interests as well if . . . . No, I really don't understand you."

"You're forgetting completely, Max," my father-in-law said with great care, "that I gave up once and for all—even in front of a lawyer—having any say in your affairs."

"I'm not talking about the business. I'm talking about Marianne."

"She's your wife, not mine."

"But you are my father and Günther's grandfather."

"Wouldn't it be better if we changed the subject?"

"You see, you're evading the issue. Everyone evades the issue and sets such great store by himself. How easy you all make it for yourselves."

"That's as it may be. I can't counter your reproaches in any way. And the only advice I dare to give I've already given—have it out with her."

"But Father, you must understand. The business grows from year to year, almost from day to day. The figures will prove it to you. It isn't to my credit—it's to yours. Everything expands by itself, inevitably, that's all. If I'm to continue everything you began, if I'm to control it all . . . . Please don't think I'm complaining; my whole heart and soul are in it . . . . But if I accept the responsibility, then I must also have the assurance— the ab-so-lute assurance—that everything here in the house is running smoothly. I can't see to everything. Is that asking too much? My God, what does it take! And let's face it, all of you profit. Because I . . . yes, why? I could make it easier on myself. I don't know why you can't see that."

"We do see it, Max. There's no way to refute what

you say. But . . . yes, tell me, what is it you're afraid of?''

"Afraid? I'm not afraid of anything. I can take care of myself. I do not want people behind my back—"

"Are you afraid of something specific? Or—let's put it into words—of tonight?"

"Tonight? Why?" Max was filled with suspicion.

"I'm just asking. If there's a particular problem, one can take a position, that's why I asked. To the best of my knowledge, Herr Möncken is not here. The newspaper reported that he was ill."

"What do I care about that fellow! And even if he were here . . . ."

"All right, all right. Shall I go to bed? Would you prefer being alone with Marianne?"

"No, please. Why? On the contrary, stay a little longer."

"Whatever you like. You mustn't have any wrong ideas about me, Max. You'd best think of me as someone who has declared himself incompetent, as it were."

"You keep bringing that up. All that is long forgotten."

"So much the better. I simply want to avoid any misunderstandings. In spite of everything, I'm still a very level-headed type."

At that moment I came down from upstairs. I'm sure it was high time. The two men abruptly broke off their conversation.

"Well, is Günther asleep?" Max called, much too loudly. His shrill voice made me realize that they had talked about me and that they had quarreled. But they shouldn't quarrel over me—I did not want that. I even felt sorry for them. I had decided that it was best to speak to them quite openly about everything. I was tired of the whole business. I was exhausted.

"How nice that you'll keep us company for a little,"

I said to my father-in-law. "Why don't you sit down, Papa? It's still early."

I glanced at the clock. It was a little past nine thirty. My father-in-law sat down in one of the armchairs. I smiled at him.

"Well, and what did the Kauer woman want?" Max asked.

"What do you think she wanted?" I countered. "To pump me."

Max started slightly but quickly recovered. "A nasty person."

"They all want the same thing, Max. By the way, I refused her invitation for Monday, with thanks. Because of our trip. I hope that's all right with you."

"Yes, of course. It really would be too much. We do have to stay on good terms with her husband; we might need him someday. But in this case—"

"You mean, to blunt all the gossip? Yes, but I'm sure at the party they'll talk about the opening night, and that might be unpleasant for you."

"That doesn't concern me at all," Max said, irritated. "None of that has any reality for me, and in connection with us, it cannot have any reality for anyone else, either. And not for the Kauer woman—I'll see to that."

"Shall I call her and tell her we'll come after all?"

"Oh, let's leave the woman alone."

"I don't want you to be displeased with me."

"What a way to talk."

"No, I mean it. It's not just an empty phrase. For example, I didn't go to the theater."

"If you cared so much . . . it's all right with me."

"Perhaps I cared, but it would have been unfair to you. How about a drink?"

"Yes, a good idea," Max said, getting up. "What will it be?"

238

"Pernod, of course." I laughed. My laugh made Max very angry. He was angry that I was able to laugh.

"That poison," he said, just as he had earlier.

"They say it shrinks your liver. But considering how little I drink . . . . And you, Papa?"

My father-in-law had been lost in thought. He was startled when I addressed him. He must have been thinking about me.

"Nothing for me, thanks," he said. "Or all right, if you insist, a drop of cognac with a lot of soda. That can't do any harm."

"I feel parched," I said. "Was supper too salty? Or maybe it's the weather."

"I'm sure it's the weather. There's a dry wind."

"It's too bad we couldn't have left for Italy a few days earlier," I said.

Max, who was standing behind us by the refrigerator pouring the drinks, had heard enough of the conversation. "Unfortunately that was quite impossible," he called over his shoulder.

"I know, I know. I was only thinking of you, Max. I would have liked to spare you having to talk about these things. Because afterward—I mean, if we had learned about it after the fact . . . . Yes, perhaps I should have alerted you in time. But I was afraid that you'd take it amiss."

"It isn't necessary to talk about it even now," Max suggested.

"But I am talking about it, Max," I said. "I'm talking about it because I don't want you to think I have any secrets from you. Because even Blanck won't be able to explain it all to you properly."

"Just leave Blanck out of it. Here, here's your glass."

"The papers said that the author was prevented from attending the performance."

239

"Surely that would have been the most outrageous tactlessness."

"Or does Blanck have more specific information?"

"Blanck's job is the business. He has nothing to do with our private life. Why don't we talk about something else?"

"Yes, cheers. Cheers, Papa. Why are you so stingy with the Pernod, Max? Just put the bottle on the table. If I were an alcoholic, I could understand, but as it is . . . . Oh, but I feel like going out. To the Excelsior, for example."

"The Excelsior?" Max asked mistrustfully.

"Oh, not for that reason. I'm sure at the Excelsior we wouldn't run into anybody we don't want to run into. From the theater, I mean. It's much too expensive. No, it was just a thought. Different faces, and music, and perhaps you would dance with me."

"Why didn't you say so earlier?"

"Because you would have thought that I . . . . All right, let's not. But it's true, Max, it would be fun to have a night on the town. We're not so old yet."

"If you really want to . . . we could still go. Nothing really gets going until midnight at the Excelsior."

"We have to wait for Fräulein Gerda," I pointed out. "It's not even ten o'clock."

"But I'm here," my father-in-law said. "I'll stay up until she gets back."

"No, thanks, Papa. I don't want you to stay up on our account, just because we feel like making a night of it. And Max is right, we can go later if we still feel like it. I'm all ready and dressed. I bet you can't stand to see a woman drink Pernod."

"Whatever gives you that idea?" asked my father-in-law.

"Oh, no special reason. The way you're looking at me. I have no intention of getting drunk. I couldn't if I tried. Quite the reverse. Should we have some coffee?"

240

"Not for me, thanks," my father-in-law said.

"All right, then, let's not."

"What I've been meaning to talk to you two about . . ." Max began. Clearly he had been searching for a topic he could discuss with us. He was pleased and eager because he had finally thought of something. "Yes, I remembered it earlier because of the Kauer woman's invitation, and before that, when we were talking about the danger of a strike. The bishop reproached me . . . that is, not me but all of us . . . in short, the bishop recently reproached us, from the church's point of view—"

And again the telephone rang. This time all three of us started. The ringing was much longer and more penetrating than usual. Conveying such urgency.

"Long distance," Max said. He, too, was momentarily unsure how to act. He even gave me a questioning look, as if he wanted to leave it to me to walk to the instrument and pick up the receiver.

Long distance? I thought. Supposing what the newspaper said was true—that Berthold was ill? And yet I had been so certain that he . . . .

But Max pulled himself together and answered the phone. "Hello? Yes, speaking. Who? Oh, it's you, Otto. To what do we owe the honor? No, you're not bothering us in the least. We're having a cozy evening at home, the three of us. Yes? Hm. Yes, I'm listening. Yes. Yes. Hm. I understand. Late next week, you said? Very interesting. Is it definite? I mean, can we count on its passing? Hm. Of course. No, not a word, you can trust me. It wouldn't be in my own best interest either. Thanks a lot, yes. I'm very grateful to you. And how is Lisbeth? The children? Measles? Oh, I am sorry. And now of all times, just before Christmas. Well, we all have to go through it. Best to get it over with. Yes, give them all my best. Marianne sends her love, too. We'll be back around the fifth. And drop in sometime soon when you're passing through. All right. Thanks again. Goodbye."

He was talking to my brother, Otto. My father-in-law and I had merely exchanged a brief look; then he stared into space and waited, a little subdued, for the end of the conversation.

Max was extremely pleased; he was rubbing his hands. He'd had important news, but he begged us for God's sake not to mention it to anyone, or Otto could be put in an extremely embarrassing position. There was to be a committee session at the Department of Trade—something to do with foreign exchange or import licenses, as far as I could tell.

Max did not return to his chair but asked to be excused: it was important that he speak to the Hamburg office at once. He immediately put through the call, priority and person-to-person. He asked the long-distance operator if there would be a long wait, and she said no, not at this time of night.

I knew Beermann, the man he was calling. He was our business agent in Hamburg and had visited us a couple of times. A tall, very fat man. When he laughed, the whole house boomed.

Max was in a superb mood. "They have the measles—the children, I mean," he said. Then he remembered that before the phone rang, we had been talking about something entirely different, something troublesome. "Yes, we were interrupted. What was it again?"

"You wanted to discuss something with me," I said.

"With you?" He was ill at ease.

I helped him. "I think it had something to do with the church."

He was relieved. "Oh, yes, of course." And then he told us that the church had reproached us—not us personally but industry as a whole—for caring too little about certain matters. A bishop had said that industrialists should really get around to reading Marx and Engels. Well, that was going too far, of course—it was hardly necessary to read Marx and Engels, of all people. Max laughed. No, that was not necessary, nor did he have the time. But in one sense the bishop was right, and it could do no harm if . . . .

My father-in-law and I paid attention. Max was in his element; he lectured, and we let him instruct us as if we were his employees or his children.

There was, for example, the refugee problem, to name just one. He had given it a lot of thought; one had to start somewhere. At the next association meeting he would be making appropriate suggestions. To give refugees jobs was not enough; these people would have to be made to feel that they belonged, to feel at home, as it were. Yes, and the reason he was talking to us was that he thought it only right for the wives to attend to such things. And he looked at me.

"Me?" I asked.

Well, yes, just possibly this was something I could do. "And you, too, Father." But no matter, in any case it would be advantageous for the Helldegen name to appear in this connection. What did we think?

"You have to tell me what to do," I said.

To talk about details was pointless at this stage, Max explained. At present it was only a starting point, not much more. And if it was something that I would not enjoy—

"It has nothing to do with enjoyment, Max. You only have to tell me what to do, and I'll be glad to do it."

That really was not what he had meant, Max replied. My willingness affected him unpleasantly.

"But it's what I mean," I repeated.

And anyway, before our trip . . . .

At that point the long-distance operator rang

through. "Ah, there's the Hamburg call. Excuse me, I'll go to the study. It's going to be a long conversation."

"It cuts right through me," I said to my father-in-law when we were alone. "The telephone, I mean. I can't bear any more."

I got up and poured myself another glass of Pernod. Then I sat back down and tried to smile at my father-in-law. "I'm a silly person, right?"

"But what are you afraid of?" he asked. He spoke very softly and turned to look at the door to Max's study.

"Afraid? Oh. Yes, what am I afraid of, actually? That I'll go crazy if the phone doesn't stop ringing—that's probably all. Wouldn't you like another drink too, Papa? No? Yes, a totally useless person—I know that; no one has to tell me. And not even honest. I deserve no better. That's enough. Are you sure you wouldn't like a drink, Papa?"

"No, thanks. You shouldn't, either—"

"Don't worry, Papa. And even if I did, it wouldn't do any good. Believe me, Papa, I really was determined, I tried so hard all these months. And I'm very strong-willed; I'm downright stubborn, they told me when I was still a little girl. Yes, laugh at me if you like. I laugh at myself. Because what have I got to complain about? Bad luck—that happens to other people too, so what's the point of whining? That's enough. Who cares? You know what, Papa? I should have gone to the theater. At least it would have been more honest."

"Do you mean to say that he's here?" my father-in-law asked.

"Yes, of course he's here."

"Is that right? Hm. How do you know?"

"I've known since this afternoon."

"Did he call you?"

"Call me?"

"I'm sorry I asked."

244

"No, don't be sorry. He didn't need to call. And I wouldn't have talked to him if he had; I would have had them make some excuse. I wouldn't have been at home, it's that simple. But I know anyhow. Don't laugh at me, Papa. A woman can sense that sort of thing. Each time the telephone rings, I get an electric shock. I'm glad the line is busy now. Because . . . well, you know him, you know what he's like. It would be just like him to actually telephone here. Just like that! As if it were the most normal thing in the world. That's why, as long as Max talks to Hamburg, we're safe for at least a few more minutes. And I know in advance what he'll say when he calls. 'Why didn't you come? We had it all planned, and I had seats reserved for you. Way up front, in the first row.' He'll scold me—yes, that's how he is.

"And I really don't know what I can say in reply. Should I say to him, 'No, I belong here, with Max'? He wouldn't believe me, Papa. And even if he did believe me . . . no, he wouldn't believe me. He knows me much too well. Yes, what can I say to him? And what will become of him, Papa? There he is, at the other end of the phone, wanting to talk to me and wanting me to go there . . . . I don't even know where he'll be calling from. From the theater? The hotel? But which hotel? It's already after ten." I stood up. "If we were to drive there at once, perhaps we could still catch him at the stage door."

"Stop running around so wildly," my father-in-law said. "Sit down."

"Yes, I'm sorry. I'm half crazy already. Do you want to do me a favor, Papa? When the phone rings again, would you answer it? This time it will be him, I'm sure. I don't want Max . . . . Don't pay any attention to Max. Just walk over to the phone and pick up the receiver and say that I'm away on a trip. He'll believe you. He liked you so much. Yes, he liked you very much, I mean it."

"And if he doesn't call?"

"If he doesn't . . . You think? . . ."

"There's always that possibility. You have to consider it."

"Yes, of course, that's self-evident. So silly, it never crossed my mind. But why? Then everything's all right. Then what are we getting upset about? We'll leave on Tuesday, and when we get back, the Christmas rush will be starting. I can't even think that far ahead . . . . I wonder what's keeping Gerda. Perhaps the play is taking longer than I thought it would. Please, Papa, if you can, don't leave me alone until then. But if you'd rather go to bed . . . . So you think he won't call at all?"

"How can I know?"

"No, be honest with me, Papa. At least the two of us should be honest with each other, even if I . . . even if you're disappointed with me. So you think he's forgotten everything long ago?"

"I have no way of judging that, my child. I only mentioned it from a sense of caution."

"And that's quite right. We have to think about every possibility, and I value your opinion very much. You can think about it coolly while I . . . yes, I'm very grateful to you for mentioning it."

"I'm sorry I brought it up."

"No, why? Why shouldn't he . . . after all this time? . . . For him it's an altogether different story than for me. Besides, it's the most sensible way, really it is. For him, I mean. I can't be anything to him—I've shown him that I can't be anything to him. I'm a silly goose. Don't be mad at me for boring you with this nonsense, which certainly can't be of any interest to you. It's because of all these telephone calls. How long Max's conversation with Hamburg is lasting! That fat old Beermann. He needs a lot of material for his suits, I bet.

246

"Shall I tell you something, Papa? I've got it too good, that's what it is. Even at home that's what they always said to me. My mother said it, not my father; my father didn't say things like that. Yes, and then they told me about other girls who were much worse off but were worth more just the same. Probably they were right. I ought to be spanked. I have a decent husband, I have Günther, there's plenty of money and everything else. What more do I want? Will you do what Max talked about before?"

"What?"

"That business about the church and the refugees."

"Yes, maybe I will."

"Fine, then I'll do it too. I'll do whatever you decide. I'd like to help Max. I'd like him to be pleased with me. Are you also among those who think I've got it too good?"

"Don't worry about it. My opinion doesn't matter."

"Yes, it does, it matters a lot to me. You're the only person with whom I can talk this way. Who else is there for me to talk to? Earlier, the first few years, I behaved toward you in ways I shouldn't have. I was still too silly, and I was a little afraid of you too. I didn't know anything about you. Please, Papa, don't be mad at me for that. The two of us . . . yes, all this time I could stand it here just because of you. I'm self-conscious in front of you. Really. You mustn't make fun of me. You least of all.

"Do you know how I met him? Through a single sentence. He said to me . . . but no one knows, I never told anybody . . . he said, 'You're someone worth dying with.' Nothing more, that's all he said. And I was very, very happy with him. I can't forget it, Papa. I just can't forget, that's what it is. But please, don't tell Max—I mean, don't tell him what Berthold said to me; he'd make fun of me.

"And I understand why Berthold didn't call. No

247

wonder! He assumed as a matter of course that I'd be there. He never doubted for a moment. He peered through the curtain and looked for me in the auditorium—there's always a spyhole in the curtain. And I . . . I wasn't there. Yes, that's it. It must be awful for him. Is it really such a crime, Papa? I mean that a person wants to be happy?"

Then, finally, I heard the rattling of keys in the front door. I wanted to jump up, but my father-in-law put his hand on my arm and brought me back to my senses. Because of course it was Fräulein Gerda. Who else could it be? No one else had a front-door key.

She rushed in, her cheeks bright red. "Oh, you're still up," she called.

I looked up from the newspaper I'd quickly grabbed. My father-in-law acted a little bored as we courteously listened to what she had to tell.

She was quite breathless, so excited and in such a hurry to spill it all out that her words tumbled over each other. She could have been home much sooner, she said, and her fiancé had scolded her for applauding so long—to the very end, until they dropped the fire curtain. Hardly anyone was left by then. Her fiancé had kept pulling at her sleeve, saying, "Come on, that's enough. The actors want to get some rest, and we'll miss our streetcar." But even after they'd been to the checkroom, she had run back, wearing her hat and coat, to go on applauding, and some of the people who were still there had started to applaud again with her. "I know the author personally, after all," she had said to her fiancé. Frau Riebow and her husband had been there too. And the mayor, and other people who had been to our house. And oh, how she'd cried. Could we tell?

Had it been a sad play, then? my father-in-law asked.

Yes, very. That is, maybe not; her fiancé had made

fun of her and said, "You cry at the most inappropriate moments." Because in the end everything was resolved happily, but all the time she'd been afraid that it wouldn't work out. When the young wife said to her husband, "How gray you've grown, Gianni. Is it my fault?" and made a little gesture and the husband pulled back because he didn't want her to touch him . . . she just had to cry then, but her fiancé had said that the woman was being mean, making fun of her husband on top of everything. But the woman herself begged for her husband's acquittal, and in the end he was acquitted.

What husband? I asked.

Her husband, the one who killed his wife and Paolo. Out of jealousy. It was an old story, many hundreds of years old, set in Italy, of course. But it was performed in modern dress, just like ours. Oh, Francesca's gown was gorgeous! And the whole trial had only been reenacted because Francesca was said to have declared that her husband would have to be punished for his deed— for killing her and Paolo. But she hadn't said it really, the poet had said it.

What poet? I asked.

Dante was his name, an ancient poet. That is, not ancient—on stage he wasn't old at all; on the contrary. And the young wife said he must have heard her wrong or misunderstood her in some way, which might easily have happened, since he was unconscious.

Unconscious? Who? I asked.

This Dante, at the time he spoke to the lovers. And as punishment he had to preside at the trial and pronounce the verdict. Everybody reproached him because he had told the story wrong.

"There, the phone," Fräulein Gerda said. And in fact the instrument in the living room tinkled.

"My husband is making calls from the study," I said.

"Oh, the President is still up, too?" Oh, yes, and here was the playbill. Would I like to see it?

"Yes, just put it down there. Thanks, I'll look at it later," I said.

But she'd like to have it back. She wanted to keep it. And there was a picture of Herr Möncken in it, too, and a preface by him that she hadn't had a chance to read yet. And Herr Möncken wasn't ill at all; at the end he'd come on stage—at the very end. The actors probably pulled him out.

"Wouldn't you like a snack?" I asked her. "You must be hungry."

No, she and her fiancé had gone to the theater bar during the intermission. Oh, and what a lot of interesting people were there!

"Was it a hit, then?" I asked.

"Yes, of course it was a hit. How could it not be? That is—" At that moment she spied Max standing at the door to his study. "Oh, sir, I was just telling Frau Helldegen about the play. It's too bad you weren't there. All the fine people you see socially were there, and I told my fiancé all the names. My fiancé wasn't pleased with the play at all; he said it was immoral, and he even got angry. I hope the critics don't feel that way. I'd be so sorry for Herr Möncken, and it wouldn't be fair, either."

"Well, we'll find out from tomorrow's paper," I said.

"Yes, I can hardly bear the suspense." Fräulein Gerda was ready to start all over again. "Just think, sir—"

I got to my feet. "All right, I think we've all had a long day. I'm glad you enjoyed your evening. Good night."

"Yes, I did—a lot. Thank you very much for the tickets."

"And don't bother getting Günther up at the regular time tomorrow. He got to bed pretty late," I called to her departing back.

We were numbed by her spate of words.

"Well, that's over and done with," I said. "Your call to Hamburg took a long time."

"I had to discuss the situation in detail with Beermann, but it's worth it."

"Are you still going to go out?" my father-in-law asked at last. He was probably only trying to help me; we had already been standing there quite a while, not knowing what to say.

"I think we'll forget it. Don't you think, Max?"

"I'll do whatever you say. But if you don't want to . . . ."

"Oh, I'm exhausted."

Max didn't feel like going out either. He hadn't felt like it in the first place.

My father-in-law said good night to us. I apologized for his having had to listen to all of Fräulein Gerda's nonsense. And I thanked him for staying up so late just for us. I walked to the stairs with him; he had already gone up a few steps.

Max must have thought that I meant to go up with his father. "Oh, what I wanted to say, Marianne," he called. Then he cleared his throat.

"Yes? Was there something else?" I asked. "Good night, then, Papa. Sleep well."

My father-in-law gave me a look before proceeding up the stairs.

"Yes?" I asked Max.

"You know that on principle I avoid interfering in your affairs," he said.

"But you have every right to."

It made him extremely uncomfortable to have to talk with me. He went to the table, picked up a cigarette, and tapped it at length on the back of his hand. Perhaps it was a habit he'd developed when he had to make proposals at stockholders' meetings.

"Yes, give me a cigarette too," I said.

He immediately offered me the box.

"What is it?" I asked as he held the lighter for me.

"Of course I am not indifferent to all this," he said, going back to the table with the cigarettes. I remained standing by the stairs. "You mustn't think that, even if I don't talk about it."

"I know, Max. And I'm sorry. I mean, I'm sorry that the play stirred the whole thing up again. It's my fault, I know. You're not to blame. But there was no way I could prevent it, either."

"Come a little closer, please. I don't want to have to raise my voice. It's nobody's business but our own." He even glanced up the stairs to see if Fräulein Gerda might be listening.

I took a few steps in his direction. "Did he call?" I asked.

"How did you know?"

"I was afraid he would."

"Yes, he called."

"What happened?"

"He called while I was in the study. Just when I'd finished my Hamburg call. He wanted to talk to you."

"Yes, I imagine he would." I tried to laugh. "I'm really sorry for you, Max."

"I thought it best not to call you to the phone."

"I wouldn't have talked to him. No, under no circumstances."

"I told him you were in Italy."

"Yes, you did the right thing. I would have said exactly the same thing. In your place, I mean. And it's almost the truth—at least in a couple of days."

"Yes, and since he said nothing in reply—"

"He didn't say anything?"

"No, that's why I added that you wouldn't be back

until December. Not before the middle of December, I think I said, but I wouldn't want to swear to it."

"Yes, of course. And the precise date doesn't matter. We don't even know ourselves. Yes, and then?"

"That was all."

"And he didn't say anything?"

"No."

"Nothing at all?"

"No."

"Funny. But it doesn't matter. There's not much he could say. I mean, did you have the feeling that he believed you?"

"He didn't answer. I waited a little; he was still there. I could hear him breathing."

"You heard him breathing."

"Maybe it was just my imagination. There was a lot of noise in the background. Voices; and the clatter of dishes. He must have called from some bar. And since he didn't say anything, I hung up gently. There was nothing else for me to say."

"Yes, you did the right thing. I'm sorry that you were troubled with it, very sorry."

"I made an effort to be polite to him."

"Yes, thank you."

"Or at least objective. I didn't get upset or anything. You know what I mean."

"Thank you, yes. Truly, I'm very sorry."

"I thought it best to tell you so you wouldn't think that without consulting you I—"

"Yes, thank you, Max. Yes, it's fine this way. But really, you don't have to consult me. You have every right. And you didn't have to tell me about it, either. But I'm glad that I know. One has to know what one is up against. It's really quite all right like this. Now I'd like to go to bed. Thank you."

I wanted to get away, to be alone. I didn't want him to notice how I felt, for that would have been unfair to him. I didn't want him to see me shake. Perhaps I wasn't shaking, perhaps it was only my voice. I no longer had the strength to conceal it.

"Oh, and one more thing," Max called.

"There's something else?" I asked.

"Oh, nothing special. It has to do with . . . . Please don't mind my bringing it up, but . . . ."

"You can say anything you want to me. I deserve no better."

"Well, what I mean is, a little physical aberration like that—one shouldn't place too much importance on it. One must get over it."

I stood still. I did not know what to answer.

"Forgive the expression. I only meant to say that it could happen to anybody, that's all."

"The expression is very good, actually," I said. "Really, it's splendid. Yes, thank you. Are you going to stay up?"

"There are some reports I want to go over. Because of our trip, to get them out of the way."

"Don't stay up too late, Max. Even your strength isn't inexhaustible."

"It's only ten past eleven," Max said.

"Oh, right. Good night, then."

I went up to my room, leaving the door ajar. I wanted to hear anything that might go on on the stairs— I mean, if anything should go on there. I heard Max turn off the light and go to his study, but I didn't hear his door snap shut; he too must have left it ajar.

I could hear the grandfather clock in the living room, its regular, deliberate ticking. It was so still in the house. Then I heard someone going back and forth in the cellar and the slam of a door. It could not be Max; he hardly ever went to the cellar. It must have been the cook. Who else? Berthold would never come through the cellar.

Max had heard him breathing.

254

I did not turn on the light; I could wait in the dark. Besides, my eyes ached, and the light would have made it worse. It was much easier to wait if you couldn't see yourself. But since I was thirsty, I went into the bathroom, and there I had to turn on the light. I let the water run so that it would get cold, but the faucet hissed so loudly that I couldn't hear anything else. The hiss could be heard through the whole house; the plumber had been called but had been unable to fix it. That was why I quickly turned off the faucet; though the water was still tepid, I drank it anyway. If Max, downstairs, had heard the water running, he would think that I was having a bath and going to bed. But perhaps he wasn't paying any attention. I went back to my room at once and listened to hear whether anything had happened. I left the light on in the bathroom so I could see a little.

I can't say exactly what I was expecting; if anyone had asked me, I wouldn't have known. I was much calmer than I had been at any time previously. I no longer had to think, I had only to wait. Oh, the silence! Just so long as nothing interrupted my waiting, everything was all right. No thinking, only waiting.

I knew perfectly well that I should have gone downstairs and said something to Max—anything. Any decent woman would have done so; there was still time. Max had gone to such pains to speak with me. It was all up to me, I could have responded. And if Berthold should really still come, I could stay hidden in Max's study and wait until Max had sent him packing.

But I was already much too far away, from Max and from everything. You couldn't tell that I was already so distant—everyone thought, There she is. But I no longer put up any resistance; I was being driven farther and farther away from them, not violently, very gently, farther and farther. Soon they would no longer be able to hear my voice; they would see my lips moving, but they would no longer be able to understand me. Nor I them.

Max had heard him breathing.

But perhaps Berthold wasn't going to come. Perhaps it was all my imagination. Perhaps he felt perfectly happy where he was and wasn't thinking of me. Then everything was all right, and there was no need for me to talk to Max.

For if it was only a little physical aberration, as Max called it—oh, how it embarrassed him to use such a phrase—then it really was better not to talk about it anymore, better simply to dismiss it as a minor illness not worth calling the doctor about. They wouldn't believe me one way or the other. But if I went on talking about it, they'd be sure that I hadn't gotten over it.

But why had Berthold first been ill and unwilling to come? Then suddenly come after all? There had to be a reason. Did the theater people telephone to say that he absolutely had to attend the performance, that it wouldn't work without him? Yes, maybe it had nothing to do with me. My father-in-law had raised this same question.

But then why had Berthold kept his silence when he was on the telephone with Max? I could see him standing in a phone booth—or the phone was hanging in the passageway between the dining room and the kitchen, not far from the bar—yes, there he stood, the receiver at his ear, and behind him the waiters strode past with trays, and there was the noise of the restaurant, and you could hear him breathing.

If I only knew which restaurant he had called from, then . . . . Or did Max suspect that I might call Berthold back? Was that why his door was ajar?

I grew restless again—that's what thinking does to you. It was taking too long. Poor Berthold, how could he be expected to get here so fast? Perhaps he had no money for a taxi, and it took more than half an hour by

256

streetcar. And besides, perhaps he couldn't get away. Had the clock struck eleven thirty already? I must have missed it in spite of the silence.

I walked back and forth silently; the floor was thickly carpeted. When I passed the mirror on the closet door, I saw something white. I was holding something white, a roll of something. It was the playbill. I'd forgotten all about it. I turned on the night-table light and sat down on the bed to leaf through the booklet.

There was the cast of characters, each paired with the name of a performer, and ads all around. But I wasn't interested in that. At the back there were snapshots of the production. An actress. No, there were two women, both very beautiful. Had Berthold fallen in love with one of them? He had every right in the world. Which one? The younger one? No, Berthold didn't like younger people; he always said so. But the other one?

Then I read the preface because Berthold had written it. Or I tried to read it. This is what he wrote.

It is not a matter of Francesca and Paolo. Their destiny has been fulfilled and serves as a fulfillment for us. All the great lovers of history failed in the worldly sense—a fact that may comfort the world. All the great lovers unrepentantly confess their failure and their love. Thus they are removed for all time from the human administration of justice, which is sometimes called divine justice. Even the dramatist is left with nothing more to interpret.

There is the further question of whether we who live in the present age are still allowed to depict lovers. A time that is so single-mindedly intent on sheer survival may not even dream of fulfillment. And things that cannot be dreamed of have no reality.

Francesca and Paolo were called only as witnesses. To put it more precisely, as witnesses for the defense in the case against Malatesta, since he alone is primarily at issue. His fate is pending to this day. There is no doubt that he is a tragic figure. It is only for his sake that the trial is resumed time and again.

Dante, too, is responsible. He tells us that Francesca stated that for robbing her and her lover of their lives, her husband would be sent to the Caina, the deepest circle of hell, where only killers of their own families are sent to expiate their sins. It is important here to have the exact wording. Francesca says, or is reported to have said, "The Caina waits for him who quenched our life." Malatesta, then, was still alive at the time, and the question arises whether the judgment in Francesca's sense was carried out. Or is it possible that Malatesta lives to this day?

And another question: Does Francesca's testimony have legal validity? For the law is on the side of Malatesta, there can be no doubt about that. To this day. That a more humane law no longer allows the husband to murder his wife and her lover is such an insignificant nuance that no serious judge need take it into consideration.

But thirdly: Is it really true that Francesca wishes to see her husband condemned to the Caina? In this regard we are wholly dependent on Dante's report, and Dante was a poet. Should a judge accord credibility to a poet?

From time immemorial this outburst of hatred has seemed a blot on the delicate image of the young woman. At the very least it is a distortion. And how about Paolo, who, according to the report, floats silently at Francesca's side during her testimony and may in fact have placed his arm around her shoulders? His silence is remarkable in itself, but is it not possible that by a single gesture, which may have escaped Dante in his fascination with Francesca's beauty, he signified, "What do we care about Malatesta? He's been punished enough by having the world on his side, by being successful, by having to go on living"?

Nor should we forget that at the crucial moment of her testimony, Dante, the only witness, fainted dead away.

The verdict is appealed by Malatesta, since the rumors that are circulating are apt to damage his reputation. The appeal is denied, not because Malatesta is thus meant to be declared in the wrong, but because the application was made on completely unreliable and, as it turns out, false premises. For there never was a trial against Malatesta, no verdict was ever pronounced. Malatesta must be content with that truth, even if it means an uneasy, suspended state of living for him.

He is left with the possibility of applying for an injunction against the poet, an action that would have a good chance of success. Francesca, called as a witness against Dante, would surely, in her dovelike gentleness, try to protect him; but even she would have to admit, smiling, that he fainted during their conversation. Yes, and why? Some will say compassion, while others will say submission to the supreme law. That may be, but is it not also conceivable that what made him fall to the ground was the devastating realization that he would never be able to partake of a fulfillment of destiny such as he saw before him in Francesca and Paolo? That the most that would be granted him would be to write about it?

Dante is not free of blame, for a poet has no right to lose consciousness, neither from compassion nor from submission; he falsifies his truth. And if he breaks down from despair, he must remain silent.

But who would be foolish enough to bring a poet to the bar of justice—it's not worthwhile. The poet is undoubtedly a tragicomic figure.

Yes, that's what it said in the playbill, and I tried to understand. I believed that Berthold was making fun of his audience, and that wasn't good for him; they would be angry. Why did he write things that would damage him?

As far as this Francesca was concerned, it was quite obvious: Dante was jealous . . . . Dovelike gentleness?

I don't know how long I sat thinking about everything. I did not look at my watch then or later; it no longer mattered. It may be that it wasn't very long, only a few minutes perhaps. I had been very far away, as in a deep sleep. Then I started up.

Someone was knocking at the window, very softly, but I heard at once; it was as if someone's finger were touching me. Come! And again. I was not mistaken.

The night-table lamp was still lit. I turned it off at once, but I remained on the edge of the bed, not daring to move. It sounded as if a bird were pecking at the windowpane, a little bird, at first very softly and timidly, as if waiting after each peck to find out if I had heard, and then with increasing rapidity. Many little birds, maybe titmice.

Or was someone throwing gravel at the window? Had Berthold gone crazy? Max would hear. Everyone in the house would hear, in the cellar and up on the third floor. And where had he found the gravel? He was throwing it with both hands.

I stood up. I felt heavy, as if I were made of lead. Slowly I sneaked to the window, step by step, often stopping to listen. The noise continued on. The curtains were drawn, and I did not want to open them; I stood behind them and listened. I didn't want to give myself away.

Finally I peeked through a narrow slit. And I came close to laughing out loud. It was hailing outside! How could it be hailing? Nobody would have thought of that. In the corner of the sill a pile of white hailstones had already accumulated, and still more were pecking at the window and bouncing off the pane.

How strange that it was hailing. What weather! And now, in November. All day it had been much too warm, and now this sudden hail. Probably downstairs Max was just as surprised as I, and he too was standing by the window to see what was going on.

Under these circumstances Berthold would not be coming, of course. In such weather—no, no way. One should not count on his coming. I'd probably better busy myself with packing for the trip with Max. Otherwise I might forget something important. I'd postponed it all this time so that my things wouldn't wrinkle so much. I meant to pack at the last moment, and it really was high time.

And that was the moment when the front doorbell rang.

What a ring it was! First just once, fairly long. Then he waited a little. But he was much too impatient to be able to wait properly. With the best will in the world no one could get to the door that fast, not even in broad daylight. He rang again at once, three short rings one after another. Sound the alarm! The whole house would wake up. That really isn't necessary, Berthold. I had to laugh. Not out loud, but my heart was laughing.

I heard Max come from the study, walk through the living room, and turn on the light over the stairs. I was standing behind my door, which was still ajar. A wedge of light fell through the crack into my room. I

261

couldn't see what was going on outside—the door opened inward and not toward the stairs—and I couldn't be seen, either. But I could hear everything.

Max went out into the vestibule. The chain rattled on the inside of the front door. And outside Berthold's feet were kicking at the iron shoe scraper. Oh, how impatient he was. Could he see that it was Max who came to the door? Surely he thought I would open it, but perhaps he could make out Max's silhouette. And was Max able to see that it was Berthold? How might he respond if Max simply refused to open the door? Would he go on ringing? Would he rattle the doorknob? It was an antique knob made of brass, and it had cost a lot of money.

"Well, finally," I heard Berthold say. His voice sounded outraged, and yet he apparently wiped his feet on the mat. The current of air blew my door open a little more, but I held it back; there was no need for them to know that I could hear everything.

"What do you want?" Max asked.

"You can't leave me standing out in the hail," Berthold complained. "That's some weird weather you have hereabouts."

"Allow me . . . ." Apparently Max was running after Berthold, who had simply walked into the living room.

"What? Has she gone to bed already?"

I had to choke down my laughter. Yes, that's how evil I am, but I came close to laughing out loud. At Max. Everything was so funny. His face in particular. I would have loved to see his face.

"May I point out to you—" Max began, but he got no further.

Berthold interrupted him at once. "Shall I wake her?"

"This is my house," Max said. Now he sounded much angrier.

262

"Yes, why not? No one will dispute that fact." Berthold was astonished. "A beautiful house. And you keep it nice and warm, too. Filthy weather outside."

"I told you on the telephone that my wife—" Max tried again.

"Man, you can't expect anybody to believe that," Berthold interrupted once more. "And you can smell it—Arpège, isn't it? Haven't smelled that for a long time. You don't have to be a dog to sniff it out. Fine, fine. It suits her splendidly. Shall I drag her from her bed?"

Oh, but I mustn't laugh. So that was why Berthold had breathed on the telephone—because of my perfume.

"I'm telling you for the last time—"

"What's going on? What's the point of all the fine phrases? We don't have time. The whole gang is waiting for us. I promised to be right back. I just came to fetch the most important person. Nice people. Especially the wife of Malatesta, the second lead. She knows her way around. And what a pair of lips on her. A true glory. She'll gulp you down and ask for more. If I'd known that girls like that work in your local theater . . . . Come on, let's the two of us get her out of bed. Some surprise!"

"I must ask you to—"

"Let go of me. What is it you want? I've never liked people to touch me."

"I must ask you for the last time to leave my house—at once."

"I have no idea what you mean. Why? I have no intention of staying here. The sooner Marianne comes—"

"You're forcing me to call the police."

"The police? What have the police got to do with it? I'll leave without the police. For Christ's sake, man, take it easy. You're the big industrialist. Or executive. Or whatever. Facts, my good man, facts. Imagine my having to explain them to you. Police? You're turning out to be a romantic. That won't get you far in life. That ends in nihilism. Believe me, I know more about it than you do.

"And why spoil Marianne's fun? Don't be like that. I rushed five hundred kilometers in barely eight hours. In that old rattletrap. See if you can do as well. And only so as to get here in time. What? And then she isn't even at the theater? That can't be. I came within a hair of calling the police myself. What do you think of that? There you are, working yourself to a frazzle . . . . What was the point of writing the play? For my own enjoyment? I can think of easier ways to have fun. Why? Look at me. I'm a famous man right here and now. Just ask around; it's not only what I say. And how can the police change that?"

I thought it best to make myself visible. Or they might have gotten into a serious quarrel. Until now it had all been funny.

Laughing, I stepped to the balustrade. Downstairs, the two of them stared up at me, openmouthed. No, not openmouthed, that's just a figure of speech. Max stood by the newel post, his mouth very narrow and pursed. Berthold had already taken the first two steps to get me out of bed. There he stood; I saw only him, and he looked the way he had to look. I, too, was speechless; I could only smile.

"At long last, my darling," Berthold said. And he added immediately, turning to Max, "Surely you do not object, sir, to my calling her darling? We are used to it." He addressed me again. "Why have you kept us waiting so long? We were about to get you out of bed."

He was a little drunk but not very, and it wasn't annoying, as men's drunkenness usually is. He was like a little boy. He was wearing his old raincoat, and his hair was wet and plastered to his forehead. He was beaming all over in the excitement of seeing me again.

264

I moved to the top of the stairs. I thought he would run up to meet me, but instead he went backward down the steps without taking his eyes off me. Was he planning to go ahead into the vestibule because I was sure to follow? No, that wasn't it. He came to a stop at the foot of the stairs. Max must have been somewhere to the right, already way to one side. I knew that he was still there, but I could no longer see him. I did not take my eyes off Berthold.

"Slowly, slowly, my darling," Berthold whispered. "One step at a time, just like before. And all the while smiling like a fine lady. Yes, that's it. Oh, it's beyond bearing. Just look at that, sir. You can't imagine anything like that, and you can't describe it and you can't put it on stage, you can only . . . . I was privileged to experience it once before. You weren't there at the time, sir; I believe you were still on the road. But to think that I'm allowed to witness it a second time . . . . Really, my darling, my legs are shaking. All this time I thought, What trash, what's left to me after having seen such a sight once. And now . . . and the same dress, too. Well, what did I tell you, sir? She's already put on the dress from that other time. A wonderful dress! But it isn't the dress that's responsible, though your husband won't believe me. Oh, my darling, why didn't you come to the play? I waited and waited for you. Wouldn't he let you come?"

I shook my head; I could not speak. I did not want it to be thought that Max had forbidden me, but that was how Berthold understood it.

"What an old spoilsport! But don't pay any attention. Come, we'll celebrate now."

"Wouldn't you like me to make some coffee first?" I asked.

"Coffee? What do I want with coffee?"

"I've had a couple of drinks myself," I said. It wasn't at all what I had meant to say.

"So much the better. We can have coffee there, too. I'll order demitasse and champagne for you, and then you can stay up all night long."

"I've had some Pernod."

"It doesn't matter. Maybe they have Pernod there too. What are we waiting for? We've wasted enough of our time."

We were facing each other now, though I was still one step above him. He was wearing a red-checked muffler, which I straightened as best I could. I'd already brushed his hair from his forehead. All this time we hadn't stopped looking at each other. His eyes were the same. And his mouth. He seemed to have no doubt that I would go with him.

"Where is your party?"

"In the Playhouse Cellar, of course. Where else would we go? All of them are nice people. One of them treated us all to champagne. I don't know his name. Some rich guy. Why not?"

I, too, had no doubt that I would leave with Berthold. I was just postponing the moment.

"Marianne . . ." I heard Max's voice.

I tried to turn my eyes in his direction, but I couldn't.

"Don't delay us now with your pretty speeches, sir," Berthold answered in my stead. "My God, how can one man get so worked up! If we acted that way—but he least of all has any reason to get excited."

"You mustn't shout, Berthold. You'll wake up the whole house."

"Am I shouting?"

"Yes, you are."

"That's because of the excitement. First the opening night, and then . . . . Why? Is the old gentleman still living with you?"

I nodded.

"I thought . . . ."

"Marianne," the voice from the right began once more, "if you want to discuss our private business with this inebriated gentleman . . . ."

"Inebriated gentleman? That's what you call inebriated? Three or four glasses of kirsch and a drop of champagne? Man alive, if you're ever as sober as we are when we've had a couple—then you'd know the meaning of sober. We're a different breed. Do you think I'm drunk, my darling? You know me. Better than anyone on earth. Am I drunk? . . . Nothing doing, your honor. I know exactly what I want. If I never knew before, this time I know; trust me."

"Don't shout, Berthold."

"What does it matter? He's only angry because—why are you angry, sir? Why don't you come with us? It'll be good for you. And I'll give you a couple of ploys for your advertising department—on the side, without charge. Wait until you see how you can double your sales. There's no trick to it, just a little psychology, that's all . . . . What, my darling? Let's show your President that we're not drunk."

"Where did you get that ugly scarf?" I asked.

"Scarf? What scarf?" Startled, he reached for his neck. "Oh, that. I just put it on because . . . my darling, I have a Volkswagen." He was beaming with pleasure. "It's parked right outside. I've had it a couple of weeks. On time. And secondhand, of course. The finish has seen better days, but it can still get up speed. Even uphill. Now we're quite independent."

"Max," I said, trying again to look to my right; but I could not. Though my head turned a little, my eyes remained with Berthold. "Where are you going, Max?" I asked at random into the room.

"Surely you don't expect me to stand here listening to this," his voice came back to me. It had already retreated much farther.

"Hey, don't run away, sir," Berthold called. "We have no secrets from you."

But it was no use. Max had gone to his study; I think he even closed the door.

"There he goes. Like a sulky boy. Oh, let's leave him alone, he'll come to his senses. Do you think he's calling the police?"

I shook my head.

"He'd just make a fool of himself. Why should he make a fool of himself?"

"I suppose he'll telephone Blanck," I said.

"Oh, yes, the famous Herr Blanck. He's still around, is he? I'd forgotten all about him. Oh, my darling, it's true, I am just a little bit drunk."

"I know," I said, brushing his hair from his forehead again.

"But not a lot. I drank too fast, that's all. And then all the excitement tonight, and you weren't there, and I haven't had anything to eat since this morning—I just took off."

"Should I fix you something?"

"Oh, who's talking about eating. It's only because of the police. Those pigs could take away my ignition key. But I had to have a drink, my darling. With the cast. It would have been rude—"

"Was it a hit?"

"A hit? What?"

"Your play."

"What do I care about the play? Perhaps it was a flop. Who cares? Come on, everyone's waiting for you. I told them you were coming. Where is your coat?"

I nodded upward.

"Shall I get it for you?"

He was ready to run up the stairs, but I held him back. "Don't bother. There's a raincoat down here in the coatroom. The one I wear in the garden."

"And the car has a heater. My God, maybe I left

the engine running. If the police notice . . . . Come on!"
He grabbed my arm to pull me along, but he remained
rooted to the spot. And oh, how he looked at me. "Do
you know what I want?"

"Not here," I said. Again I had to brush his hair
back; it wouldn't stay put.

"I felt you all these three months. Or was it longer?
Really felt you, I mean. Your breasts, here in my hands.
Your nipples, you know. What's wrong? It's all right
to say it. He can't hear us. I nearly went mad. I didn't
write you because you didn't want me to. Why didn't
you come on your own?"

"It wasn't possible, my darling. Truly, it wasn't
possible."

"Well, it doesn't matter; we're together now. And
just think, I almost didn't come at all. I was afraid; I
thought you might not like it."

"And I thought you were ill."

"But that was just an excuse. Suddenly, this morning, I couldn't stand it anymore. I drove here in one
stretch, without stopping on the way. Almost five
hundred kilometers. I just got in the car, just the way
I was—I don't keep it in a garage, it's always at my
door—and off I went. Without anything. Without a
toothbrush—yes."

"I knew," I said.

"And I knew that you knew. Did you think of me
sometimes?"

"Yes, but let's not talk about it here."

"The Volkswagen is wonderful, my darling. You'll
see . . . . What is he doing in there? Doesn't he want
to come along?"

"Do you want him to?"

"If he wants to—why not?"

"He won't want to."

"He'd rather sleep?"

"Maybe."

"It's all right with me. Let him sleep, then. Do you know that it was hailing? Peculiar weather in your part of the world. I was surprised this afternoon. Up there in your mountains—I don't know the name of them— over there on the other side of the river, before you can see the town . . . ."

We were still standing at the foot of the stairs, just as before except that we had moved closer. He was speaking much too rapidly; he was very worked up, and he wanted to tell me everything all at once. He had quite forgotten that we were in a strange house and that Max was in the next room telephoning. Once again I adjusted his muffler. He paid no attention. I listened to what he was telling me. I didn't understand every-thing, but I said yes and smiled. It was wonderful to hear his voice and to stand there with him; it was won-derful that he was so happy and excited, and his face was wonderful, and everything was wonderful.

He was telling me about a yellow sun under a black cloud bank, a bright yellow sun, and above it only black. For the final stretch the sun had been right in front of his windshield, sending its brightness into the car. Even his sunglasses didn't help, and that was why he had to drive slowly. Whenever the road curved or a hill appeared, he had felt absolutely blind, as if it had turned to darkest night. And once he was back in the clear and heading in the right direction, he was dazzled. "And all the time all I wanted was to get here as fast as I could."

None of what he told me was important, and there was no need for him to tell me now. He was here, and there was no need for hurry. But I did not want to interrupt him; I, too, was no longer in a hurry. And I had stopped being tired. That very afternoon I had ached all over from excitement. Even as a little girl I used to ache all over when I was excited—at Christ-mastime, for example, just from waiting and looking

270

forward to it. I always overdid the anticipation. But now I felt light as a feather.

And just before the road left the hills behind, Berthold was telling me, someplace up near where you got your first view of the town, there was an inn, an old half-timbered building. Probably a place that catered to hikers. Did I know it?

I nodded because that was the way he wanted it.

And there was a garden attached to the building. Probably where they served coffees. Did I know it?

Again I nodded.

Now the garden was bare and leafless, and a girl was hanging tablecloths or white sheets on the line. "And what do you think?" he asked with a cunning look.

"Why was she hanging up the laundry in the rain?" I asked.

"It wasn't raining yet, and maybe she wanted to bleach the sheets. The girl was standing on the other side of the line, and I could only see her figure; the sun was silhouetting it on the sheet. Then I saw that it was you—just like you. I put my foot on the brake and almost fell down the hill. The wheels don't brake simultaneously. The car has cable brakes, the old-fashioned kind. That's why I got it so cheap."

"It's been a long time since I hung up laundry," I said.

"Quiet!"

"What is it?"

"The phone clicked. He's finished making his calls."

"Forget him. I'm thirsty."

"Me too. We have to . . . ."

"I'm parched."

"That's what comes of so much talking. Shall I . . .?"

Looking past my shoulder, Berthold's eyes traveled

271

up the stairs. I too turned around. My father-in-law was standing at the banister. He had put on the robe with the blue and red stripes that Max and I had given him for his birthday a year ago. My father-in-law was a simple man, very undemanding; he thought of such things as unnecessary luxuries. But the robe was very becoming to him.

He had taken off his collar, and perhaps he was wearing slippers, too. I couldn't see from where I stood. He leaned slightly over the banister, looking at us. And he gave us a friendly smile; then I knew that Berthold had smiled at him.

"We didn't wake you, did we?" Berthold asked.

"Oh, no, Herr Möncken; I wasn't asleep yet. On the contrary, I've been expecting you, in a manner of speaking."

"I'm so glad to have another chance to see you. I wanted . . . " Berthold went up the few steps to shake hands with my father-in-law. He bowed deeply, but he wasn't making fun of the old man; he really meant it. It almost looked as if he were about to kiss his hand.

"I've been wanting to tell you—you're right. Writing books, that's no way for a grown man to spend his time."

"Did I say that?"

"Perhaps you didn't, but I'm certain you thought it. And if you didn't think it, I thought it for you. That's what I've wanted to tell you for a long time, to set your mind at rest. I myself am relieved to be over it at last. I'll join a newspaper as an editor, or I'll work for the radio or as literary manager at some theater. Something like that. They're jobs like any other; you work eight hours and get a fixed salary. Everything is much simpler, and it leaves me more time for her."

"We have to leave, Papa," I said.

"Yes."

272

"We're going to the party. We're only waiting for Max."

"Yes?"

"It would be a great honor for us," Berthold said, "if you would participate in our humble celebration." How graciously he could express himself. And so respectfully. "But I do not dare to invite you."

"I am beholden to you, Herr Möncken"—my father-in-law was equally gracious—"but I'm just a little too old for that sort of thing."

"Berthold has a Volkswagen," I said.

"That's marvelous. Drive carefully."

And then another funny thing happened. So many events of the night were funny, quite different from what one might have imagined. Suddenly Fräulein Gerda appeared above, at my father-in-law's side. She must have been standing in the corridor for quite a while, behind the pillar, and now she couldn't bear it any longer and came out of hiding.

"My compliments, Herr Möncken. I was at the theater tonight. Would you like me to get your coat for you, madam?"

Amused, we turned to look at her, even my father-in-law.

"No, thank you very much, Fräulein Gerda," I replied. "I'll wear my old raincoat."

"But how about a hat?"

"We don't need hats, my girl," Berthold shouted cheerfully. "I've never owned a hat in my life. Madam can wear my old cap if she's cold." He pulled a crumpled beret from his pocket to show Fräulein Gerda. "And if she wants, she can have my scarf as well."

We all laughed—all except Fräulein Gerda, who seemed to feel consternation.

"All right, let's go," Berthold shouted, running down the stairs.

Then we saw Max standing in the doorway to his study.

"Ah, there he is, our President. Well, how about it? Are you ready?"

Max was white as chalk. He paid no attention to Berthold.

"Herr Möncken," my father-in-law called.

"Yes, sir?"

"I do not wish you to insult my son."

"But surely I'm not insulting him. On the contrary, I've asked him to join us. We'd be so pleased."

"One moment, Marianne," Max said, moving two steps closer.

"Yes?" I asked.

But Berthold was at the end of his patience. "You can talk to us on the way."

"Would you please let me speak with my wife?" Max said.

"What is it, Max?"

"I presume you realize what this means?"

"Yes, of course, Max. It means that I have to have some coffee first. Why don't you come with us?"

"Yes, let's go," Berthold exclaimed. "There's room for everybody. In a pinch the car can hold five people if they're not too fat."

He ran ahead into the coatroom to fetch my rain-coat. My father-in-law was still standing at the upstairs banister, Fräulein Gerda next to him. I remained downstairs, next to Max, who wore an angry expression.

"Don't be like that, Max." I gave an encouraging little laugh. "We'd been planning to go out anyway. We don't have to stay long."

"Is this it?" Berthold called, coming back with a raincoat.

Yes, it was my coat. Berthold helped me on with it. Max stood still, not speaking.

274

Then the front doorbell rang again. Max moved; he was about to go to the door and open it.

I stepped into his path. "Who is that, Max?" I asked.

Not answering, he tried to get past me, but I would not let him. "Who is ringing the bell?" I asked again.

Max shrugged. "Blanck, of course. What did you imagine? I need a witness." Max's voice was hoarse.

I stepped aside. "Blanck, of course. Fine, then I know the score. Come, Berthold."

We walked into the vestibule. We were moving so quickly that we almost got ahead of Max. Berthold pulled the door wide open and gestured invitingly. "Hello, if it isn't the renowned Herr Blanck. And how are your horn-rimmed glasses? Why don't you join us at the Playhouse Cellar too? And try to persuade your boss."

Blanck stood in the angle of the door, pressing himself as flat as possible to let us pass. His coat collar was turned up. He looked like a clean-shaven owl.

"Come," I said to Berthold to keep him from talking any more nonsense. I pulled him down the steps.

And then the door closed behind us.

A wind was blowing outside. Berthold took my arm to keep me from stumbling, but I almost stumbled anyway. I was wearing very thin shoes.

We had to walk down the driveway. Berthold's car was parked outside, on the street. And I was cold.

He took a deep breath. "It was much too hot in there," he said.

I didn't want him to notice that I was so cold and that I had almost tripped, but after a few steps he stopped and said, "Is something the matter?"

"No, let's go."

But he held both my arms. "No, my darling, tell me. Are you sad?"

"It's nothing. We'd better go."

"Did I act foolishly? Did I insult someone? You have to tell me; sometimes I act badly."

"No, you did nothing wrong. I'm glad you acted the way you did. I'm glad you finally came. We can't go on standing here. Come on."

"Your shoes are too thin, that's what it is. What pretty shoes. I've never seen them before. Come, be careful, or you'll get your feet wet. You see, there it is." He pointed to his Volkswagen.

My feet were already wet. A heap of hailstones had accumulated at the bottom step, and I'd accidentally stepped into it; immediately my feet got wet.

He really had left the engine running. Berthold laughed because no one had noticed. The windows were misted over on the inside.

"Hurry up and get in. It's nice and warm inside. Wait!" With his fingers he scraped off the hailstones stuck to the car door. "Now."

It really was nice and warm inside the car. There was a strong scent of gasoline. Berthold used a glove to wipe the windshield on the inside. He was proud that we had a car of our own and had no further need of taxis. He stepped on the accelerator to show me how well the compressor was still functioning. And he touched my hands.

"Don't you have gloves?"

"I was in such a hurry I forgot."

He wanted to give me his, and he suggested that I warm my hands at the edge of the windshield, where the hot air from the defroster blew. Tomorrow he'd buy me some gloves, he said.

"I have all the money we need," he added, patting his breast pocket.

"You should turn on your lights," I said.

"Oh. Right."

Then we drove down our street and then left, down

the street that led to the main road. No one was out, probably because of the weather. Besides, it was quite late; there's never much nighttime traffic in our town.

I kept very quiet, I did not want to disturb Berthold. But after a few moments he shifted gears and stopped at the side of the road.

"What is it?" I asked.

"You're not sad?"

"No, not at all. I'm happy to be with you."

"Truly?"

"Yes, absolutely. Please drive on. We've got to get away from here."

"Don't let it upset you."

"No. It's just that this time I'm sure I won't be able to go back."

"Why should you? There's nothing there for you."

"No."

"And now you have me. Everything will be quite different."

"Yes. Please drive on."

So he drove away, but very slowly and hesitantly. Past two crossings, then we took a right turn onto the main road leading to the town center. There, too, Berthold drove slowly, much too slowly. A few cars were going the other way, and one streetcar; it must have been the last one of the night. And one car honked and passed us.

Berthold placed his right hand on my knee, and I put my hand over it.

"Are you warm enough?" he asked.

"Yes," I said, pressing his hand.

"Do you know what I'd like?"

"What?"

"I'd like to sleep with you."

"Yes, I know."

"I don't want you to think that I . . . I can manage

277

without it quite easily other times. For years on end; if I have my work, it doesn't bother me. But now . . . ."

"Why don't you speed up?"

But he didn't speed up; we were still crawling.

"You know what?"

"What?"

"Why should we go to the Playhouse Cellar?"

"I don't feel much like it either."

"I bet the others are thoroughly drunk by now, and we'll get there too late anyway. Why don't we drive straight there?"

"Where?"

"The place where she was hanging up the laundry. I think it's a place where people can stay overnight."

"And if they're closed?"

"We'll get them up."

"Maybe they haven't turned on the heat."

"Then we'll drive on. We have all the time in the world; it doesn't matter anymore. Or do you want to stop for coffee?"

"No, I don't need coffee now. I'm wide awake again. Just drive."

Then he finally speeded up, and after he had shifted gears, he put his hand back on my knee. I noticed that he was happy, and I held his hand. We had no further need for talk. Everything was the way it had to be.

A few cars were still traveling in the opposite direction, but no one passed us. At this late hour no one was headed downtown. Ahead of us the bluish-white garland of streetlights stretched straight ahead, toward its end like a pale line along the sky, and finally a thin hook lost in an indistinct darkness. The farther we got and the faster we drove, the less my thoughts clung to what I had left behind.

The wind howled through a crack in the window onto Berthold's shoulder, rising and falling, rising and

278

falling. And then Berthold started whistling softly to himself. First I thought I was just imagining it, but then he pinched my knee gently, so I knew that it was him and that he was whistling the lullaby I'd taught him. He had not forgotten; he was whistling it correctly, and he was whistling it now because he was happy and because he wanted to make me happy and because we belonged together. And I was happy.

Then the car began to fly—there, where the garland of light curved into the dark. We were floating. How light we were! Light as feathers. We were wafted over to the pillar of the railroad bridge. Faster and faster. I clung to Berthold's hand. And he clung to my knee. We did not want to be separated again.

Yes, and then we were blown to quite another place. It did not hurt. No, all the pain had been before.

In the meantime—that is, while we were driving and while we were sleeping and while we were being blown away or whatever it was that happened to us— of course I don't know exactly what was happening at home in the meantime, but I have a general idea. I had lived with them quite long enough to be able to imagine everything very well, and I hardly believe that the truth was much different. Why should people change just a few minutes after I left them?

Yes, so that man Blanck was there. We'd let him in the door ourselves, and he had closed the door behind us. So there he was, in the vestibule. Since the situation was quite embarrassing to him, he hesitated. And there was another reason, a very funny reason— just like everything else that night, so funny you could hardly keep from laughing. Blanck had turned up his coat collar and was holding it anxiously to make sure that it would not open. That was because he was no longer wearing his collar. He was not properly dressed.

As soon as his boss had telephoned, he had put his trousers, suit coat, and overcoat on over his pajamas and had rushed to the house in a taxi. Very commendable, but of course it robbed him of his self-confidence to know that he was not correctly dressed.

"Come in, come in, Blanck," Max called from inside. As far as Max was concerned, it was almost more important to have Blanck with him now than it had been before, when I had still been with him.

He immediately apologized to Blanck for calling him so late and possibly waking him out of a sound sleep—and on top of that, quite unnecessarily. Max stressed the word *unnecessarily* with great sharpness, so that it came out sounding a little affected. Then he motioned to the empty living room. Blanck for his part apologized for having taken so long to get to the house; he had been unable to get a taxi right away even though when he called, he had insisted on the urgency of the matter, and the dispatcher had assured him that she would send a car at once.

Max said that he'd never forget Blanck's willingness to rush right over, but . . . .

The reason it was so important to Max to have Blanck at his side was that otherwise he would have been alone with his father and Fräulein Gerda. And how was he to face those two, who had unfortunately witnessed everything? Yes, if only that could have been avoided.

"Fräulein Gerda," Max called up the stairs.

"Yes?" the frightened answer came back.

"Would you be so kind as to look after the child?"

Upon which Fräulein Gerda disappeared without a word, so that Max was able to turn his full attention to Blanck and explain that all he had cared about was a reliable witness. "An absolutely reliable witness," Max repeated, raising his voice slightly. But as Blanck could

280

see for himself, the matter had taken care of itself in the meantime.

"Max," his father called to him after this exposition. He even came down the stairs—that's how much importance he attached to it.

"Yes, Father, what can I do for you?" Max was polite but annoyed.

"Wouldn't it be better if you followed them to the Playhouse Cellar at once?"

"Them? Who?" Max asked. He raised his eyebrows in astonishment.

"And without Blanck. Forgive me, Herr Blanck," his father continued, ignoring Max's question.

"I really do not understand you, Father," Max said.

"I think that's the only chance you've got."

"Whose chance did you say? *Mine?*"

"Or your duty. Let's not argue about words."

Max did not answer. Instead, he looked up the stairs. "Well?"

"Günther is asleep," Fräulein Gerda whispered.

"Fine. Thank you. You may go to bed," Max said, and Fräulein Gerda obeyed at once.

"Max, I asked you a question," his father reminded him.

"Yes, one moment, Father. How about it, Blanck? Won't you at least let me get you a drink? How about a cognac?"

"Listen to me, Max. I have a feeling that we mustn't lose any time. I'd go myself, but . . . ."

"Really, Father, I must ask you not to interfere in my private life again. Yes, forgive my bluntness, but you leave me no choice. And besides, I don't consider this the right moment, here and now, to discuss *my* chances. I hardly think that *my* chance is waiting for me in the Playhouse Cellar, if you'll forgive my saying so. As far as I'm concerned, the case is—"

281

Max did not finish the sentence because in the distance he heard the hysterical wailing of a police siren. The squad car must be rushing along the main road; at night noises were audible a long way off, especially when the wind came from the right direction. The three men listened nervously, their heads cocked slightly to the right. Only when the siren faded away did they turn back to each other, acting as if nothing had happened.

"I believe that I can claim for myself," Max continued—strangely enough, his voice was much more assured, as if the howling of the siren had restored his superiority; his lips even took on a sneering expression—"that in granting chances, as you put it, I've been more than generous. But there are limits to everything. We simply cannot afford more, Father. We have to think of our good name; it would damage our reputation. Therefore I wish . . . ."

By now Max was speaking as if he were addressing a stockholders' meeting. That was the role in which he felt most confident. In it, no one could touch him; there was no contradicting his clear and decisive proposals. To lend his words more emphasis, he even hit the back of a nearby armchair with the flat of his hand—not very hard, no, and by no means to express anger, but only because he believed that such gestures were part of the role if it was to be played well and effectively.

"Therefore I wish all of us to consider this matter as settled once and for all—as of this moment, tonight. Once and for all, do you understand, Father? Yes, let's draw a clear line. And Blanck, please, I expect your utmost discretion."

"Of course, sir."

"Not a word about tonight's events. Not even to your esteemed wife. You know, women . . . . Are you sure you wouldn't like a drink?"

"No, sir, thank you very much."

"Well, all right, then I don't want to keep you. Good night, then. And take a taxi. Your wife will be worried."

Max held out his hand to Blanck.

At that moment the doorbell rang, and Max dropped his hand.

"Now who can that be?" he said softly, looking at his father as if the old man could enlighten him. For a moment it seemed that he would go to the door himself, but then he thought better of it. "Please, Blanck, won't you see who it is?"

As Blanck went out into the vestibule, Max tried to maintain his superior stance. "It seems that we're not destined to get any rest at all tonight."

Max heard Blanck opening the front door, and then the voice of a strange man trying to speak softly. But Max did not wish to listen—such behavior was beneath his dignity—and so he continued talking. "Seriously, Father, we really cannot afford this. Surely you will agree. It never hurts to face facts . . . . What is it?"

Blanck had returned to the living room. Alone. Uncertain of what to do, he looked at my father-in-law. He didn't know whether it was all right for him to speak in the old man's presence.

"Well?" Max asked.

"The police, sir. They want to speak to you in person . . . ."

"I'll go," Max said, moving to the vestibule.

My father-in-law gave Blanck a questioning look. A murmur of voices and the scraping of feet on tile could be heard from outside. One of the patrolmen never stopped shuffling his feet as he addressed Max.

"They drove into a pillar of the railway bridge," Blanck whispered. "Apparently at top speed. The car must have skidded. They say it's totally demolished."

"Both of them?" My father-in-law was whispering too.

Blanck nodded his head.

Then they waited. They had nothing more to say to each other.

Max came back shortly. The front door had been left open, and the draft was so strong that the ashes blew out of the ashtray across the tabletop.

Max behaved admirably. Anyone who claims differently is lying. Max is always admirable in a crisis.

He had already put on his hat and was about to pull on his coat. He had grabbed his things from the coatrack in passing. Max truly is admirable. No need to fear for him.

Blanck ran to help him on with his coat.

"Thank you. Please go at once—" Max began, but his father went to him, eager to say something. "I don't have time now, not one second, Father. They're waiting for me outside. I'll go to the emergency room with them; they've kindly offered to drive me. I'll see to the arrangements. Please go to bed. There's nothing you can do anyway, and your health is more important to me . . . . All right, Blanck, you'll go to the press office immediately. We'll have to beat the newspapers. Put out a release, a very short one, something to the effect . . . ." Max reflected for a moment, wording the announcement.

Blanck looked at him expectantly, careful not to let a single word escape his lips.

" 'Suddenly and unexpectedly,' " Max began before interrupting himself. "No, not like that. That sounds like the official obituary. Let's say, 'A tragic accident'—yes, let's begin like that—and then, 'took the life of the wife of the well-known . . .' and so on. You know—the usual. Not a word about the other one. But hurry . . . . All right, gentlemen, I'm coming."

My father-in-law was left alone in the living room. He heard the squad car starting, he heard the squeal of tires as it turned the corner. Then there was total silence.

284

An anxious whisper floated down the stairs. "Sir?"

Calmly my father-in-law looked up.

"Did something terrible happen, sir?" Fräulein Gerda asked.

My father-in-law shook his head.

Yes, that's more or less how it was.